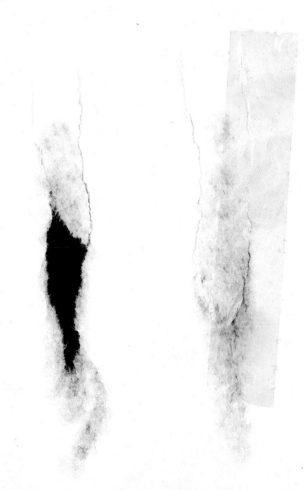

WHO CARES?

The Crisis in Canadian Nursing

Sarah Jane Growe

M&S

Canadian Cataloguing in Publication Data

Growe, Sarah Jane, 1939–
Who cares? : the crisis in Canadian nursing

Includes bibliographical references.
ISBN 0-7710-3446-6

1. Nursing – Canada. 2. Nursing – Canada – History.
I. Title.

RT6.A1G7 1991   610.73′0971   C90-095494-9

Printed and bound in Canada. The paper used in this book is
acid free.

McClelland & Stewart Inc.
The Canadian Publishers
481 University Avenue
Toronto, Ontario
M5G 2E9

The unique function of the nurse is to assist the individual, sick or well, in the performance of those activities contributing to health or its recovery (or to a peaceful death) that he would perform unaided if he had the necessary strength, will or knowledge.

And to do this in such a way as to help him gain independence as rapidly as possible.

International Council of Nurses, 1960

Contents

Acknowledgements   *ix*

1   Patience   *11*

2   In the Shadow of the Grange   *26*

3   A New Sphere of Usefulness   *44*

4   System Failure   *63*

5   The Crisis   *78*

6   Turf Wars   *96*

7   Women's Work: It Ain't Necessarily So   *113*

8   The Highest Respect for the Law   *132*

9   Education by Degrees   *155*

10   Back to the Future   *175*

11   The End of the Rainbow   *199*

12   The Health-Care Armageddon   *222*

Bibliography   *241*

Index   *253*

Acknowledgements

This book reflects the contributions of more than two hundred thousand women – the nurses of Canada.

I thank, in particular, Win Miller, Elva Armstrong, and Trudy Staley for sharing their files on the Vancouver revolt; Irene Goldstone, Phyllis Jensen, Judith Hibberd, and Marie Campbell for their unpublished graduate work; Christina Power, Suzanne Bowley, Jeannette Gallant, Nancy Avery, Delrose Gordon, Briget McGrath, Jessie Mantle, Judy Grabham, Pauline deVette, Rosemarie Riddell, Cindy Carson, Mary Glavin, Dilin Baker, Mae Reardon, Bernadet Ratsoy, and Dianne Simms, for opening their workplaces to me; and the three hundred and some other nurses, men and women, unionists and academics, who opened to me their thoughts and feelings on this painful era in nursing history.

There have been other reports on the crisis in Canadian health care; this is the first one committed to giving nurses their say.

Others who helped, with professional expertise or with emotional support or with both, are Mary Wickens, Brooke Forbes, Joyce McKerrow, Jackie Smith, Linda Hossie, Veronica Doyle, Kathe Lieber, Vivian Macdonald, Margot Gibb-Clark, Olivia Ward, Carole Yawney, Ken Clowes, Dani Singer, Tara White, Jessica Growe, Adam Growe, Eric Miller, Wendy Barrett, Linda Zarytsky, *The Toronto Star*, and Dinah Forbes.

I acknowledge with thanks the research assistance of the *Edmonton Journal*, the Public Archives of Ontario, the Staff Nurses' Association of Alberta, the Wellesley Hospital, the Registered Nurses Association of British Columbia, the College of Nurses of Ontario, the Registered Nurses' Association of Ontario, and the office of Dennis Mills, my Member of Parliament. I am also grateful for financial assistance from the Ontario Arts Council and the Explorations Program of the Canada Council.

Sarah Jane Growe

1

Patience

It's only nine o'clock on this stormy Newfoundland morning and Chrissie Power has already done the work of three people.

All yesterday they were one nurse short. Today is Saturday, which means three fewer staff than usual. Power should be out on the floor by now, but she's had to go on rounds with the doctors in place of the head nurse and she's had to do the paperwork usually handled by the ward clerk. On weekdays the night shift would have had all that organized before they signed off in the morning. Today everything is late and Power, an hour into her twelve-hour shift, is backed up.

The 148-bed Charles S. Curtis Memorial Hospital in St. Anthony is experiencing the worst nursing shortage in recent memory. The hospital has had to close beds, shut down the emergency room from midnight to 8:00 a.m., and scrunch up two wards into one. That's serious business in this remote corner of the world, a good twelve-hour drive from St. John's, Newfoundland. The closest hospital, in Corner Brook, is two hours southeast by Air Nova and connecting bus; the 450-kilometre car ride is four and a half hours. And it would take Grenfell Regional Health Services' leased Twin Otter at least an hour to get to its other hospital in Goose Bay, Labrador, if the winter weather doesn't ground the plane, as it often does.

Today at least no one will have to be "prepped" for the operating room, thank God, because it's closed. But otherwise

11

there's as much nursing work to do on Saturday as on any other day in the week, and as luck would have it many of Power's thirty surgical patients are "completes," the hospital's nursing term for total dependence. The hospital has a formula, based on patient volume and severity of illness, for determining the number of nursing hours required, but in these days of short supply, the patient classification system is a joke.

A buzzer sounds. "Bet you ten to one that's Henry," Chrissie Power says. Today Henry, a bucolic young man with his leg in traction, may be the last straw.

There is no polite way of describing Henry. He was drunk when he broke his leg driving his snowmobile around – apparently not an uncommon occurrence because two other young men are in traction in nearby rooms for exactly the same reason.

"They think they should be waited on hand and foot and that doesn't go too well with me," Power says. At twenty-three, she is a small slip of a thing. But she is formidable. The other two snowmobile casualties, however, are not Henry's equals in terms of nursing time, if you call answering a buzzer every five minutes "nursing." Power would just love to tell Henry's mother a thing or two. Henry is twenty-nine.

"Button up, Henry. Your pill's not due for another hour yet." It's the third time he's rung in an hour.

Power is in charge of organizing the workload for the four other nurses in her ward on shift with her today: one other registered nurse and three registered nursing assistants. Because the other RN and one of the RNAs finish at 4:00 p.m., she has to assign and finish the routine temperatures, blood pressures, dressings, and medicines in the first eight hours so that the skeletal staff on evening duty can be free for emergencies. The hospital emergency room isn't open on weekends so Power's only back-up is the one nursing supervisor "float," who could be anywhere in the hospital carrying a beeper on her waist. Power must be prepared for anything.

General surgical rounds went well this morning, but orthopedic rounds took too long; there was a lot of fiddling with scissors and casts and traction pressure. The morning medications are due at ten o'clock and, according to law, RNs are the only nurses who can administer drugs. A car accident victim is a paraplegic who has to be turned every two hours. The orthopedic surgeon must treat the circulation problem in a diabetic amputee's one remaining leg. And a lot of the bedridden people in Power's charge are in pain.

Out on the floor an intravenous line is running dry. Power presses a plunger two or three times in quick succession and goes for a new plastic bottle to hang, stopping for a moment to write it all down in a notebook she carries in her pocket. She runs down the hall to remove the diabetic patient's urine catheter and inject a sedative ordered by the orthopedic surgeon, returning to the station to find the other RN close to tears. She's removed a suture by mistake. "Don't worry. Nothing can be done now. We can't suture her up again," Power tells her.

It's after 10:00 a.m. but Power is only now setting out yellow, brown, and pink pills in small paper cups. The buzzer rings again. It's Henry. "I'm coming, my God." He's complaining about the pain her "big claws" have caused him. Now the telephone rings; the wife of a patient who is about to be discharged wants to know if he can cut wood and shovel snow. Power chats with the woman for a while. The medical resident tosses off a comment about "saving nurses' asses" as he sits down to change the suture order to conform to what has already been done. His remark falls on deaf ears.

At 11:00 a.m. the three RNAs on Power's nursing team aren't even halfway through the floor with the morning care – making beds and bathing. Power's on the phone again, this time to the "girls" upstairs in obstetrics, begging them to come help. Even the required twenty-minute coffee break would be a relief, but no one has the time.

"You have to do everything, see. You're maid. You're everything. Honest to God, I had no idea what I was getting into." Power entered the diploma course at a hospital-based nursing school in St. John's. She was fresh out of high school, too young to take stock of the responsibility and stress. That happens to a lot of young women. The provincial pay scale is one of the lowest in Canada, ranging from $25,000 to $31,000 a year. The only place to live in town is the Grenfell low-rental residences for singles.

Most days Power likes the job. Halfway into the second year of her first nursing position, she isn't ready to quit. "I'm not sick of it yet. Some days I dread coming to work but it turns out not to be as bad as I dreaded. I can't really say what I'll be doing after the summer."

A doctor has changed an order without telling her, but his directions aren't clear. She doesn't understand the new order and phones for the doctor. She checks "the rectal bleeder" who's been sent into hospital for investigation. She changes a dressing – RNAs aren't allowed to change wet dressings any more – and puts on rubber gloves to "disempact" the paraplegic patient's bowels. It's a dirty job. Because of the woman's paralysis her feces have to be massaged and pulled out by hand. A buzzer rings. "What's the matter now, Henry? Are you in that much pain?" "Yes, ma'am." And she goes to help the RNAs make the beds. If suggestions coming out of government commissions for a more rigid division of tasks between RNs and RNAs ever come to fruition, the women staffing the surgical ward in St. Anthony will never get through the day.

"Have you got a second?" It's the orthopedic surgeon. "Well, just a second." He's putting a cast on the diabetic patient's leg. Although he has his medical resident to assist him he calls Power over to ask her where the scissors are and starts handing her the garbage as he wraps the gauze around the leg. The procedure is messy, so he sends Power out for more hot water and sterile bandage packs that he claims he couldn't find for the life of him. The resident watches as Power goes out into the hall and back several times. "You don't need me any more?" Power asks. It's a hopeful question that doesn't get answered.

Henry is threatening to pee in bed, so Power takes him the bedpan. He makes noises about getting out of bed to smoke in the lounge upstairs, one of the few places it is permitted. She's not even going to try to restrain him, she says. He's not a two-year-old and he's been told what can happen to him if he stops the traction. "I've got tons of work to do," she says to him. She can barely control her impatience.

Lunch is late and hurried. But when she returns, the obstetrics nurses are there to help the RNAs, so Power can start writing up her charts. Since she's responsible for her every action, as well as the actions of the three RNAs working under her today, she's vowed to do that at least twice a day "just to cover myself." Someone wants Demerol for pain. She draws it up, phones, and sets it aside for another RN (probably the supervisor) to cross-check before running out of the narcotics room. Then she hurries back, remembering she's forgotten to lock the door.

The RNAs need help with blocks to lift up the bottom of the bed for the patient with a bowel inflammation who is having problems with her inner ear; Power stops to flush out a patient's intravenous tubing on the way, ending up in the room of one of the other young men with broken bones thanks to a snowmobile accident. Also strung up in traction, he has lost the elastic stocking used to stimulate circulation in his unbroken leg. She gets a fresh stocking and stretches it on. "Turn the TV down will you?" "No," she answers with a shake of her curls and starts to leave the room. "Say please."

"Puuulleeees," he answers.

"I likes to be said 'please' to."

Then she's coaxing food down an elderly woman who is hard of hearing, telling her the doctor should check her ears while she is in hospital. The diabetic patient is awake and troubled; she doesn't understand how the cast got there, and it hurts. After stroking her, explaining why she must try to move her toes, Power runs to the nursing station again to get hold of another doctor whose order isn't clear. "I have to think what else to do," she says, more to herself than to anybody else.

Henry's buzzer signifies his continuing obsession with the upstairs smoking room. "It means nothing to me," she tells him. "I don't have to live with a bone infection, you do." The diabetic woman is in real pain now. She wants Power to take her cast off. "The doctor wants it on," Power says, and tries to soothe her. "He doesn't have to suffer the pain," the woman says, getting churlish. "Give me something for pain," she begs. A pain killer has been ordered, so Power goes out to draw up the syringe.

"I keeps it still," the woman says.

"I know, love." The motherly reply is from someone who is one-third the woman's age.

"I'm in pain all the time, all over."

Power draws the curtains and bares the woman's hip. "I can't take it off, my love. The doctor wants it there." She injects the sedative.

"The doctor can put it on his own leg."

"It's not going to do you any good on his leg."

"I wouldn't care right now if he cut it right off."

Power strokes her again. That and Demerol is all the nursing she can do. She leaves a glass for urine to be tested for blood sugar at another bedside, again writing it all down in her pocket notebook. A buzzer rings. Henry is getting more aggressive; he wants a cigarette. "It's fine to say you are taking the responsibility. I know what can happen to a leg like that. I'm sorry. I'm not taking the responsibility." A nine-year-old in pediatrics is more mature than he is, she mutters on the way to the intensive-care unit next door. It's break time, and since she's now the only RN on the ward she has to leave the narcotics key with the neighbouring RNs. She stops to joke with an old man at the nursing desk, kidding him about his addiction to candy. "It's so much nicer at night when you can stop and talk."

By early evening the diabetic patient still hasn't urinated; it's been eleven hours – since just before the orthopedic surgeon ordered her catheter taken out. The catheter would have prevented any urinary complications, and Power is worried. She tries to get the doctor on the phone. "You can't be sluggish. You have to keep your wits about you." She's just spent almost twelve hours whirling around, electrifying everyone with her bristling energy. The first doctor still hasn't returned her call, and since she has a third patient who is refusing medication, she dials the staff doctor on call. The only hospital physician on duty tonight has been sent out in the ambulance to rescue a seven-year-old who is choking.

Outside, a storm has been building all day and navigation is treacherous. The women are starting to arrange to double up with nurses who live in the hospital residences rather than try to make it to their own homes and return tomorrow. During the storm season the bank across the street often closes, but the nurses always manage to get into work.

The bedpan of the patient with rectal bleeding has blood in it and the woman's blood type hasn't been cross-matched. The doctor admitting her should have attended to that and Power, concerned, makes a note on the woman's chart. Then she begins to tape record her report on all thirty patients for the next group of nurses on duty. The woman with a bowel inflammation now has a distended stomach, the diabetic woman still hasn't urinated, and a man in the third room to the left won't take his medication. There is, however, at least one good piece of news for the night shift; Henry's girlfriend has come to wheel him out, flat on his back – traction and all – for a smoke.

Suzanne Bowley is a gem. A nine-year veteran in medicine's most highly specialized and newest science, Bowley was recruited from Nova Scotia for the Mount Sinai Hospital's neonatal intensive-care unit, one of only three such units in Metro Toronto. In 1988, out of the unit's seventy-four full-time nurses, fourteen resigned within a period of eleven months.

Interrogation room 101 in George Orwell's *1984* couldn't have been more intimidating than the neonatal intensive-care unit in Toronto's Mount Sinai Hospital; it looks and sounds like something out of *Star Wars*. The ventilators mark each tiny breath but trust in the steady rhythm is shattered by an ominous hiss that permeates every corner of the room. Red computer numbers flash over each little isolette, a temperature-controlled crib, unemotionally spelling out vital signs. The room is hot. It's white bright. It's noisy. And then there are the alarm bells, each attached to a different machine, a hundred or more of them. They go off so often that after twenty minutes it becomes impossible to hear them.

Each alarm is a cry for help from a baby too small and frail to send up a signal that something is amiss. So the nurses, respiratory therapists, biomedical technicians, pharmacists, and resident doctors must react to every sound. Every action in here is an heroic measure; twenty years ago the newborns being treated here now would have died. Ten years ago the mortality rate for a 1,500-gram, thirty-two-week fetus was 75 per cent; today it's only 5 per cent. Now, of the premature babies born weighing more than 700 grams, 90 per cent survive – an incredible scientific achievement, although the rate dips considerably lower, to 55 per cent, for babies born under that weight. But there is a price: a twenty-four-hour stay for one baby – counting the oxygen, the medication, the tubing, the high-tech machines, and the people to watch them – costs $40,000 to $50,000.

A few years back new graduates were not considered experienced enough for this kind of nursing. Now, with the current nursing shortage, there is no option. But the group of ten new nurses now going through ten weeks of orientation won't be able to make a full contribution to the staff for another year. So even after this initial ten-week investment – about $60,000 in wages – the hospital will still need to pay the new nurses during another eight months of on-the-job training. Within two years a lot of them will have quit; the turnover here is astonishingly high. The constant shortage of nurses means there is not enough expertise to keep these specialized units operating at full capacity; every other month it seems another high-risk mother in Metro Toronto is sent away to deliver her premature baby in Kingston or Buffalo, New York.

On this mid-November day, Bowley and her 1,172-gram patient are both walking the fine line between life and death. The baby girl in the isolette is the second of twins born twelve weeks early, and she can't breathe on her own. The tube attached to the computer-monitored pump that is breathing for her passes behind her vocal chords, temporarily paralysing them so she can't even cry.

One of the other babies is so small, at 560 grams, he looks like a newborn bird. Bowley's baby is big enough at least to resemble a human being. The infant even tries to peek up as the nurse reaches her arms into the holes in the isolette's plexi-glass sides. "Hi there, my little friend."

The baby is very sick. Just after her breech birth, the ventilator pump had to be set so fast and at so high a pressure that it caused a blowout (pneumothorax) in each lung. Two tubes, one on each side of her chest, now drain the blood, fluid, and air out so that her lungs can re-inflate. She is on 100 per cent oxygen, but no matter how high they turn up the pressure they can't get enough to her blood. So a brand new last-ditch drug requiring consent from her parents is pumping through her veins to dilate her blood vessels. A feeding tube runs from her mouth to her stomach. Ten separate leads on her body give out readings on blood pressure, body temperature, heart rate, respiration, carbon dioxide, oxygen, and pH levels. Bowley isn't going to do a lot of the routine hands-on tasks because they want to disturb the infant as little as possible. They have inserted an arterial line into her umbilical cord to draw blood without having to poke her – arterial blood provides more accurate results than blood drawn from a vein. The line requires expert care because it can damage the circulation.

Yesterday screens surrounded this isolette all day, enclosing clusters of specialists deciding where to set the ventilator pressure, what tests should be ordered, and how much of the experimental drug the baby could tolerate. Today the doctors order an ultrasound to assess the extent of bleeding into the head. It may be necessary to ask the family's permission for less heroic action.

Bowley has rarely seen a doctor give up on a child. They have been taught all their lives to try to save patients, she says, and it's hard for them to let go of the prospect of curing.

In 1986 nurses participitating in a Vancouver seminar on women in women's work reported doctors' reluctance to deal directly with death as one of the biggest problems on the floor. For doctors, death equals failure. When the end is near, nurses are often the ones to tell the patient about it, despite not being permitted by law to do so.

Nurses' tenacity can also be a problem. During a run of deaths on the Mount Sinai ward last fall, some nurses were so worked up about a parent's decision to let her suffering child die that the hospital sent a staff psychiatrist to talk with them.

Today Bowley is in charge of only one baby. A primary-care nurse rather than a member of a nursing team like Power, Bowley would normally have been given a second baby this assignment, or perhaps even three babies, if none of them was on a ventilator. But this infant is too ill for anything other than one-to-one nursing. Suctioning a baby on a ventilator is a sterile procedure requiring a nurse with a special certificate of competence earned by putting in the required number of supervised hours on the job.

Bowley's mind is always working. She must keep a constant watch over the machines, changing the tubes and probes and recalibrating the measurements. Too much oxygen can cause blindness. Infection is a constant danger, and the wrong dose of an antibiotic can damage kidneys or hearing. Improper suctioning can perforate a lung. She must test the blood gases to measure the oxygen, carbon dioxide, and pH levels. She must read vital signs – blood pressure, heart rate, and body temperature, writing each reading down carefully on the hospital chart. She alone must decide whether to call the doctor, the resident, the medical graduate student or specialist "fellow," the pharmacist, the respiratory technologist, or the social worker; she is the patient's voice. The consequences of doing nothing can be fatal. For all this, for twelve-hour shifts – nights and weekends too – Bowley earns $32,000 a year.

The staff neonatologist on duty this month stops by and asks Bowley to turn down the pressure on the ventilator. Bowley is concerned. The baby isn't looking good; she seems to be struggling harder than usual for breath. But Bowley knows there is no room for discussion. This doctor won't listen.

The hospital hierarchy is still as rigid as it ever was, despite efforts to tone it down by relaxing the rules about caps, uniforms, and the deceiving, disarming custom of using first names instead of titles. A few years ago nurses had to stand up when a doctor came onto the ward. Now they are made aware in more subtle ways that the doctor is in charge, even though nurses are not the doctor's employees.

Nursing students are still trained to correct doctors in a way that manipulates the physicians into thinking they knew the right answers all along, a strategy coined by a U.S. psychiatrist in 1967 as "the doctor-nurse game." "What the doctor-nurse game is all about is that nurses know but they can't let the world know they know," Queen's University vice-principal Alice Baumgart told *The Canadian Nurse* in January 1985. As Bowley puts it: "It's tricky sometimes; you have to have a lot of tact to get yourself listened to. All the nurses are considered way below the residents. You have to coddle them along."

Ros O'Reilly, nursing administrator of Mount Sinai's neonatal intensive-care unit, has had several talks with the staff neonatologist who is pulling rank on Bowley. The situation is not improving. But one of the two new male nurses on the unit has at least succeeded in persuading the doctor to allow nurses to change endotracheal tubes. The restriction was a longstanding policy O'Reilly had been trying to reverse for years. The male nurses are more ambitious than the women, O'Reilly has noticed. "Nurses have got to start speaking up for themselves."

Bowley, meanwhile, has turned up her baby's oxygen and made a point of writing it down. The carbon dioxide level is still too high. It may be that the probe she changed isn't giving an accurate reading. Should she call the resident? Should she wait for him until after lunch? Or should she do a blood gas so she'll be able to prove to him that it's really the baby and not the probe? She injects chloralhydrate, the medicine that has been ordered, hoping it will settle the baby down.

The resident fellow assigned to the unit comes by before she has to decide. Bowley goes for ice to get the blood-gas procedure started. By the time she has drawn blood from the arterial line into her syringe, the resident is back, offering to porter the sample to the lab for her. The buddy Bowley chose at the beginning of her twelve-hour shift this morning is back on the floor so Bowley can go for lunch. But she says, "No, thanks anyway." Her baby isn't looking good.

By now, the chief neonatologist is at the bedside, although no one has called her. She notices the new equipment. "What's all this, Nurse?" Nurse is said with a capital N, a generic substitute for Bowley's first name. The probe has just been changed but the doctor doesn't listen. She orders it changed again. Bowley complies and calls a respiratory technologist to check the machinery. A slip of pink paper arrives from the laboratory confirming Bowley's judgement: this baby is sick and getting sicker.

There are now four experts surrounding the baby: Bowley, the resident fellow, the neonatologist, and the respiratory technologist. It's a silent signal. People start moving in rhythm like a mime troupe without a director. The "charge nurse" walks around from behind her desk at the front of the unit; the "float" (the one nurse on duty who has no assignment so she can handle admissions or emergencies) arrives unsummoned out of nowhere; Bowley's buddy leaves the neighbouring baby to wheel over the crash cart; and O'Reilly comes out of her office, without a word, to hover at the fringe of the tense circle. They are four simultaneous actions.

The nurses are calling readings out to the resident, as he fiddles with the tubes and turns the dials. They are trying all kinds of procedures, the neonatologist on one side of the child, the resident on the other, the three nurses and the respiratory technologist on the outer ring, the second bulwark in the line of battle. The baby's temperature-controlled isolette has been exposed to colder air for almost an hour, so Bowley wheels over an electric heater.

"Get that baby warmer away, Nurse," the neonatologist says.

"It's not for me; it's for the baby." Bowley calls the doctor by her first name.

"It doesn't matter. We're going to close the door soon. And the warmer isn't over the top of the baby anyway. It's not keeping the baby warm."

Bowley complies – again. These babies catch cold very easily, she thinks to herself, and infection is just another stress. She knows the baby warmer makes the doctor too hot, but the nurses always put up with it. The resident orders an x-ray and removes the ventilator tube from behind the baby's vocal chords. Someone has put a screen around the child.

Now, with no ventilator to breathe for her, the baby must be "bagged"; the resident presses the black rubber suction bag in and out, air in and air out, four times by hand. The heart rate is dipping. The blood gases with the oxygen, carbon dioxide, and pH levels come back from the lab, one, two, three times. Each reading is worse than the one before. The resident keeps "bagging," in out, in out. The neonatologist thinks it's another pneumothorax; Bowley and the charge nurse, Eileen Scott, wonder if it could be something else. Maybe it's a plug at the end of the tube.

The intravenous tube is leaking. Bowley is afraid it's going to go interstitial (into the tissues) and the valuable drug inside will not reach her baby. "Don't touch the baby, Nurse." Those are the doctor's instructions.

This baby is dying. She is breathing in but she can't breathe out; that's why the carbon dioxide level is so high. The resident takes a suction catheter and inserts it all the way down the tube. A huge plug of mucous is blocking the tube. A plug that big and that deep isn't very common; that's why it took so long to find. "Don't touch the baby, Nurse." These are the neonatologist's final instructions.

"Ahhhhhh," Bowley screams to anyone who can hear her. "If I only had a small scissors right now." She is a responsive, intelligent woman of thirty-two who is almost always calm. She's been with many babies who have "crashed." If she knows it's coming and it's inevitable, she finds death fairly easy to accept. This death, however, she would not have liked at all. The baby had been stable all morning; her condition was correctable; there was no reason to believe she would not thrive.

What would she have done if the baby had died? Blamed the doctor? "If that baby had died I would have gone home and blamed myself. I would have blamed myself for not doing my best for that baby. I should have stood up to that doctor. I should have kicked that doctor in the shins."

Competent and compassionate, Power and Bowley are both excellent bedside nurses, trained to deal minute by minute with pain, illness, and death. Attuned to cope with emergency, yet also adept at managing routine, they bring to the job a level of commitment that outstrips the usual nine-to-five employee mentality. On these particular days, neither has been off her feet for more than an hour during her twelve-hour shift. Neither goes home from work free of the stress she has experienced; the instant life-and-death decisions, the charting, the exhaustions, the raw nerves among the conflicting personalities in the hospital workplace.

Neither Power nor Bowley is likely to be working at the hospital five years from now. They are not paid much for the work they do; they aren't respected; they have little control over their own nursing practice; and what job satisfaction they get doesn't measure up to the kind of energy, responsibility, and personal risk they put in. Hospital patients are sicker than they used to be, and more and more nurses are needed for each patient bed. But fewer and fewer women seem to be willing to stay at the hospital bedside for any length of time.

In the spring of 1987, *The Canadian Nurse*, the monthly magazine of the Canadian Nurses Association, predicted "It is unlikely that the current shortage will ever be resolved." The mobility of nurses and an imbalance between supply and demand used to explain the high turnover and shortages, but now research suggests a growing malaise in the profession. Hospital administrators are worried, and for the first time patients are expressing concerns about their own safety.

No single event in the 1980s alerted more Canadians to the increasing concern about patient safety than the Royal Commission of Inquiry into the mysterious deaths at Toronto's Hospital for Sick Children. The inquiry was televised live in 1983–1984, and viewers watched open-mouthed as doctors and nurses paid testimony to the complexity of nursing practice, to the stress, to the large number of inexperienced nurses having to take on more technical responsibility, to the lack of communication among doctors and nurses, and to the overall distrust of nurses' judgement. Eight years ago, the whole country knew something was wrong.

2

In the Shadow of the Grange

Thirty-six babies on cardiac ward 4A/B died at Toronto's Hospital for Sick Children between July 1980 and March 1981. Code 25. Cardiac arrest. The call over the public address system summons nurses, doctors, and technicians into the room from every corner of the hospital. One arrest can draw in as many as nineteen people – shouting, suctioning, injecting, listening, wheeling, dialing, chestbeating, fetching, probing, and crying.

At the Hospital for Sick Children in that nine-month period, the cardiac arrest calls, six times the number normally experienced, all went out from the same ward. Three years earlier the hospital's executive director, J. Douglas Snedden, had warned the country that the pressure on nurses was becoming so great many had threatened to quit. At the time Snedden was responding to the fourteen-month revolt of eight hundred Vancouver General Hospital nurses, worn out by chronic staff shortages, who were creating a furor about hospital care on the coast. The nurses on cardiac ward 4A/B in Toronto did try to sound a similar alert. At a fall 1980 in-hospital conference on the baby deaths, they "identified the need for a more open communication between nursing staff and medical staff," expressing their frustration "that the medical staff did not trust nursing judgement." Like their colleagues in Vancouver, they were worried about the safety of their patients. But nobody listened.

Night supervisor Kathy Coulson was on duty for twenty of the twenty-seven baby deaths that occurred between 2:00 a.m and 4:00 a.m. She says she tried to make waves; she talked to as many people as she could, but she didn't know then how to make people listen to her. Nobody listened in Vancouver either, until the nurses there took their message to the street. Ignoring nurses seems to be the norm in Canadian hospitals. That's why, when Kevin Pascai died at the age of twenty-five days on March 12, 1981, staff nurse Susan Nelles was relieved when the coroner was finally notified. "Because now the doctors will listen to us when babies are really sick. Now, maybe they will come when we call them in the night," Nelles said, according to a police statement from her colleague Phyllis Trayner. Trayner told police she felt the same way.

Hospital officials *were* looking at the situation, insists the hospital's former director of nursing services, Anne Evans. But mortality and morbidity reports were hand-generated then and not correlated, not like the computerized reports they have now. "The nurses might have been dismissed," Evans acknowledges. "But, pardon me saying so, it could also be the way nurses presented it. Maybe they didn't have good facts to say, 'We have had twenty-eight deaths in six months and compared to this time last year, that's five times as many.' ... I think we all know a lot more than we did then."

The strain among nurses in all parts of the hospital that winter was palpable. There was a steady influx of inexperienced nurses, and the hospital's short-staffed intensive-care unit had to transfer patients out onto the wards too soon, leaving 4A/B nurses to cope with many more babies who were much sicker than usual. The baby deaths were as much a function of the nursing shortage as anything else, Coulson and four of the ward's other five senior nurses told CBC broadcaster Steve Wadhams in January 1985. In an interview for CBC-television's *Man Alive* that same month, Nelles said: "It's hard to describe to other nurses or to other medical people, let alone to people who have never been in that situation, the stress of looking after very ill babies. The stress ... is high anyway, and then you put death on top of that."

Nurses had been speaking of murder in hushed tones in the non-doctor section of the hospital's segregated cafeteria months before the police investigation began. They all "knew something was happening up on the cardiac ward because, for one thing, whenever there was an arrest, a nurse from the emergency had to go with the crash cart," recalls Deborah LeBaron, then an emergency room nurse.

The nurses' first reaction to the investigation was to try to help. Socialized to serve and used to conforming, they talked to police openly without seeing the need for protecting themselves. Evans says she was "wowed" by the homicide officers. "We were all slightly horrified that it could be murder, and so if they said to me, 'We need these records,' or 'We need to interview these people,' I said, 'Fine'."

But when police charged Susan Nelles with murder on March 25, 1981, the nurses were shocked. They felt betrayed by the paternalistic behaviour of hospital administrators. "I think it is interesting to see how an institution rises to that challenge or doesn't from the very beginning," says Carol Browne, a clinical nurse specialist on ward 4A/B at the time. "We asked and asked, 'What's going on? Help us know what is happening.' The hospital lawyer came in and patted us on the head like little children. What it came down to was defending ourselves as nurses, and we don't have a good track record of pulling together and supporting one another."

Everyone thought the hospital would protect its employees. It couldn't. That assumption, dubbed "employeeism" by N.K. Grand in a 1971 article on Nightingalism and nursing, is the flip side of paternalism. It is the attitude of a perennial child. "We were all so innocent then," Coulson says. "We were told the hospital lawyer would look after us. All I wanted to do was the right thing. I expected he would be with me while I was being interviewed by the police. And I didn't know any better. *I didn't know any better*."

Nelles had nowhere to turn for help. She was not a member of a trade union. The powerful 54,000-member Ontario Nurses' Association has tried, and failed, many times to organize the Hospital for Sick Children. Nelles had not joined the professional association, the Registered Nurses' Association of Ontario – Ontario is the only province in the country where membership in such an organization is not mandatory. When Nelles went to the RNAO for advice, they turned her away. "In all fairness, a nurse was charged with murder. It hadn't happened in our history before," says Diana Dick, an RNAO staff member at that time. "The association was severely criticized for not helping, but it was a brand new and very severe situation."

After five days under heavy guard in a segregated cell at the Metro West Detention Centre, Nelles was released on $50,000 surety put up by her parents. Her bail conditions said she must live with her family in Belleville, Ontario, and they prohibited her from talking with any members of her nursing team or from practising her profession. The financial burden of her defence was enormous. "We'd go into the lawyers' office and they'd say, 'Next week, we want $75,000,'" Nelles said in the *Man Alive* segment. "It just gave me a terrible feeling. Again, I had no control. I had no money. I had to totally depend on my father for that kind of support."

The forty-four-day preliminary hearing cost $104,850. Nelles sued former Ontario attorney-general Roy McMurtry, two of his prosecutors, and the Metro Toronto police, arguing that a proper investigation was not completed before the charges were placed. At best, police had spent thirteen days examining the evidence before they arrested Nelles; it was more likely as little as four. Three years later, Mr. Justice Samuel Grange exonerated the police. But many nurses, including the RNAO, still insist Nelles's assertive conduct towards the two policemen who arrived on her doorstep had more to do with her arrest than it should have. In a 1988 college term-paper LeBaron held Nelles up as the prototype of an "insurgent sister": "The fact that Nelles did not 'co-operate,' *as the rest of the nurses had done*, was seen as a strong indication of her guilt. Susan Nelles did not behave submissively, as befits a woman and a nurse, and thus, on a grand scale, she was labelled a troublemaker and a murderess." (My italics.)

Nelles's discharge on May 21, 1982, was a further blow to the equanimity of the hospital. The fact that there was insufficient evidence against her was disconcerting enough. Provincial court judge David Vanek then dropped a bombshell by establishing the cause of death as "deliberate massive overdoses of the heart drug digoxin." The hospital announced the decision as if it were a "national disaster," LeBaron says. With no tidy ending to the baby death mystery, the crisis continued for another four and a half years.

In the spring of 1983 the Royal Commission of Inquiry into Certain Deaths at the Hospital for Sick Children held the country spellbound for fifty days. In Toronto the drama played all day to the local cablevision audience. Some two years after Nelles's arrest, the inquiry put 42,039 nurses on trial, 39 from the hospital's cardiac ward and 42,000 from all across the province. On trial was the very act of nursing.

Cardiac ward nurses had already been placed under strict supervision: no new admissions; restrictions on transfers; digoxin, not a controlled drug, put under lock and key; staff nurses forbidden to administer it. When the inquiry opened, fifty lawyers sat behind rows and rows of tables piled high with papers: lawyers for the commission, for the attorney-general of Ontario, for the solicitor-general of Ontario, for the coroners, for the Crown attorneys, for the police, for the hospital, for the doctors, for the parents of the dead children, for the Canadian Civil Liberties Association, for the nursing assistants, for the ward clerks, for the registered nurses, for the RNAO, for Nelles, for Trayner. They all grilled the nurses: What drugs are "controlled" drugs? Where are they stored? How are they labelled? Who double-checks the dose? What are the chances for error? Why were nurses on the ward team fighting? Who resolves the conflict? What does a nurse do if the hospital policy tells her to do one thing and Ontario's standards of practice another? Why didn't they report the deaths? Why didn't Nelles cry when the babies died?

For the nurses, reduced to tears and sullenness on the witness stand, it was an identity crisis. They were being labelled unco-operative and incompetent, charged with changing their stories and withholding information to assist the accused. "It was so belittling," says Browne, the first nurse to testify and the highest-ranking of the fourteen Hospital for Sick Children nurse witnesses. Soft-spoken and slim, she tried adjusting herself to be nearer the microphone, but her voice still appeared unassuming, deferential, and very, very small, no match for Barry Percival, the merciless lawyer acting for the police. The legal representatives at the inquiry were not bound by standard rules of evidence. To Browne, "It felt like rape. We became public property. We were paranoid. We thought our phones were being tapped. We were afraid we would never find work again."

Coulson still remembers "the big guy," commission counsel Paul Lamek who is, in fact, huge. She could almost see the wheels turning in his head. On her last day of testimony she thought, "Dear God, you know and I know. I didn't do anything wrong. I didn't kill those kids." But she said the way Lamek was building up the case, "I felt it was like Perry Mason." Coulson strains to speak past the catch in her throat. The words, when she finally gets them out, are a passionate whisper. "The way he was building it up, I thought, 'He's going to accuse me of murder.'"

But Coulson wasn't going to let nursing down. At the Grange inquiry in front of 1.3 million people, she was not Kathy Coulson; she was up there for all of nursing. To this day, it is still a matter of pride for her that not once during the brutal four days on the witness stand did she cry.

The Grange inquiry's significance to the future of nursing in Canada was not as apparent then, even to nurses, as it later became. The RNAO did come to realize nurses and nursing had something important to lose and should be represented. But Canadian nursing leaders were also paranoid. Gail Paech, then president of the RNAO, remembers spending hours on the telephone talking to more than a hundred nursing managers and educators across the country looking for a nurse willing to try to qualify as an expert witness. When Paech reached Marian McGee, the associate dean of health sciences at the University of Ottawa, McGee refused. She said her field was public-health nursing, which gave her an expertise not likely to shine in an acute-care pediatrics inquiry. Alice Baumgart, then dean of nursing at Queen's University, phoned McGee back and told her nobody else would do it. Baumgart told her that Canadian nursing leaders were afraid, and McGee finally agreed. But then the commission had to be convinced of the need for such an expert.

On the surface, Paul Lamek's opposition was a rational argument against something illogical and unnecessary. The Hospital for Sick Children's practices were one thing, he said. But the commission need not be concerned with "general nursing matters, with the nursing profession, or with nursing practices in any way," he argued. "I have heard suggestions for months now that your report is going to change the face of nursing and nursing practices throughout this province .... That has always come to me as something of a surprise, as, no doubt, it has to you, sir." Mr. Justice Grange, as he revealed four days later, agreed. "If a nurse is arrested for drunken driving, is that a matter of concern for the Nurses' Association?" But nurses today suspect the legal objection was really a rejection of the whole idea of an expert nurse.

The inquiry had been going on for almost a year when Marian McGee, after many challenges, did win the right to testify as an expert on May 14, 1984. Nurses to this day are still stung by the way McGee was treated. She came across as the exact opposite of the typical nurse, who is everything feminine and womanly in her white uniform. McGee didn't look like a nurse. Outspoken and somewhat of a visionary, she didn't sound like a nurse.

She was crucified all the same, despite her thirty-one years of experience. When RNAO lawyer Fran Kitely tried to elicit McGee's expert opinion on nursing matters such as factors affecting a nursing team leader's memory or when it would be reasonable to assume a coroner would be called or if the nursing team should have been split up, she was thwarted at every turn. Mr. Justice Grange took to questioning McGee's qualifications: "You see this is a good question for a psychologist, I suppose, or a psychiatrist, but even those we don't allow in the court." He invited the other lawyers – Lamek, Lamek's associate, the hospital lawyer – to assist him in attacking her credibility. And they did.

The inquiry was an opportunity to expose the failings of the beleaguered Canadian hospital system. "System failure" is how McGee described it in her testimony. She was the only one of sixty-four witnesses to focus on the organization and conduct of nursing work. But by the time the public proceedings had captured the political spotlight, murder had far outstripped "system failure" in the public imagination.

"It was a hell of a lot easier for the Crown to charge some dumb kid with murder than it is to modify Sick Kids, I can tell you," McGee explains. "After all she is only a nurse. Thank God Susan Nelles, bless her heart, didn't behave like the passive little darling. No, she wasn't a dumb kid. She ended up being perfectly strong and intelligent." In the kitchen of her Ottawa home, McGee exudes a warmth and comfort that belie her public image. She takes more pride in Nelles's demeanour on the stand than she does in her own. "I decided when I was walking out of there, I wasn't aggressive enough," she says. "I was ashamed of myself for not being more aggressive."

Once Ontario nursing leaders saw nurses "being battered to death," the RNAO finally did get organized, Gail Paech recalls, and "took the road show out." Beth Symes, Fran Kitely, and Liz McIntyre, the trio of feminist lawyers hired to represent the RNAO and thirty-nine individual nurses, would get in their car at 5:00 p.m. and drive all over the province giving pep talks. They raised $400,000 for the legal costs. It was the first time in history nurses had ever done such a thing.

But the events leading up to and including the Grange commission scarred the thirty-nine cardiac ward nurses for life. The official investigation is not what has scarred them; they, too, want to know how the babies died. It's the way the inquiry was carried out. From the start, only nurses were treated as suspects. Metro police staff inspector David Boothby, former head of the homicide squad, suggested in an interview that mistaken or deliberate drug overdose is a common occurrence in Canadian hospitals, "where patients receive dosages they should not be receiving either by a mistake or to cover up from within. There is no doubt in my mind." Only nurses control access to addictive or potentially lethal drugs. It had to be a nurse, Mr. Justice Grange said, "It's almost impossible to conceive of anyone other than a nurse being responsible."

The Grange nurses are survivors, and like all survivors they still have the guilt, the trauma, the lack of satisfaction with the way they acted. They are tormented by the fact that no one – parents, hospital, nurses, or justice – has been served. Kathy Coulson appears to have fully recovered. Squeezed out of the nursing department after two wards merged, Coulson applied for other positions and was rejected. After finding a niche for herself in the research department, she hung on at the hospital for two years before resigning in the fall of 1985. Then she would have abandoned nursing for social work if friends had not made her sit down and talk. She decided to use the Grange experience as a catalyst and enrolled in graduate school.

"I've learned since then to be more political, to speak out, to make demands," she says. She never saw herself as a feminist; now she finds feminism is not as negative a term as she had thought. Looking back, she realizes nurses lacked credibility at the Grange inquiry because they are women. The experience is still very much part of Coulson's life, and she says it probably always will be. "It's still so terribly painful," she says, and although she is uncomfortable, now she isn't ashamed to cry. Five years after the inquiry into the mysterious deaths at the Hospital for Sick Children, the memory is still so fresh, the emotions still so intense, tears are rolling down her face.

The release of the Grange report on January 3, 1985, marked the national launching of nursing's age of awakening, as if from a hundred-year sleep. The report concluded that deliberate overdoses of the heart drug digoxin killed at least eight if not twenty-three babies. The suggestion that the drug overdoses were the result of error was "preposterous," Mr. Justice Grange said. "Accidents will happen, of course, even under the best regulated procedures, and they did happen in the administration of digoxin at the Hospital for Sick Children, as we have seen, but the theory of multiple, repeated, concentrated, fatal error must be rejected as untenable."

The judge also dealt summarily with the question of Nelles's arrest: "I think it is clear that staff sergeant [Jack] Press did not arrest Susan Nelles because she said she wanted to see a lawyer. He arrested her because of his previous high suspicion and because she gave him no explanation to allay that suspicion." The judge concluded his report by quoting from a remark made by defence counsel Austin Cooper to deputy Crown attorney Robert McGee after Nelles's discharge: "You did your job; I did mine. The police theirs: the judge his. *The system worked.*"

Hours later the RNAO held a news conference blasting the report for its single-minded preoccupation with murder. The male-dominated medical and legal system had treated nurses unfairly, the RNAO said, and that amounted to wholesale discrimination. Alice Baumgart, in a January 20, 1985 interview with *The Canadian Nurse* she is sure will be carved on her tombstone, called the Grange inquiry "the highest-priced, tax-supported sexual harassment exercise that we've ever witnessed."

Nurses all over the country soon realized they had to examine their rights. The Manitoba Organization of Nurses' Associations, renamed the Manitoba Nurses' Union in 1990, asked Nelles to come to Winnipeg to speak in May 1986. The nurses had thought they were protected as employees of the hospital, says the union's former communications officer Shirley Popadiuk, but that didn't turn out to be the case. Nurses have always been legally accountable for patient care.

Until the Grange, however, it was common for them to mini-
mize the extent of their own liability, deferring to the doctor
as the person ultimately responsible. The national press coverage of the arrest brought that "error in belief" to the attention of every nurse in Canada, says Winnipeg nurse and
lawyer Sherry Wiebe. In a chapter on legal issues in a new
nursing textbook, Wiebe writes: "Nurses across Canada have
personalized this ordeal [the Grange] as their own and have
raised a hue and cry for education and advice on legal matters." Most nursing unions now include liability insurance
with membership, and non-union nurses are being urged to
buy it through their professional associations. The 1985
Canadian Nurses Association code of ethics sets out a nurse's
first duty as being to her patient rather than to the doctor;
now she is required to challenge a medical order she deems
is inappropriate.

The Grange taught nurses that minute-by-minute charting
is their best defence. Hidden in the same lesson, says Marie
Campbell, a nurse systems consultant in Ottawa, is the knowledge that if there is a choice between documents and patient
care, it is dangerous to choose the latter. The hospital structure holds nurses responsible, accountable, and legally liable
for decisions they frequently have no authority to make.

The only remaining alternative is the same worn-out solution nurses have been using for more than a century: self-
doubt. They torment themselves. What else could I have
done? What could I have done differently? What if I had been
there at the time? "The nurses themselves believe they are
guilty," Campbell says. "They aren't where they are supposed
to be. They can't be. They can't be in two places at once."

The long and short of where Canadian nurses found themselves after the events at the Hospital for Sick Children was
the realization they do not have the power to enact their most
sacred commitment – the care of patients.

The six senior nurses on cardiac ward 4A/B – Browne,
Coulson, Bertha Bell, Elizabeth Radojewski, Mary Costello
Tynan, and Lynn Johnstone – formed a group after the
Grange. They arranged private therapy for themselves, they

met regularly, they did speaking engagements. They even started drafting a book.

Enraged by a September 1987 newspaper story describing the Grange nurses as "casualties," they decided to test their new-found ego strength. The front-page article listed several unidentified nurses who had attempted suicide, dropped deeper into drug and alcohol abuse, suffered a nervous breakdown, or been fired for administering the wrong drug as a consequence of the Grange. Browne, Coulson, Johnstone, Radojewski, Tynan, and Bell, at the centre of the crisis, said the story implicated them by not naming the nurses. The RNAO had no plans for action so they contacted their lawyer, took the reporter to the Ontario press council on their own, and won.

In the psychology of abused women, going public, pressing charges, making someone accountable for his actions: these represent an act of healing. That is exactly how Browne describes it. Taking the reporter to the press council was a turning point for them; they had proved they aren't passive victims after all. "I think there was health in our response," Browne says. "I want to tell you that prior to that, for whatever reasons, we didn't feel that we had the energy to respond. Or we thought that by responding, we made ourselves more vulnerable, or more visible, or whatever. So, that was really a positive thing for us to do."

The survivors of the Grange are, in many ways, even more committed to nursing now than they were before, even though their lives are haunted, especially those who have elected to stay in nursing. Trayner, who was transferred off the ward in 1981 and then forced to take a leave of absence, officially resigned the day the Grange report was released in January 1985. Still registered as a practising nurse with the College of Nurses of Ontario, she has dropped out of sight. The rumour is that she has had to change her name to continue to work in her profession.

Nelles agreed in October 1985 to accept $190,000 compensation from the province of Ontario and abandon her suit against the police. But as a matter of principle she went ahead with her suit against McMurtry and the two prosecutors, claiming a further $800,000 in damages. Although two Ontario courts gave the prosecutors absolute immunity, the Supreme Court of Canada overturned that decision, giving Nelles the right to continue. But neither the longest pre-trial hearing ever heard in the Canadian courts nor the subsequent Royal Commission inquiry into the baby deaths could commute the sentence already handed down. Nelles, who went back to Belleville to live with her husband and children, still waits in vain for police to clear her name.

No more than three of the fourteen Hospital for Sick Children nurse witnesses remain at the hospital, and one of those three, former ward 4B registered nursing assistant Meredith Frise, was working as an office manager in radiology. Nelles, after fighting to be reinstated in July 1983 following a forced leave of absence, stayed on until the fall of 1988, longer than almost any of the others.

That kind of turnover rate is not uncommon for any hospital, Evans says; lots of employees stay only a year or so. There was no concerted effort to get rid of nurses, says Nikki Rankin, one of four senior nurses who rotated through the top administrative position in nursing during the shake-up following the baby deaths. The nurses left of their own accord, she says. "If you were in that position and you were a nurse on that unit and you felt that you had given the best care that you could have given and that you did your best and that you were painted in a certain fashion, don't you think that you might want to start new in another area?" Rankin asks.

To this day, no one knows how or why the babies died. CBC journalist Steve Wadhams had speculated in 1985, "In five years' time, the knowledge of digoxin will be so much more advanced, the way it has been treated at the Grange inquiry will be a joke." Four years and three months after that prediction, scientists at a national news conference in Vancouver announced further research supporting the idea that certain immune reactions in sick infants can produce substances that imitate the drug digoxin and are easily mistaken for it. Maybe it wasn't a nurse after all.

Meanwhile, the nurses who survived the Grange have their own task at hand. "We all feel that there are a lot of things the profession should know," Carol Browne says. "There is a sadness through all this that people still want to compartmentalize the Grange. 'It's over here; it wouldn't happen to me.' We all have a wish to be naive and comfortable. We see it as anything but that.

"It's not paranoid to realize that no one is going to protect you. That's one of the messages we really hoped nurses would learn from the Grange. We don't think they have."

The Royal Commission of Inquiry into Certain Deaths at the Hospital for Sick Children was without precedent in its implications for nursing. It penetrated the veneer of the profession, exposing its unprotected centre and piercing it straight to the core. It was the point in history when the largest organized group of women in Canada lost their innocence. The Grange inquiry exposed how powerless they really were. Nurses across the country suddenly realized they were at the bottom of the totem pole and were being blamed without any examination of the health-care system itself.

But at the same time as the Grange telegrammed the increasing complexity of nursing to the country at large, the inquiry made it painfully apparent how little influence nurses have over what they do. Despite laws in every province of Canada allowing them to regulate themselves, they have no control over their own nursing practice. They lack self-esteem; they lack the status to command esteem from others; and they work in hospitals under conditions of terrible stress.

The RNAO's lawyers tried to get the commission to look at the management of the hospital and at the doctors. But Mr. Justice Grange deferred to an earlier report by a committee already appointed for that purpose. Chaired by Mr. Justice Charles Dubin, the committee had just released its findings in January 1983.

The Dubin report had been highly critical of the hospital. Singling out an inbred administration and a faulty reporting system, Dubin suggested sweeping changes. But his ninety-eight recommendations received little public attention. The RNAO put out a response as one of its in-house publications. Several downtown hospitals in Toronto made some internal changes. And although Dubin had made a point of extolling hospital nurses as providing "the single most important element in patient care," subsequent remedial measures taken by the Hospital for Sick Children did little to change the structural oppression of nurses there.

The RNAO waited two years after the Grange report to announce its response. The document came out with three recommendations reflecting longstanding RNAO positions: legislate nurses into policy-making positions on hospital boards, flatten the hospital hierarchy to bring nurses "on an equal plane" with doctors, and require all nurses entering the profession after the year 2000 to earn university degrees. A fourth recommendation, buried deep in the forty-two-page report, was quite out of keeping with the organization's traditional conservatism; it urged nurses to become aware of their complicity in promoting the negative image of nurses, which was simply a mirror reflection of the negative image of women.

The RNAO stated that nurses must begin to understand the politics of sexism that exists in the hospital bureaucracy and recognize they are not inherently inferior but have been so defined by the dominant culture. The way out is to develop a broad power base with women. Nursing education, practice, and research should facilitate this connection by introducing "feminist goals as the philosophical backdrop." Nurses must overcome their aversion to power.

It was Nelles's refusal to answer questions without the presence of her lawyer that the police officers zeroed in on as highly suspect, the RNAO said, despite the fact that such action would likely be accepted as par for the course for a man. Nelles also did not always cry when the babies died. Her stoicism was interpreted in court as showing a lack of feeling, an interpretation "steeped in sexual stereotyping . . . . Because Nelles showed other than the stereotypical female reaction to the deaths, she was viewed by the Crown as unfeeling, cold-hearted and, therefore, capable of murder."

The RNAO, which had dithered seriously before taking a pro-nurses stand, was not altogether unambiguous in its analysis. It did not choose to take on the doctors directly. But it did reflect the enormity of the Grange inquiry's impact by stating, "Nurses and nursing will never be the same."

The first conference on Canadian nursing history convened in Charlottetown, Prince Edward Island, in spring 1988. A group of nurses was listening to a paper, "Attitudes and Practices Towards Families at the Hospital for Sick Children from 1935 to 1975." Several were ex-alumnae of the Toronto hospital. At lunch, out of the blue, someone said: "Oh my God. No wonder the digoxin problem happened." The paper made no reference to the baby death epidemic. But its portrait of a rigid institution with all its double standards was immediately recognizable. "No wonder an institution with that kind of history couldn't respond," says Irene Goldstone, director of nursing at St. Paul's Hospital in Vancouver. "That's a study in itself. Look at that. Look at the Grange report."

The hospital organization is the real culprit of the Grange. Hospitals are monstrous bureaucracies that breed their own pathologies, Alice Baumgart says. The hospital structure supports an historical division of labour based on nurses in a subordinate role, with no separate and distinct professional identity. Employeeism was supposed to have gone by the wayside in the late 1950s with the emergence of collective bargaining for nurses, but the Grange inquiry illustrated that employeeism still flourishes. The message for nurses across the country: you can't rely on the institution to take care of you. "We have all had our eyes opened – we cannot let this happen again," acting editor Judith Banning wrote in a *Canadian Nurse* editorial in March 1985.

For the younger nurses who now comprise the bulk of the general-duty staff at hospitals around the country, Susan Nelles is no longer a household word. But the nurse from

Belleville succeeded in doing what nursing unions and professional associations had not. She shook 200,000 registered nurses by their shoulders, fanning an anger that had been smouldering for years. The Grange was not only an event that precipitated a crisis; it was a symptom of what lay underneath, a metaphor for systemic abuse. Susan Nelles, head buried in the back of a friend, cringing from the press the day she was indicted for murder, is still a national image in the nursing psyche. She represents the nurse who fought back. In that respect the RNAO was correct when it said "Nurses and nursing will never be the same."

But Gail Paech, now a consultant for Coopers & Lybrand in Toronto, is worried the lesson has not sunk in. "We rallied to the cause," she says, "and once the cause went away, we forgot what the essence of it was." Nurses' ability to work together to master the hospital system is the real lesson of the Grange, Paech says, a lesson that is still unlearned. Marian McGee, during her testimony, had suggested that "a forced self-examination of both the system and the discipline" would be the inquiry's *positive* effect on nursing. "An increased militancy on the part of nurses in their protection of themselves" was what she said would be its *negative* impact. Given the "tremendous area of responsibility that apparently exists," it is essential for nurses now to have more control, McGee told the inquiry. "Nurses are going to have to become more self-interested than they have been in the past. . . . In fact, we are going to have to address with more care what seems to be manifested as system failure."

During the two years from 1988 to 1990, more than two hundred cardiac operations were cancelled at the Hospital for Sick Children due to a shortage of intensive-care nurses; the high cost of living and the intense pressures drive nurses out of downtown Toronto. That exodus had reduced pediatric intensive-care beds to thirteen from the normal twenty-two. When there aren't enough cardiac intensive-care beds, too many too-sick patients must remain on the wards. The hospital, still the only major downtown hospital facility without a nurses' union, is raising the salaries of intensive-care nurses to try to keep them. "It's a lot like taking a bucket of water and throwing it on the Hagersville tire fire," Glenna Cole Slattery, the provincial union's chief executive officer, told the newspapers.

The original version of a nursing textbook co-edited by Alice Baumgart of Queen's University and Jenniece Larsen of the University of Manitoba devoted an entire chapter to the Grange inquiry, until the pair sent the galleys out for review. "Why on earth would you want to do this?" was the reaction. "What lessons are there in it for us?" Baumgart was amazed. There is, however, no Grange chapter. Nurses refuse to acknowledge their own history, says Phyllis Jensen, a contributor to the book.

Nurses must take collective action. Leaving the resolution of system failure to individual nurses does nothing to change the traditional medical and nursing authority relationship. The problem is how.

How will nurses begin to protect themselves – either by "increased militancy" or "forced self-examination" – if they don't acknowledge their own history? Many women work in occupations where responsibility greatly exceeds either prestige or rewards. But none of those occupations has a history like nursing. Without facing the source of nurses' oppression, even if it – like the Grange – is almost too painful to record, how is nursing ever going to grow up?

3

A New Sphere of Usefulness

Ask any nurse why she chose this high-stress, dangerous, low-paying, and often dirty job. Invariably she'll answer, "to help people."

"To nurse," from the Latin verb to nourish, is a commitment to stand by and be present through joy and pain, through sickness and health, through birth and old age, through death. That duty was at one time a woman's innate responsibility to her family, a labour of love for which she expected no earthly reward. It has since become the modern rationalization for a cheap labour force. In 1901, 100 per cent of the nurses in Canada were women; in 1989, 97 per cent of the nurses in Canada were women. Veteran nurses say the same kind of women entered nursing in 1989 as did a hundred years ago – "women who need to be needed." Nursing academics are now calling this centuries-old ethic the "compassion trap." The twentieth-century nurse's historical attachment to self-sacrifice is the key to understanding the current crisis.

In the early days, nursing was a calling. Pre-dating medical science by centuries, to nurse meant to care. When mothers, wives, and elder daughters were unavailable to fulfil this domestic obligation, members of the community, called "born" or "professed" nurses, came in to help, using the skills they had acquired in tending their own families. In Canada in the early seventeenth century, these self-taught lay nurses were assisted by the Roman Catholic nursing sisters trained in France. Cloistered nuns trained in strict monastic discipline and the concepts of Christian charity, the Catholic sisters founded Hôtel Dieu Hospital in the town of Quebec in 1639 and twenty years later took over the Hôtel Dieu Hospital in Montreal. As historian Abbé Casgrain pointed out, the "spirit of [their] vocation [was] the love of God.... Hospital work exacts of every nun that she sacrifice herself for the service of the sick poor."

In 1671 the hospital commissioners began to stop bringing in the French sisters, and by the end of the seventeenth century Canadian-born nuns outnumbered them. The first Canadian nursing order, the Grey Nuns, was formed in Montreal in 1738. Non-cloistered in the tradition of Vincent de Paul, Les Soeurs Grises visited the sick at home as well as caring for them in hospitals. They were the forerunners of the well-known visiting nurses established 150 years later as the Victorian Order of Nurses. Trained in the use of herbs and nutrition as well as in spiritual healing, the "Sister Doctors" began moving west after the battle of the Plains of Abraham in 1759, nursing settlers, soldiers, and Indians.

The French Catholic nursing tradition did little to forge a professional identity for nurses. But the French settlers of the sixteenth and seventeenth centuries fared better as hospital patients than the British who, according to John Gibbon and Mary Mathewson in their history of Canadian nursing, were left to the mercy of female volunteers because no one outside the religious sisterhoods trained nurses. The uneducated women, impoverished widows, immigrants, and domestic servants who took up the task were driven by need. The early hospitals – dirty and crowded facilities reserved for those unable to afford treatment at home – paid these "nurses" only room and board. Even then, the nurses often had to fight the sick for food and a place to sleep.

Enter Florence Nightingale, the wealthy British spinster who broke the bonds of upper-class Victorian womanhood to study in Germany. Seeing women in drawing rooms and country houses going mad "for want of something to do" prompted Nightingale to change the face of nursing throughout the English-speaking world. In those days a woman who chose nursing as a job was taking a revolutionary step. Nice girls did not become nurses; nursing for money was as disreputable as whoring. Nightingale's parents refused to let her train as a nurse, and she had to study in secret.

In 1854 Nightingale and thirty-eight other trained nurses were sent abroad by her friend Sidney Herbert, secretary of war in the British cabinet. The Crimean War was on and wounded soldiers were suffering in makeshift military hospitals behind the British lines. Nightingale's work, based on discipline, stamina, and skill, dramatically reduced the mortality rate from almost one-third to 2.2 per cent. By the time she returned home the Lady of the Lamp was a heroine to all Victorian women. Because she embodied the very heart of womanly virtue – courage, character, discipline – nursing became not only respectable but also romantic, even glamorous, an occupation for women capable of eliciting both deference and awe. As Susan Reverby writes in her synthetic history of American nursing, during Nightingale's time nursing not only provided a livelihood but was also a "virtuous state."

Nightingale, determined to make nursing a high-status profession for women, began raising money for training. There was an oversupply of middle-class women in Victorian England; many of them would never find men to marry; they needed some kind of meaningful work. "Mark what by breaking through customs and prejudices Miss Nightingale has effected for her sex," British Colonial Secretary Lord Stanley said in promoting the Nightingale Fund. "She has opened to them a new profession, a new sphere of usefulness." In 1860 Nightingale organized a training school for fifteen female probationers at St. Thomas' Hospital in London. It became the prototype for nursing schools throughout Britain, the United States, and Canada.

Philosophically too, Nightingale was a woman before her time. The holistic notion that humans and the environment form an inseparable unity dates from Florence Nightingale;

she challenged the prevailing belief that every disease must have a scientific cause. Committed to promoting health rather than simply nursing illness, Nightingale emphasized the total environment, and as a consequence medical intervention was not nearly as significant to her as care. It was not as an acquiescence to his larger talents that she left the task of cure in the hands of the male physician; nursing had more important things to do.

A division of labour based on gender presented no ideological problems for women living in nineteenth-century England; in fact, the "separation of the spheres" carried the weight of strict moral dictum. So it was not surprising that in the hospital, modelled on the Victorian home, there was little overlap between the medical arena, under the exclusive rule of men, and the *separate but equal* department of nursing services, governed by women. The essence of Nightingale's nursing reform was to take all power over nursing out of the hands of male physicians and administrators and put it into the hands of one female trained head. Thus would a strong female hierarchy become an invincible bulwark for nurses, ensuring they would never be exploited. Nightingale's nursing matrons were powerful women; in the smaller cottage hospitals, they did not have to answer to the administration, they *were* the administration.

The first school in North America founded on Nightingale's principles was New York City's Bellevue Training School for Nurses, established in 1873, followed closely by schools in Boston and New Haven. Many Canadian women went to the United States to study: some stayed on to play significant roles in the development of the nursing profession there; others came home to establish a similar network of Canadian training schools. The first, directed by two nurses who had trained in Britain under Nightingale, was the Mack Training School (named after its founder Dr. Theophilus Mack) established in 1874 at the Central and Marine Hospital in St. Catharines, Ontario. Its motto, "I See and I am Silent," became a watchword for nurses for the next hundred years. There nurses learned technical procedures by doing them, at the same time conveniently completing all the nursing tasks the hospital required.

The hospital-based schools, not very different in ambience from the earlier cloisters, achieved respectability by providing a decent place for unmarried women to live and by organizing nursing apprenticeships on a paramilitary structure designed to build character. The mandatory live-in arrangement provided a refuge from the dangers of fending for oneself, and the work offered good training for the domestic role expected of a woman if and when she married. The "ideal lady" transplanted from home to hospital was to show wifely obedience to the doctor and motherly self-devotion to the patient, Judi Coburn notes in her nursing history of Ontario. The family was the institutional model for the hospital-based schools, with student nurses, who were not to marry during their two to three years of training, acting as the elder sister. Susan Reverby points out that in 1917 the Chicago Hospital Association could comfortably declare: "Nurses in training are not employees in the sense that they are wage-earners. They are a part of the hospital family, and are cared for as a father cares for his children."

At the time when Nightingale reforms were having an impact on England and the United States, the public sector in Canada was small, and hospitals, funded by donations and municipal grants, were financially hard-pressed. Hospitals quickly realized the economic advantages of setting up their own schools, where students could be used as unpaid nurses. By 1909 there were seventy hospital-based schools for nurses in Canada. Recruitment was not a problem; Nightingalism was attractive. But gruelling working conditions, exhaustion, and illness meant the dropout rate was seldom less than 30 per cent and often as high as 40 per cent.

The regimen, according to Reverby, combined "the domestic order created by a good wife, the altruistic caring expressed by a good mother, and the self-discipline of a good soldier." The idea was to turn out virtuous women willing to serve as soldiers for humanity by nursing the destitute. Turn-of-the-century hospitals regarded the care of the "sick poor" as charity, and they treated their employees in the same paternalistic way. The nursing novices were indentured into apprenticeship, paid room, board, and ten dollars a month pin money, and awarded the supreme privilege of caring. Virtue was its own reward. Although the nursing reformers shocked society by insisting on medical instruction for the new nurses, lectures in anatomy, physiology, pathology, and nursing arts were thrown in at the end of twelve to nineteen hours of unpaid labour. Nurses' training was a bargain at the price; it was free. But calling it "an education" was a hoax.

The majority of the trained nursing graduates, 85 per cent of them before the year 1909, went out into the community and were paid directly by their patients as private-duty nurses, either in the home or in hospital. There they had to compete with the thousands of "professed" or practical untrained nurses. But at least they could control their practice in the same way doctors did, making their own decisions on which cases to accept for how long and establishing a professional contract with each of their clients.

But as medical care in hospitals grew in complexity, treatment at home came to be seen as risky. In the 1890s, medical science was overshadowing Nightingale's reliance on good care to promote healing. With new treatment methods, the age of technology had arrived, and hospitals rapidly turned into large corporate enterprises no longer reserved for the poor. Health care was becoming institutionalized.

The doctors who had staked out new territory now guarded it jealously. One attempt to close the gap between the home and hospital – the Victorian Order of Nurses set up in 1897 by Lady Aberdeen, the wife of the governor-general – was vigorously opposed by the Canadian Medical Association. According to Dorothy Pringle, a former VON director, groups of physicians from Halifax to Victoria "predicted dire consequences for the population receiving care from VON nurses, despite the fact that they all were fully trained nurses with additional preparation in midwifery and six months' training in district nursing." As a consequence, VON nurses were permitted to practise midwifery only in emergencies when a doctor could not be summoned. The "lobby and influence of the Ontario Medical Association was strong enough in 1897 to force the government to retract its earlier promise to provide substantial financial aid to the new organization," Pringle writes in a recent nursing text. Today, VON nurses work under far more restricted circumstances than their founders ever intended.

The growing hospital bureaucracy also got the better of Nightingale's nursing matrons. They soon had no choice in their financial negotiations with the new administration but to abandon the nurses below them. Nightingale had not trained nurses to be used as coolie labour; she had envisioned nursing schools as financially and administratively independent with their graduates commanding high wages in a free marketplace. She did not foresee her two-stream, separate-but-equal hospital hierarchy collapsing into one, leaving the matron, her invincible bulwark, to play a no-win game placating the doctors and buying the support of the administration by underfunding nursing services. The matron hung on as the head of her own department, but the doctor as "captain of the ship" commanded a much higher position. Progress in medical science put doctors in control of hospital work, reducing nurses to serving the new science.

A nursing authority structure with an independent power base might have protected the hospital nurses from some of the exploitation, Reverby writes. But the male-dominated family structure worked against them; becoming one of the family is *not* a positive image. Instead of growing into their own, hospital nurses took what the doctors gave them: the more routine and less intellectually demanding jobs, taking temperatures, changing dressings, and sitting up all night with critically ill patients. As medicine developed, caring was left to nurses because it was no longer considered important.

No one then could have predicted that the far-flung network of Nightingale-inspired nursing schools would turn into a warehousing system designed to indoctrinate handmaidens and process cheap labour; the perversion of Nightingale's vision of a separate *but equal* cadre of self-employed professional nurses has been called an "historical accident." Now Nightingalism, used interchangeably with the "compassion trap," is a pejorative. "Florence Nightingale may well be given the credit for establishing nursing as we know it – including low pay, long hours, and subservience to men," U.S. nurse Marlene Grissum writes.

Nightingale's famous prescription for nurses – "Every woman has, at one time or another of her life, charge of the personal health of somebody, whether child or invalid; in other words, every woman is a nurse" – is blamed for giving birth to the idea that nursing is simply a female instinct springing from the soul of every woman, trained or untrained, like Venus from the sea. In fact, Nightingale's *Notes on Nursing: What it is and What it is Not*, published in 1859 and designed "to give hints for thought" to women nursing their families at home, may be the foundation for a more inherently feminist ideology that, after 130 years of disparaging the value of caring, is only now coming home to rest. Florence Nightingale at least began with the premise that caring is the most important single ingredient in the delivery of health care. A creature of her time, she based the concept of caring on gender and the ideology of service. But she never once made the mistake of suggesting that nurturing was an inferior attribute of a weaker sex. Quite the opposite. Encouraged by proper training, discipline, and essential good character, feeding, bathing, coaching, and cajoling the sick was a *forte*, a skill of such intrinsic worth that no man could ever hope to master it completely.

In Canada the deplorable conditions in hospitals reached a crisis point at the turn of the century. The nurses were inexperienced and unsupervised students; the only licensed graduate nurses were the matrons. Administrators, facing an increasing call for support services for the new medical technology, were discovering that medical and surgical skills alone were not enough. They needed a large labour force to maintain the newly invented sanitary environment. And they realized expertise in disciplines such as nutrition-enhanced rehabilitation. Hospitals soon began to take a second look at the graduate nurses they had been throwing out onto the street.

Nursing leaders of the day were also worried about the quality of nursing care in hospitals, although their agenda was different. They were concerned with qualifications. But unlike Nightingale, who opposed registration in her determination to open nursing to all women of good character, nursing leaders were intent on consolidating. Commanding professional wage rates would be dependent on enforcing minimum standards and restricting entry. Nursing leaders, in short, had a vested interest in reducing the supply of graduate nurses rather than expanding it.

The institutionalization of health care at the end of the century had created two opposing needs – the need of hospitals to "proletarianize" a semi-skilled and cheap labour force and the need of nursing leaders to "professionalize" nursing into a skilled academic discipline with full professional status. The battle lines were drawn on three fronts: who could practise as a nurse, where she would be allowed to practise, and what she would be allowed to do.

Nursing leaders began their drive for control by pressing for registration and licensing. In 1908, representatives of sixteen nursing bodies met in Ottawa to form the Canadian National Association of Trained Nurses, renamed the Canadian Nurses Association in 1924, and officially incorporated as a federation of provincial registered nurses' associations in 1947. Because health in Canada is a provincial matter and a national association can only recommend standards, nursing associations had to be set up in the provinces. By 1924, nurses in every province had formed an organization committed to improving the status of nursing and to enforcing minimum standards of education. Professional associations were determined to mark the difference between those nurses who were trained and those who were not.

The first task was getting nursing regulations in place at the provincial level; it began with Nova Scotia's 1910 nursing

act and ended with Ontario's 1922 act. The long and dis-
heartening fight is still unfinished. Provincial governments,
involved in the financing of hospitals, had a vested interest in
preserving the existing economy of nursing. Doctors and hospital administrators argued that passing registration acts was
bound to reduce the already limited supply of nurses, and
there was concern that registration would exclude many fine
women from nursing.

As a result, the registration procedure established by legislation was voluntary. Although the laws identified the registered nurse as someone who had met accepted criteria, they
failed to prevent those who did not from working as nurses.
Nursing associations had no control over who called herself a
nurse, only over who could practise as a "registered nurse," a
symbolic title hospital employers were not required and often
preferred not to honour. The politicians believed employers
could impose enough restrictions on non-registered nurses
to ensure patient safety without jeopardizing their employment in the way that licensing would. And the practice laws in
no way reflected the real scope of nurses' work.

The nursing leaders had tried to establish a professional
monopoly in the same way doctors had forty years earlier. But
their success depended on a high level of co-operation from
governments. In the end they collapsed under the weight of
their own gender-based history; there was an unwillingness
not to allow any woman to work at nursing. Canada's licensing regulations have lagged behind those of the United
States, where mandatory licensing began in the state of New
York in 1935, more than a decade before Canada's first provinces, Newfoundland, Quebec, and Prince Edward Island,
passed mandatory statutes. In at least two provinces in Canada, professional associations have not succeeded in getting
regulations passed limiting who can use the title "nurse." In
Ontario, "physician" is still the only health-care provider
defined in the Health Disciplines Act. Ontario nurses have
been pressuring the government to change that situation
since 1921, and a commitment for protection was being
debated at Queen's Park in 1989.

Nursing's second task was improving education, a battle also still not won. In all provinces except Alberta, Ontario, and Quebec, the provincial nursing acts passed between 1910 and 1922 included requirements for admission to nursing schools and made provincial nurses' associations responsible for defining and maintaining standards. Ontario did not pass a law giving the professional nurses' association (The Registered Nurses' Association of Ontario) full power of admission and certification until 1951, eighty-two years after granting it to the Ontario Medical Association. Now the government-funded College of Nurses of Ontario, created in 1963 and responsible to the minister of health, has a contract with the Ministry of Colleges and Universities to monitor the diploma programs, and the Ontario region of the Canadian Association of University Schools of Nursing is in charge of the university programs. In Alberta, the Universities' Co-ordinating Council administers university nursing schools. The Quebec Ministry of Higher Education and Science has jurisdiction over the nursing programs in that province, although a mechanism for professional approval was being developed in 1989. In three provinces of Canada, nursing education is still not under nurses' control.

The first target for education reform was the hospital-based nursing schools. They were not the independent educational institutions Nightingale had intended, so incorporating them into the Canadian education system and subsidizing them with government funds was one of the most urgent recommendations of the Weir Report in 1932. Five years earlier a joint committee of the Canadian Medical Association and the CNA had appointed Dr. George Weir, professor and head of the University of British Columbia's education department, to conduct a national survey of nursing education. Weir called for sweeping changes, stressing the need for nurses to have a liberal as well as technical education and to end the disadvantages of being trained in a service-based setting. Nursing education in Canada, however, remained largely under hospital control for another forty-five years.

Despite the success of an independent Metropolitan Demonstrations School for Nursing established in Windsor, Ontario, in 1948, it was not until 1960 that a second independent
school, the Nightingale School of Nursing in Toronto, was
established. In 1965, over 95 per cent of Canadian nurses
received their initial preparation in hospital-based diploma
programs. In 1988, more than sixty-five years after the Weir
report, at least twenty hospital-based schools remained open.
Establishing other diploma-granting nursing schools in post-
secondary education settings did not begin in earnest until
the report of the Royal Commission on Health Services in
1964 which, in addition to promoting university nursing education, asked for the change in jurisdiction for the two-year to
three-year diploma programs. The "Ryerson Project" in 1964,
promoted by the RNAO, was the first diploma nursing education program at a post-secondary institution in Canada,
inspiring other programs to be set up outside hospitals.

In 1973 the government of Ontario announced that all
diploma schools of nursing in the province would come
under the wing of the Colleges of Applied Arts and Technology. In Quebec the same process occurred from 1967 to
1972, as hospital schools closed and the community colleges
(CEGEPS) began to offer nursing options. Saskatchewan
closed all hospital-based schools, locating diploma programs
in the rapidly expanding community college system. In New
Brunswick and Prince Edward Island, diploma nursing education became the responsibility of regional and independent schools, but in British Columbia, Alberta, Manitoba,
Nova Scotia, and Newfoundland, the transfer, still not complete, occurred piecemeal.

The administrative transfer, however, is not going to wipe
away a hundred years of living history. Nancy Nadalin
attended a two-year community college nursing program at
St. Clair College in Windsor from 1982 to 1984, doing her
practical training at the Hôtel Dieu Hospital in that city. She
says, "I was told during my training you must have your cap
on when you are in the hospital. That even included riding in
the elevator up to the floor. That kind of mentality, I found

very confining. The whole idea of it." Nadalin recalls having to say, "Yes doctor, no doctor." There was no encouragement of independent knowledge. The atmosphere was oppressive.

Her nursing instructors, who had trained fifteen to thirty years earlier at the hospital-based nursing school in the Roman Catholic hospital, used to speak of those days. They had gone into the regimented dormitories right out of high school, Nadalin says. "It was like entering a nunnery. They couldn't entertain men except on certain days." As recently as twenty years ago, nurses-in-training at some hospital-based schools could be expelled for getting married.

The first university-based nursing school opened at the University of British Columbia in 1919. But although five other universities started certificate courses in public health between 1920 and 1921, initiatives to establish a foothold for nursing education at universities did not get off the ground for another twenty years. The UBC prototype for university education for nurses, emulated by several Canadian universities, was a six-year non-integrated "sandwich" model: two years of university followed by twenty-eight to thirty-two months in an affiliated hospital school with a final year back at university. The program led to a diploma in nursing from the hospital school and a baccalaureate in the applied science of nursing. But the crust of the sandwich, university-controlled academics, had little do to with its filling, hospital-controlled service.

The first integrated baccalaureate nursing program in Canada, called "generic" or "basic," was not established until 1942 at the University of Toronto. The new feature of this thirty-nine-month program was independence; the faculty of the university, administratively separate from the hospital, would now assume responsibility for the student's education, prying her loose from staff service to be a true scholar.

The report of the 1964 Royal Commission on Health Services suggested that all "non-integrated" programs be eliminated and, in accordance with a 1957 Canadian Nurses Association position, recommended expanding university-based nursing education by promoting ten more "generic" programs. But the idea of basing all nursing education in universities by the year 2000, as the professional associations wish, is now one of the most explosive issues in nursing.

Meanwhile, the hospital administrators in the first decades of the century had their own agenda. With the hospital system expanding at a breakneck pace to accommodate advancing medical science, more nursing support service was an urgent need. They began a concerted campaign to woo graduate nurses back into hospitals with the promise of full-time salaried employment.

During the Depression, private-duty nurses had a hard time surviving. Most people were unable to afford nursing care, and only 60 per cent of graduate nurses (as opposed to an earlier 85 per cent) were able to find work in the community. On the other hand, giving up the one-to-one contract of private practice for assembly-line nursing on hospital wards was not an attractive option. Nursing leaders, anxious to define nursing tasks, and hospital administrators, only too happy to save money, held out the promise that registered nurses in hospitals would be reserved for professional work. Private-duty nurses had invariably been asked to substitute in the home as housekeepers or maids. Now hospital administrators were going to hire cheaper unskilled and semi-skilled subsidiary workers to do the more routine chores. The idea, in keeping with the economic theories of good management in fashion at the time, was to create a rigid hospital hierarchy in which the lesser-trained workers would be kept in lowly positions and registered nurses would climb to a higher administrative status. The workers taken on as nurses' aides were to be trained on site and supervised by the smaller group of graduate nurses.

The associations in charge of licensing and registration in the provinces monitored the new class of non-professional worker, taking care to keep the lesser-trained nurses outside the profession instead of including them by creating a secondary category. The rationale may have been to protect the public, but Judi Coburn suggests the newly formed nursing associations could "be accused of falling prey to that characteristic instinct of professionals, the desire to assert a monopoly in a field."

The reorganization of health care mounted by hospital administrators, government, doctors, and the nursing elite between the Depression and the Second World War was devastatingly successful; by 1943 only 29 per cent of the graduates remained in the community as self-employed entrepreneurs. The change in setting shattered nurses' commitment to care. As hospital employees they no longer controlled their relationship with the patient. Now nurses had three competing loyalties – the doctor whose orders they were required to implement, even though they were not his employees, the hospital administrators who employed them, and the nursing managers in charge of assigning and supervising their work. And the nursing team concept that had evolved to use the two different classes of nurses now fragmented the work of registered nurses even further.

The decision to transform a nurse from an independent contractor to an employee restricted the range of her duties and responsibilities. In fact, the move into hospitals marked the end of nursing independence. In 1986, 81 per cent of all Canadian nurses worked in institutions (hospitals, nursing homes, or homes for the aged); fewer than 10 per cent were employed in community health (clinics, schools, public health, visiting homecare); the remainder practised in doctors' offices, taught in community colleges and universities, or were self-employed. Less than 2 per cent of registered nurses in Canada in 1986 were in private practice; medicare does not pay for private-practice nursing. Professional status implies legally sanctioned autonomy. As employees working under close supervision, nurses came to be seen as a "semi-professional."

Indeed, before the institutionalization of health care in the early years of this century, nurses enjoyed more power, autonomy, and status than they ever have since. In a 1980 article David Wagner labelled the process of creating a nurs-

ing labour force the "proletarianization of nursing," stating
that it created an economic shock analagous to driving the
peasantry off the land to accept factory work in the eight-
eenth and nineteenth centuries in England. "Hospital nursing, stripped of its prestige from close association with
doctors and medical technology, bears strong similarities to
factory work," Wagner argues. Hospitals achieved a great deal
of their prosperity in the postwar years "through an organized rape on the nursing field."

The entry of government into Canadian health care in
1958 created an even more oppressive hospital bureaucracy.
National hospital insurance gave birth to a new hospital sub-
culture in which every hospital patient was a public patient
and every hospital nurse a civil servant. The move to less
than professional status was enhanced by the introduction of
medicare in 1966. With the coming of third-party payment,
there was no longer any way to measure how much each
nursing task was worth. Medicare essentially buried the value
of nursing services at the same time as it elevated the value of
doctors' services with an exclusive fee-for-service insurance
plan. The result was a nursing underclass in a hospital system in which the number of patient beds, the type of patient
occupying them, and the length of time they stayed was controlled by doctors. Nursing departments were not administratively distinct; doctors as gatekeepers made decisions based
on medical science rather than on the moral values of the
former charitable institutions; and hospital trustees kept the
public trust in name only since most hospital policies had to
be based on money.

National health insurance made the hospital system more
cumbersome to administer without easing the financial pressure. Because nurses now depended on government funds to
pay their salaries, higher wages for nurses would require tacit
government approval. And with government involved in hospital funding, the traditional two-way wage consultation
would no longer suffice. Government insurance increased
the significance of union activity in Canadian hospitals.

Labour disputes had erupted sporadically among nurses in

Canada, in Montreal in 1878 and in Newfoundland in 1931. But self-employed nurses had no common employer; it wasn't until postwar nurses became employees that they began to realize they had an interest in taking collective action. Medical associations had been able to improve working conditions for doctors as self-employed professionals without resorting to trade unions. But nurses' associations were not going to have the clout to protect registered nurses in their new employee status. The professional associations had failed to remove nursing education from hospitals; they had failed to distinguish professional nurses from the new non-professional nurses' aides; the associations had failed to limit the massive government-financed immigration of nurses launched after the war. And in 1941, the average salary of a hospital nurse was less than a female factory worker's.

The Canadian Nurses Association had condoned collective bargaining for nurses in 1944 only if it were done by nurses using the provincial professional association as the agent. In 1956 the CNA issued an anti-strike policy, condemning any nurse for taking any strike action for any cause, a stand so contested it was repealed in 1972. While the Ordre des Infirmières et Infirmiers du Québec was the only provincial professional association to set out a formal anti-strike policy (still in effect), the professional associations in other provinces resisted the "shop-floor culture" that treated nursing as a job rather than as a profession. Professional associations endeavoured to prevent massive unionization among nurses by adopting a cautious and circumscribed collective bargaining function themselves.

The first group of nurses to negotiate an employment contract, in 1939, did so through a professional organization formed by a nursing sister in Quebec City. But when a group of French nurses in Montreal asked the provincial professional association for help in bargaining, they were turned down. The francophone nurses turned to the Quebec Federation of Labour and in 1946 founded the first true nurses' union in Canada, the Nursing Alliance of Montreal, which later became the Federation des Infirmières et Infirmiers du

Québec, still the most politicized and militant group of nurses in the province, if not the country. In 1945 the Registered Nurses Association of British Columbia, fearing that nurses would affiliate with the trade unions organizing other hospital employees, became the first professional association to apply successfully for certification as a bargaining agent under a labour relations act.

Professional nurses' associations in the rest of the country did not formally establish a collective bargaining function for another twenty years. Because the postwar labour laws in provinces outside of British Columbia did not extend to nurses, the professional associations continued their low-key collective bargaining function, publishing a non-binding annual personnel policy suggesting optimal salary levels and improvements in working conditions. It wasn't until the early 1960s that they organized, forming employment-relations committees to advise nurses on salary increments and standard hours of work, training staff nurses in collective bargaining, and setting up the agency staff associations that eventually became the bargaining units certified under new provincial labour acts.

The writing was on the wall, however, even before the Supreme Court of Canada ruled in 1973 that professional associations could no longer act as bargaining agents for nurses. The legal issue had surfaced when the Service Employees International Union challenged the right of the Saskatchewan Registered Nurses' Association to apply for certification as a bargaining agent. But rank-and-file registered nurses, already alienated by registration, were having problems with their associations. They wanted to improve their wages and working conditions, yet the bargaining group they belonged to also represented the management nurses who hired and fired them. The legal ruling escalated a separation that had really begun fifty years earlier.

In some provinces the move was bitter, with staff nurses storming out of association committee rooms, taking their cartons of files and staff people with them. Ontario nurses had enough trouble dealing with a binding arbitration law

passed in 1965; when the 103 independent staff-nurses' bargaining units merged to form the Ontario Nurses' Association in 1975, relations with the professional association were
amicable. The RNAO had given up its licensing authority in
1963 when the government formed the College of Nurses of
Ontario, and depended solely on voluntary membership. But
the Supreme Court ruling made it impossible for professional
associations to continue bargaining for nurse employees;
they needed a trade union.

The trade unions that separated from the nurses' organizations in each province were, like the parent groups, made up
entirely of registered nurses. Small pockets of registered
nurses, especially in Quebec, had been organized by health-
care trade unions; registered nurses working for government
in public health or in correctional institutions had to belong
to government employee unions; a rival nurses' union organized RNs at provincially run hospitals in Alberta; and nurses
teaching at the university level joined faculty associations. But
the majority of unionized nurses in Canada came to be members of a provincial nurses' union.

The last provinces to spawn such a union, British Columbia and Prince Edward Island, did so in 1981, the same year
an umbrella group, the National Federation of Nurses'
Unions, was born in Winnipeg, and the new regroupment of
three nurses' unions was formed in Quebec. By that year,
over 75 per cent of active nurses in Canada were union members, with the highest number, 84 per cent, in Manitoba and
the lowest, 57 per cent, in Ontario. Their numbers now
include most hospital nurses below the rank of head nurse,
some public-health nurses, and nurses employed in government-run clinics. They do not include nurses working in
private clinics or in doctors' offices. In all provinces except
Ontario, to be licensed to practise these unionized nurses
are also required to pay membership in the provincial professional association – thereby creating a financial overlap in
which tension is inevitable.

4

System Failure

Nursing supply and demand, always characterized by cyclical ups and downs, has reached a critical turning point in its hundred-year history. Until now the economy has effectively controlled the numbers of nurses, and hospitals and nursing schools, dependent on government funds, have simply budgeted full-time nursing equivalents and nursing school spaces accordingly. Whenever supply dipped too low, governments managed the short-term crisis by jiggling the enrolments, and hospitals would temporarily close beds and tap into the facility's "on call" supply pool: permanent part-time nurses or day-to-day "casuals" kept standing by to fill in as needed. The hospital system has banked on the fact that nurses want to help people.

But when bed closures are frequent and excessive, when nurses are chronically overworked, and when hospitals are receiving too many poor safety reports too close together, it is clear the nursing shortage is one the system isn't able to manage. These are the tell-tale signs that today's crisis is more pervasive and more permanent than any before.

A lack of money to pay nurses is not the new supply problem. Hospital administrations have had to conserve funds ever since the institutions were built. Today's hospitals continue to be strapped for money. They face constant demands for more equipment, more operating room space, more beds, and many of them have developed these medical services beyond their financial capacity. In the past ten years, Ontario hospitals' share of the province's allotment for health care has shrunk from 52 to 44 per cent. This decrease does not affect doctors' income; while doctors' billings are part of the overall cost of health care, they are paid for by the provincial insurance plan. Between 40 and 50 per cent of that dwindling budget in every hospital in Canada, however, must be set aside to pay the wages of registered nurses, orderlies, aides, and registered nursing assistants. The quickest way for hospitals to expand their medical programs, and some are still erecting the buildings to do so, is obvious: control salaries. The hospital system has always depended on inexpensive labour. And it still does. By artificially depressing nurses' wages, province-wide hospital rates have eliminated the necessity for free-market competition.

By confining and controlling the labour supply in this way, hospitals have been able to use a "variable" nursing workforce to be expanded or contracted as required. Women could be counted on to enter easily and exit early, with no aspirations other than to pass the time until they married. Many of them would also jump at the chance to work part-time, and nurses working part-time were more economical. They earned a pro-rated salary considerably less than full-time workers, with little access to benefits. Statistically they proved to be less tired, less sick, and less burned out. The variable method started out as a reasonable approach to around-the-clock staffing.

But the traditional "captured labour market" is no longer working. Now study after government study is trying to figure out a way to cultivate full-time career nurses. One British Columbia report recommended decreasing the casual ratio, "where the greatest degree of movement occurs," and increasing full-time and part-time components by 5 per cent, working them longer hours if necessary. The 1988 study said, rather drily, that the registered nurse workforce can "no longer be considered an 'inexhaustible resource' by the pool of hospital employers in the province."

That is the new problem in nursing supply. Women today aren't as willing to begin, or stay in, a job with such limited salary and career potential. The "appliance nurse" who filled in a few shifts a week to buy a dishwasher is now a relic. The nurses who used to be satisfied with waiting to be called in at any time now have other options. The ones who still want day-to-day work can register at a private agency, where they are not only paid more but where they can also choose shift times and type of nursing. Agency nurses are expensive. And because the hospital's on-call nurses are now working less than if they had been put on the regular schedule, even they are no longer economical.

Governments used to be able to turn out nurses like widgets, turning the tap on and off at will. Doctors were in short supply in the mid-1970s, so they set up nurse-practitioner programs in universities to ease the strain. As soon as doctors became more plentiful, the courses were withdrawn. When Ontario's health minister, Frank Miller, proclaimed a surplus of nurses in 1976, spaces in community colleges were cancelled. Now they can't get enough people to fill them. "Three years after the surplus, they said there was a shortage. There never was a surplus; let me make that very, very clear," says Anne Gribben, chief executive officer of the Ontario Nurses' Association for the twenty years prior to 1986. "There is a lack of funding but there has never been a surplus of nurses. It was an artificial surplus."

Words like surplus and shortage are taking on an increasingly political connotation. An unmanageable shortage of neonatologists in 1986 prompted Ontario to start turning out clinical nurse specialists trained to do more or less the same work as residents in neonatology. If and when that specialty becomes more popular among medical students, the nurses with that status will likely be as expendable as the nurse practitioners now are. Time is running out on this kind of manipulation. Enrolment in nursing diploma schools is holding steady in some provinces; in others, the bottom is dropping out. Regardless of numbers, educators are acknowledging the declining quality of applicants. It is unlikely that

Canadian universities can provide enough new spaces – a minimum estimate of 9,000 to 10,000 nurses a year – to meet the demand in the next twenty years, even if the women could be found to fill them, which is equally unlikely.

With the entire industrialized world facing the same crisis, importing nurses is not an alternative. In addition to the difficulties presented by Canadian immigration laws and unacceptable education standards, foreign nurses are now being encouraged to stay home. And Canadian nurses are being courted abroad. The Canada-U.S. free trade agreement now makes it easier for nurses to get temporary work visas in the United States, where private multi-million-dollar health-care businesses offer annual salaries 33 per cent higher, night shift differentials as high as five dollars a shift (Ontario hospitals pay their night nurses an extra forty cents), subsidized accommodation, and fully paid tuition.

The attempt to create a continuous and managable supply of nurses has backfired. Facing a crunch in recruiting and keeping nurses, hospitals are breaking ranks. Toronto's Hospital for Sick Children, where RNs do not belong to the provincial nurses' union, is offering intensive-care nurses a $10,000 annual bonus. Nursing agencies, brokering for the nurses on their registries, are also creating a wedge in salary controls. Pay-equity negotiations in Ontario are threatening to blow apart that province's uniform wage rates. Full-time career nurses, now in high demand, are pressing unions to become more militant.

This urgent demand for nurses is probably even more significant than the dwindling supply. Doctors, encouraged by the lifesaving potential of the new technology, are admitting more acutely ill patients to hospital, people they would likely have given up on years ago. "Every empty bed is an insult to the profession," says Dr. Trevor Hancock, now at York University but formerly with the Toronto public-health department. A doctor wears the hospital size and the sophistication of its high-priced equipment on his sleeve. "It's like flashing," explains Lorine Besel, vice-president of nursing at Montreal's Royal Victoria Hospital. "I have a 600-bed hospital. I have an 800-bed hospital," Besel mimics, opening her arms out like an accordion. "That's what these men are like."

Some U.S. insurance plans have tried awarding bonuses to doctors for *not* doing surgery. But Canadian medical insurance continues to give doctors a licence to print money. While the hospitals' share of the provincial health-care budget has decreased during the last decade, the Ontario medical-insurance plan's portion (92 per cent of which goes directly to doctors) has climbed to 32 per cent from 24 per cent. Trevor Hancock suggests the only way the system can expect to reduce the number of hospital beds is by literally chopping them up and throwing them out the window. As former federal minister of health Monique Bégin told the Canadian Hospital Association's annual meeting in June 1988: "The biggest single force driving the entire health-care system in our country, and in the industrialized world in general, is modern medicine itself as a science growing at an exponential rate, supported by constant technological developments and by pharmaceutical discoveries. You may think that you are running your hospital, that you are in charge.... But you are not."

Frances Picherack, former policy analyst for the College of Nurses of Ontario, calls the assumption that every medical service must be right and good "the provider ethic." Doctors race to give everyone equal access to the same high-tech care without assessing if the patients really need it, she says, and nurses are not far behind them. The provider ethic created by national health insurance and new expectations for a longer life supports the use of high-tech heroics. "Gimme my transplant. Gimme my dialysis," is the way Lorine Besel describes the current consumer mentality. "The pressure is to save lives rather than help you through it, and nurses are getting sucked into that more than we want to be."

Instead of treating more people, hospitals are "overservicing" the same number of people too intensely. The patients who a few years ago would have died now live out of a tube;

those who used to be in the intensive-care unit are now out in the general surgical unit; those who used to be in the general surgical area are now out on the street, and more and more critical-care nursing needs to be done. The number of full-time equivalent RNs needed for every hospital bed in Canada rose by 36 per cent from 1981 to 1986. Health-care policy analysts are predicting that every general hospital in Canada in the year 2000 will resemble one big intensive-care unit. With unfettered control to admit patients and the exclusive opportunity to profit from them, doctors are "hot bedding" patients in and out of hospital as fast as possible, creating a short-term in-hospital population that is much sicker than it has ever been before. What used to be a 33 per cent proportion of severely ill patients in hospital now is close to 90 per cent.

The new technology not only requires more nurses but also more specialty nurses with expensive on-the-job training. Soon all information from patients, laboratories, radiology, and chest x-rays will be on line in an electronic chart. If a nursing department maintains a turnover rate of 20 per cent, and if the in-service computer and other specialty training continues to take each nurse twenty to forty hours, it will cost one hospital an additional $20,000 a month to maintain a 500-member nursing staff. Soon hospitals will not be able to afford to teach nurses at all.

The 1988 Medicus Systems Corporation report on Toronto's Wellesley Hospital illustrates the unmanageable growth plaguing Canada's beleaguered hospital system. While the number of patients remained the same between 1981 and 1986, there was a staggering increase in the resources being marshalled for each patient: a 72 per cent hike in salaries, a 110 per cent increase in expenditures for medical and surgical supplies, a 165 per cent increase in funding for the expanded programs, and a 63 per cent increase in staff benefits.

Doctors introduced procedures without making sure nurses knew how to use the equipment and without accounting for their effect on the nursing workload. In the four years between 1983 and 1987, the use of agency nurses increased by 18 per cent. The financial impact of the climb was much higher: in 1987–88, hours for agency nurses, whose salaries rose from sixteen cents an hour *less* than full-time staff nurses in 1983 to $5.10 an hour *more* than staff nurses in 1987, cost the hospital $472,000 more than the same number of nursing hours performed by nursing staff. By the end of January 1988, doctors' orders for one-to-one nursing care, executed without any apparent criteria, had reached a total of 79,542 hours, four times higher than expected.

The report did blame irrational inequities in the Ontario government's hospital funding process. But it also castigated the downtown Toronto hospital for bad planning, unbudgeted expansion, and gross mismanagement. In-patient nursing was singled out as the area in which the most money could be saved. Turnover rates as high as 48 per cent in some units and the uncontrolled growth of special-care nursing made it necessary for expensive agency nurses to fill in the gaps, the report said, with the high payment to agency nurses compounding the dissatisfaction of the regular full-time nursing staff.

The report revealed that the hospital provided only one housekeeper to do urgent clean-ups for the entire institution at night, that doctors were unwilling to spend enough time training residents and interns, and that nurses had to give that kind of instruction. On one unit, 33 to 50 per cent of the patients were long-term-care patients awaiting placement rather than the acute-care patients nurses had been trained to tend. The high staff turnover, estimated in 1981 to cost hospitals $3,000 a nurse, forced new nursing graduates to perform tasks without the proper certification, since "every new gismo and pump needs someone who knows how to maintain it."

The list went on. Nursing administrators did not have enough authority, the report said. Absentee doctors left nurses to make medical decisions, including how long patients were to stay in hospital. Closed beds reopened without enough notice. Nursing administrators were unwilling to jeopardize their relationship with doctors by documenting such incidents.

Virginia Sinnott, the vice-president of nursing at Wellesley, says corrective action has already been taken and that Medicus turned up similar deficiencies in other Ontario hospitals. Wellesley staff doctors with big plans for technical procedures are now being sent back to find the money for the equipment in their own departments, Sinnott says. Special-nursing hours at the Wellesley have been cut by 25 per cent by closing beds in the intensive-care unit, so that the hospital's sickest patients are no longer sent out to the care of inexperienced nurses on the floor. In other words, fewer sick patients requiring high-intensity care are being admitted to the Wellesley Hospital, presumably leaving them for another understaffed institution to manage.

When nursing shortages reach a certain level, hospitals say they close beds to maintain a safe level of care. They don't say what that level is, on what criteria it is based, and who decides which beds should be closed. Mount Sinai Hospital nurses in Toronto tried to get beds shut down in February 1976. Three nurses on the night shift refused to admit a critically ill patient because they thought the intensive-care unit was already overburdened with too many too-sick patients. Doctors had to take care of the patient, and the nurses, disciplined as insubordinate employees, were suspended without pay for three days.

The message: doctors control patient admissions and nurses are hospital employees who must obey first and grieve later. The unions' "obey and grieve" remedy is only a way to fight disciplinary penalties against the nurse; filing a grievance does nothing to correct unsafe staffing quotas. Hospitals rarely point out that bed closures are often an administrative tactic to control costs. The Moncton Hospital closed beds in 1989 just to save enough money to get beyond the end of the fiscal accounting period. It reopened them six months later.

Meanwhile, the nursing problem is being ignored rather than solved. Wellesley Hospital nurses are furious at Medicus for calling the nursing department on the carpet instead of blaming doctors for expanding programs. They say any changes accepted by the hospital focus on saving money rather than on patient safety. What the budgeted shortage of nurses amounts to, in effect, is mediocre care, which is even more demoralizing for nurses than overwork. While Virginia Sinnott won't go so far as to say hospitals are no longer safe, she has no problem stating that there now is a "much higher potential for risk."

Anne Gribben is not as cautious. Gribben put her foot down at the Ottawa Civic Hospital a few years back. The director of nursing tried to persuade her to allow the operating-room nurses to violate their contract by working longer hours on coronary bypass operations, but Gribben refused. They were "asking me to allow that nurse there to start scrubbing at 7:20 a.m. I'm not sure whether you are going to put a catheter in her so that she can piddle because she is not going to be able to unscrub. And you want her to do two bypasses of five to six hours each. That's going to be ten hours of standing, feeding her a sandwich, while one patient goes off the table. Let me be the 8 o'clock operation, thank you very much, not the 2:30."

Dianne Simms, nursing director at the Curtis Memorial Hospital in St. Anthony, Newfoundland, describes patients coming in from St. John's hospitals with their toenails uncut, with dirt between their toes, and no skin care. Nurses in Montreal, spooked by a 1988 hospital fire, still go into work at night praying. Some of them, women weighing little more than a hundred pounds, are all alone on a floor with totally incapacitated patients, some weighing as much as two hundred pounds. Although there is supposed to be a fire plan, they couldn't get the patients out if they tried. Mavis McKenzie, a nurse for thirty years, believes hospital practices at York-Finch General Hospital in Toronto hastened the death of her eighty-one-year-old father, Arnold McKenzie, of bronchial pneumonia and pulmonary embolism in May 1989. McKenzie saw her father strapped into a hospital bed with a canvas and mesh restraining jacket for the six days leading up to his death, and she claims he was given the wrong intravenous medicine and was improperly monitored. The family was concerned enough to get an inquest ordered. Many of today's nurses are choosing to nurse loved ones themselves rather than leave them in the care of the system.

Because of the nature of the work they do, nurses are the first to feel the negative effects of the Band-Aid strategies now being used to cover over the financial wounds in the failing hospital system. Government cutbacks and hospital bed closures control the shortage only temporarily. While politicians and hospital administrators, reluctant to decide who will live and who will die, toy with the prospect of rationing the number of patients doctors can bring into the system or of limiting how much high-tech surgery will be available at public expense, only patients and nurses understand the crux of the matter: that nursing care, "the single most important element in patient care," has been rationed for years.

Hospitals spent almost thirty years developing a formula to "ration" nurses. Before 1966 they depended simply on patient volume and the global standard of care established in the mid-1940s. The fixed nurse-patient ratio was arrived at by multiplying the number of occupied beds by that standard – 3.5 hours per patient per day. The head nurse would sometimes alter the numbers slightly based on her intuitive assessment. But as the science of medicine grew in sophistication, health-care administrators began to have some concerns about the subjectivity and imprecision of these methods. The global average of 3.5 hours had a better chance of being correct when spread over a hospital stay that included not only acute care but also a few weeks' recuperation. That was no longer the case. Even more important, rising costs of medical treatment made it impractical to continue supplying nurses according to patient demand.

So in the late 1960s North American studies came up with a more scientific and objective tool for *predicting* how many nurses would be needed, and now well over a dozen private consulting firms are marketing patient classification systems. Operating on the principle that some patients need more care than others, the idea is to get nurses to group patients in clusters according to some quantifiable standard of measurement. Using categories like personal care, nutrition, level of activity, teaching and emotional support, treatment and observation, the bedside nurse assesses the level of nursing task required, assigns it the numerical value indicated by the commercial classification system in use at her hospital, and adding up the numbers, classifies the patient into one of four or five standard types, ranging from the least amount of nursing care required to constant nursing care. The head nurse then uses the hospital's budgeted time-conversion formula, "target hours" representing the average or standard care time per patient per day the administration has *predetermined* for each class, to come up with the magic number of nurses to staff the unit over the next twenty-four hours.

Target hours *pre-set* at 2.80 (.70 hours *less* than what the Alberta Association of Registered Nurses called the "inappropriate and irresponsible" global standard) for Ward 9Y East at the Edmonton General Hospital on January 10, 1989, yielded a recommended staff of 9.2 RNs and 2.4 RNAS over twenty-four hours. That was for thirteen patients with an expected acute-care level of 2.43 to 2.97. On any given day, the staff level on a ward may have to be "topped off," either with a hospital "float," with a permanent part-time staff member, or with a nurse from the hospital's "casual" pool of temporary part-time nurses. The new "controlled variable staffing" system diminished the need for a full-time workforce at the same time as it increased dependence on part-time nurses. The United Nurses of Alberta calls these in-and-out employees "technical machines."

Patient classification systems measure the severity of illness by using medical diagnoses. Unfortunately, that diagnosis often does not reflect the intensity of the demands the patient makes on nursing time. Pre-established indicators of care are also unreliable in accounting for non-direct nursing tasks like filling in charts, briefing the doctor, teaching, counselling, explaining side-effects of drugs, or comforting a family member. They make no allowances for the varying levels of professional skill each nurse brings to the bedside or for how a patient's medical condition changes during the twenty-four-hour period. And while the predetermined target hours are supposed to fit the real nursing needs of the ward, they are often adjusted to what the hospital can afford, speeding up the nurses much in the same way as a manufacturer might turn up the pace on a parts assembly line.

"Things got much worse in 1983 and 1984 when they decreased the target hours because of the budget," explains Laverne Gallagher, a nurse at University Hospital's cardiology ward in Edmonton. "They went down to the bare bones and then we saw a lot more nurses dissatisfied working. That's when professional-responsibility committees started coming in. The patient complaints rose dramatically during that period. There just wasn't the staff there to deliver the care." Target hours at the Edmonton hospital have since increased but to a level lower than before the cutbacks. Because nursing labour is the hospital budget's most expensive single item, it stands to reason nursing time will be the first place to cut costs.

Provincial governments are not allowed to control hospitals directly, but money transfers and hospital accreditation give governments an opportunity to make hospitals demonstrate effective management: many of them do so by "encouraging" the use of a commercial classification system. "Our government in Ontario says we must have them," says Virginia Sinnott, who thinks the systems are a farce. " 'There is no such thing as acuity of illness.' That's what they say. But there isn't a head nurse in any hospital across this country, and I am a surveyor across the country, that can't eyeball her patients and say, 'I need five staff or I need eight.' They know it in their gut."

Patient classification systems provide an empirical rationale for a desperately practical decision: meeting patients' nursing needs in Canadian hospitals today is just too expensive. In displacing the nurse's working knowledge of the patient, the standardized formula may not be providing a scientific basis for what is *actually* needed as much as justifying the hospital's *expected* level of production in terms of cost-efficiency. The best way to save money is to ration nurses' time, forcing them to give fewer and fewer services to more and more patients faster and faster.

Hospital nurses now are being asked to "prioritize" their tasks to eliminate any unnecessary or wasted action, and "prioritize" in the jargon on the floor is just another word for unpaid overtime. "You always have to do what is needed and do the polishing later," explains Linda Silas Martin of Moncton, New Brunswick. "It's always like an emergency, even on the floors." Having to choose between what is necessary and what is extra care means leaving one person unattended to look after another. Or skipping a lunch break, or putting hospital schedules and doctors' orders ahead of one's better judgement.

In its brief to the Premier's commission on future health care in the province, the United Nurses of Alberta blames patient classification systems for entrenching temporary staff shortages to the extent that they have become chronic. Union objections to these workload measurements contributed to the UNA's illegal nurses' strike in 1988. In 1980 three nurses' unions in Quebec staged a province-wide boycott of the Project for Research in Nursing (PRN) classification system (developed in that province in 1974) on the grounds that it negated the patient-nurse relationship. The bedside nurses refused to fill out the forms. Ottawa consultant Marie Campbell, a nurse with a sociology PhD based on an analysis of patient classification systems, maintains they are a "management invasion of the control previously exercised by nurses." The systems have replaced individual professional discretion with mechanized work in which every step is task-directed, she says. Vice-president of nursing Inge Schamborzki has discontinued using the Medicus system at the Vancouver General Hospital in favour of a "more qualitative measure."

The workload measurements may have "gone overboard," admits University of Alberta nursing professor Phyllis

Giovannetti, whose research helped get the systems started in Canada. The "ample evidence that they are not suiting their intended purpose" is not the fault of the system but of the way administrators, fiddling with the numbers to make them conform to the budget, have misused the measurements, she says. Bedside nurses are bound to be alienated when they exercise professional judgement and no one listens. The Alberta commission has asked hospital managers to use the systems "as guidelines only, and in conjunction with professional judgement." Policies looking at the growing demand for geriatric and chronic care are calling on staffing formulas to "incorporate less tangible indices."

This tardy recognition of their intuitive skills is small comfort to nurses worried about inquests, fatality inquiries, and the nation-wide publicity of the Grange commission. In and out of hospital rooms twelve hours a day, the nurse hates having to document every action; the endless paperwork interferes with her connection to the patient. But although provincial nursing guidelines advise charting only as required, deciding against doing so is risky when the nurse, the legal "custodian of the person," is accountable for all patient care, including the actions of orderlies, nursing students, and RNAs under their supervision.

The Fédération des Infirmières et Infirmiers du Québec changed its position on patient classification systems during its 1989 contract negotiations; the union saw the value of a measurement that could be used to prove excessive workloads. The new GRASP system at Moncton Hospital has finally illustrated how short of nurses the hospital is. "We can't just wave our arms around and say things are going to hell in a hand basket at the Vancouver General," warns Pat Cutshall, executive director of the Registered Nurses Association of British Columbia. "We've got to have facts."

Overworked and underpaid Canadian nurses are worried about the long delays in treatment, the waiting lists for admissions, and other unsafe conditions that they say are jeopardizing human life. Several hundred of them marched on Queen's Park in Toronto in January 1989. Cardiac patients awaiting surgery at Toronto's St. Michael's Hospital staged an unpublicized sit-in during that same winter. Politicians and hospital administrators are blaming each other, with the government pointing to hospital mismanagement and hospitals pointing to the government ceiling on health-care spending. "It's a social question," says Gordon Cunningham, president of the Ontario Hospital Association. "Hospitals are doing the very most they can with what dollars they have available. Society has to decide to spend more money on health." But despite Mr. Justice Dubin's contention that "adequate nursing care is the single most important element in patient care," neither consumers nor governments are pressuring the hospitals to set aside more money for nursing.

Meanwhile, nurses watching conditions deteriorate in Canadian hospitals have to decide whether to see and be silent or to document and tell. The Canadian Nurses Association says, "Colleagues and professional associations are morally obliged to support nurses who fulfil their ethical obligation" to advocate for patients. But as executive director of the Staff Nurses' Association of Alberta Louise Rogers says: "The technology goes on and on creating unbelievable dilemmas for nurses. One of the reasons for the shortage is that there is not nearly enough support for nurses who are caught between the family and the physician and the patient. Nurses trying to advocate on behalf of the patients actually feel quite powerless."

Things are going to get worse instead of better. By the year 2021, there will be approximately two and a half times as many people living in Canada aged seventy or more as there are in 1990, all requiring some kind of nursing care. As Ottawa statistician Eva Ryten puts it: "There is no way a dramatic increase in the number of nurses required in the future can be avoided."

5

The Crisis

In the summer of 1977, nurses at the Vancouver General Hospital, plagued with staff shortages and worried about the safety of their patients, sounded a province-wide alert that set off a startling series of events. The next fourteen months saw a string of firings, resignations, public forums, marches, meetings, petitions, a lawsuit, and a review committee chaired by a prominent local judge. It all culminated in the provincial government stepping in to kick out the president and board of trustees and take over the hospital. Newspapers called it "the most stupendous coup in Canadian medical politics," extolling "the rebel nurses" as "unsung heroines."

What eventually erupted into a full-scale rebellion began with nurses' anxiety about patients in the 1,750 bed hospital. In the summer of 1977, a significant number of VGH nurses alerted the Registered Nurses Association of British Columbia, still their official bargaining agent, to their concerns about unsafe patient care. When the RNABC countered by asking for documented evidence, VGH nurses that fall came up with sixty separate incidents of unsafe patient care. The "hospital incidents," chronicled from September 12 to November 15, 1977, were not untypical; what was remarkable was the high number of them in such a short period of time.

On one November 1977 night, a hemorrhaging patient went without one-to-one care because his nurse was responsible for twenty-one other patients; a student nurse let two intravenous systems run dry, and she failed to recognize that a diabetic patient needed immediate insulin. On a separate occasion, another inexperienced nurse unfamiliar with high-tech equipment was assigned to three babies on ventilators in the intensive-care nursery after being told "just to make sure they are breathing." Dressings in the burn unit that required changing every four hours stayed put so long they were in danger of turning septic. An elderly patient who had climbed out of bed during the night had to lie on the floor for two to three hours because no one could be rounded up to lift him. A nurse worked nineteen hours straight because no one was available for the next shift. An RN who had developed a high fever at work had to remain on duty even though she was too ill to respond to patients. The documents, a half-day of reading stored in big notebooks, are still classified as private to protect nurses from recrimination.

The nursing administration in the fall of 1977 did not have the authority to remedy the situation. Many of the sixty complaints, tabulated by the RNABC and reported, passed through the regular hospital channels but produced little or no results. Hospital officials apparently didn't want to believe conditions could be as bad as the nurses described. The RNABC was organizing meetings with the VGH administration, and on November 21, with the provincial minister of health, when the nurses received an unsolicited boost from a keen and outspoken nursing director who had recently been promoted from head nurse.

Bonnie Lantz, a home-grown graduate of the hospital's nursing school, had been trying to get funds deflected into in-service training and orientation for the 250 surgical nurses under her supervision. Despite support in October 1977 from both the physician who headed the department of surgery and the Canadian Council on Hospital Accreditation, Lantz was not greeted with open arms by the hospital administration. In fact, she was criticized for exceeding her department's budget. Her forced resignation on April 14, 1978, was the trigger that ignited the explosion.

In 1977 the Vancouver General Hospital was in the midst of an external battle with pro-abortion and anti-abortion groups fighting for control of the board, an internal power struggle between community-based and university doctors, and salary negotiations. The administration was trying to apportion funds equitably among various clamouring departments in the face of drastic cutbacks, designed to cut the hospital down to half its size, imposed a year earlier by the B.C. government.

Larry Truitt, an American-trained hospital administrator appointed as VGH president on November 24, initially calmed things down by promising to conduct a formal review and by finding $100,000 to pay for nineteen new nursing positions. But Truitt's scheme for a new corporate hospital structure, announced in January 1978, only aggravated tensions among the nurses. His four new vice-president positions knocked the director of nursing out of the hospital's inner circle. At stake was the nurses' authority to influence patient care, and senior nurses needed only the signal of Lantz's dismissal in April to call in the troops.

For the seven months between Lantz's departure in April and the release in November 1978 of a government-ordered report that ostensibly ended the crisis, the hospital was a battleground. Within three days of Lantz's departure, a committee of concerned nurses was formed. Aided by the RNABC, it launched a campaign both for a vice-president of nursing position and for an independent inquiry into continuing unsafe conditions. On June 1, 1978, three of the four remaining clinical nursing directors (the fifth was on vacation) were fired for not signing a statement of loyalty to hospital management. One of them, given an hour to pack her bags before being escorted to the hospital door, had already given thirty years of service to the institution. Within one three-week period during the month that followed, sixteen senior nurses resigned.

Nurses were so incredulous at the firings and resignations that they were crying in the halls. The committee of concerned nurses kept gathering support, until by August 1977,

800 of the 1,200 hospital nurses had signed a petition demanding the reinstatement of the three nursing directors (Lantz was seeking redress in the courts), the creation of a position of vice-president of nursing, and Truitt's resignation. "We literally had to talk and plan in broom closets; it became a game," recalls mental-health nurse Leith Nance. "If it had not been for our union status, I'm sure we would have been fired. The directors weren't in a union."

Exposing the issue on Vancouver street corners, in the provincial legislature, and on radio, television, and in newspapers around the province, the concerned nurses had worked the VGH revolt into a grand-scale media event by the summer of 1978. By then, only an abridged version of the requested independent inquiry had been released and Truitt's offer of a conditional reinstatement for the three fired directors had been rejected, twice. Meanwhile, reports from nurses to the RNABC of unsafe patient care continued and more nurses resigned.

So when three bizarre patient deaths – two of them violent – became public on August 11, the B.C. minister of health parachuted in ex-RCMP officer Peter Bazowski as the hospital's public administrator later that same day. Bazowski was ordered to assume all functions of both the hospital's board of trustees and of its president, Larry Truitt, immediately. Although the coroner's office later failed to establish a link between the deaths and lack of adequate nursing, Bazowski's report to the provincial government the following November confirmed in no uncertain terms that there was "insufficient nursing at this hospital." As Sue Rothwell, RNABC president in 1978 and in 1988, said about one of the deaths: "People don't drown in bathtubs if there's enough nurses to keep them safe."

By flying in the face of the "I See and I am Silent" code, the Vancouver nurses paved the way for a new nursing politic. They had succeeded in toppling the administration of the largest hospital in Canada. "It started off as nurses' desire not to be an invisible minority in health care any more," says Rothwell. "We said, 'Screw it.' We do most of the work around

here and we're not going to listen to these hospital administrators tell us [as Truitt did] that hospitals don't run by petition. We're serious about patient care. We're experts on
nursing quality, and we're tired of listening to administrators
and doctors tell us how things are when they don't know."
Vancouver nurses now talk of the uprising as the forced recognition of nurses as professionals.

But it's taken Lantz ten years to land a nursing position
anywhere near the status and salary of her job at vGH. She
says she is bitter and disillusioned. "I was a non-conformist. I
wasn't acting the way a good woman and nurse should, but I
just couldn't stand by and not see patients getting good care."
Lantz, who sued for wrongful dismissal and then settled out-
of-court for $12,000, admitted to the newspapers of the day
that she was "politically naive."

The three fired clinical nursing directors ultimately were
reinstated without conditions. None of them is a vGH employee today.

Win Miller, a founding member of the committee of concerned nurses and the only nursing director who signed its
petition, admits her actions were "not good organizational
behaviour," considering her management position at the
hospital. A mental-health nurse for forty years with an
immaculate reputation, Miller, an elegant, gracious, fine-
boned woman at sixty-four, could hardly be characterized as
a rabble-rouser. But she felt Lantz's "resignation" was
"extraordinarily unfair," and she was prepared to be fired to
say so. "There comes a time when you just have to say 'no,'
and that was the time for me. I think there are times when
ethics take precedent over organizational behaviour." But
today Miller views the vGH revolt as "a much smaller step than
one would have liked to have seen for all the energy that went
into it."

In November 1978 Health Minister Bob McClelland did
direct the new hospital board to create a vice-president of
nursing affairs and sixty new full-time nursing positions. The
Medicus patient classification system initiated by Truitt to
ensure that staffing levels were assessed on a "scientific

basis" had recommended 181 additional nurses, but the hospital did not find the money to hire another 100 until the following year. Truitt was shifted laterally to make room for a new president. The interim administrator, Bazowski, affirmed in his report the premise, by now well-known to nurses, that when resources are limited, nursing services sink to the bottom of the requisition list. As Bazowski reported to McClelland: "In my view the nursing staff situation is the most significant single cause of the condition of this hospital which required you to act in August to appoint a public administrator."

Like the Hospital for Sick Children during the baby death epidemic, the too big, too complex Vancouver General Hospital was the real catalyst for the 1977 crisis. *Vancouver Sun* columnist Tim Padmore, describing what he called "Byzantine hospital politics," commented at the time on the "poisonous atmosphere" at the sprawling VGH with "its pyramid-like chain of command" encouraging factional internal wrangling rather than an open line of communication. Despite some efforts at consolidation to meet the edict issued before the crisis, the VGH in 1988 had 1,200 beds, a nursing staff of 2,200 (including 1,600 RNs), and a payroll bigger than a small B.C. city.

The new vice-president of nursing position, as it turned out, did not ease the strain. "We were politically naive," says former concerned-nurse committee member Trudy Staley. "We thought that person would help, but if [she doesn't] get sanction from the president, then nothing is going to happen." In fact, the power structure governed from the top simply shrank back like an amoeba, consolidated and re-formed, with the new vice-president of nursing emerging as a middle-management employee expected to keep staff nurses in line. "She came in and the nurses gave up," says Elva Armstrong, another committee of concerned nurses founder. "We were very tired."

Truitt's characterization of nurses as wage-earners accountable to their employer rather than to their patients had prompted an angry response from the RNABC during the crisis. The association had taken pains to steer clear of strategies like mass resignations with the express intent of maintaining a dignified image of experts with a professional interest in patient care. Former concerned nurses, however, now think Truitt was correct. "We are employees; we are not independent," says Staley, who, years after her part in the Vancouver revolt, now turns to the illegal nurses' strikes in Alberta as a model of action. "I think the nurses in Alberta who are fighting for professional wages and some normal life will advance the profession far more in some respects than this. This was a nice, clean, professional way to go. It was neat and tidy, but I'll tell you, if I had to do it again, I'd be out there doing what those nurses in Alberta are doing."

The VGH-style revolt may be a "last fling at negotiating normative relationships in patient care," Vancouver nursing director Irene Goldstone wrote in her 1981 thesis on collective bargaining in British Columbia. The alternatives to such "neat and tidy" negotiations can only be to advance wages with illegal strikes "the way the nurses in Alberta are doing" or to give up in disgust. One VGH nurse quoted in the December 1979 edition of *RNABC News* put it this way: "What happened last year [at the VGH] reflects a crisis facing the entire nursing profession. People are leaving nursing by leaps and bounds because they are not going to put up with the conditions we have worked with for so long. And they can't be bothered to go through what we did just to get reasonable improvements. A lot of people were excited when the changes were made at the top. What they don't realize is that the people involved were merely a fuse – we are still sitting on dynamite."

Canadian nurses now want formal mechanisms for blowing the whistle on unsafe hospital practices. Courts are ruling that patients are entitled to rely on nurses. But although they are accountable for patient safety, nurses have no authority to control the patient environment. The Ontario nurses' union succeeded in getting a professional-responsibility-committee clause enshrined in its contract in 1977, a year after the Mount Sinai incident. Nurses' unions in New Brunswick and Alberta have won similar clauses in their contracts. A way to advocate for patient safety was so important to Saskatchewan nurses in 1988 that they went out on strike for a professional-responsibility clause in their new contract. The British Columbia Nurses' Union, which finally split from the RNABC in 1981, got its professional-responsibility clause after its strike in the spring of 1989. In 1987, Manitoba nurses, who have no formal professional-responsibility clause, filed as many as 762 work-situation reports alerting employers to potential patient safety problems.

But these time-consuming, union-supervised alternatives to full professional status provide only limited protection to the nurse. What's more, they fail to resolve the competing values of a professional's independent judgement and an employee's silence. Accountability is one of the most critical ethical issues facing modern nursing, and the Vancouver controversy was a clear signal that the issue is not being addressed.

Today's high-tech, acute-care hospital is not the place a nurse can do what she has been trained to do: promote health and well-being. Canadian hospitals are horrible places to work.

The Hospital Council of Metro Toronto's 1988 survey of 1,240 registered nurses revealed an "overwhelming career dissatisfaction" among *hospital* nurses. More than 50 per cent of the respondents would not have recommended nursing as a career; 27 per cent would not have become a nurse if they could choose again. Half of them had seriously considered leaving their current jobs and almost half, 47 per cent, were likely to seek a new job within a year. While virtually all nurses complain about their pay, the hospital job itself is the most important reason why nurses are leaving hospitals.

A night shift at Toronto's Women's College Hospital in 1988 had Donna Cameron, a nurse in private practice who moonlights part-time for a nursing registry, in charge of fifteen patients, six of them post-operative, six on intravenous, and two of them severely ill. "If you put up with this every day, you're nuts," Cameron says she told the charge nurse. The woman, who hadn't been in nursing for long, burst into tears. "It's a totally unreasonable workload, totally unsafe, and totally unacceptable," Cameron says, "but they'll try to do it. They'll run themselves into the ground."

Burnout – low attention span, remoteness, headache, tight muscles, trouble sleeping, and a hot flushed face – was defined in the 1970s as a response to prolonged, unavoidable, and excessive stress in a work situation. But Mary Vachon, a nurse consultant at the Clarke Institute of Psychiatry in Toronto, writes in a 1982 article that burnout, "the progressive loss of idealism, energy, and purpose experienced by people in the helping professions as a result of the conditions of their work," is the combined result of idealistically high personal expectations and a willingness to sacrifice personal needs to the workplace.

Shelly Ouellette, an intravenous nurse at the Moncton Hospital, says recruits now burn out after two years. She can't think of one occasion in her nine years when she's gone home and said, "I'm satisfied with my day." Symptoms of burnout were reported by 50 to 70 per cent of the 667 Newfoundland nurses answering a 1987 questionnaire. Working conditions *per se* cannot be the only reason, a recent Nova Scotia study contends; burnout develops only when heavy workloads are combined with a lack of professional growth and strained relationships among hospital personnel. Economist Noah Meltz, in a 1988 study for the Registered Nurses' Association of Ontario, called this fractious interaction the "corporate culture" of hospitals.

Then there are the back injuries, physical assaults, exposure to hazardous substances, risk of life-threatening infection, and unacceptable noise, temperature, humidity, and air-circulation levels. Shift work is also a shock, especially for new nurses. "You can never know what it's like until you've done it for years," explains Vancouver nursing instructor Rosemarie Riddell. Now that 85 per cent of the nursing workforce is married, hospitals are being forced to find shifts to accommodate women with children. Many are reviving the twelve-hour shift, opposed for years by unions, as the best of the worst. Although 60 per cent of it means working either the late afternoon or the late night shift and only 40 per cent days, nurses have much longer stretches of time off. Few hospitals, however, are examining more radical reforms like self-scheduling or on-site day care.

In Quebec, shifts at francophone hospitals are permanent and do not rotate. A nurse must wait a very long time for one that permits a normal life outside the hospital. The required stint on the province's on-call availability list may last years. Hélène Brault has nursed full-time for ten years but has never held down a full-time job. The only day shift she could arrange at a regional hospital seventy-five kilometres from Montreal was two days a week. She's had to "work" the other three on call, waiting by the telephone every morning. Once off the on-call list, Quebec nurses face another stretch of waiting for a chance at a permanent day shift. It took Anne Marie Poitras two years to figure out the only nurses on permanent day shift at Montreal's Ste-Justine Hospital for Children had started nursing before Poitras was born. The extra pay she was earning for her permanent night and evening work bought Poitras a coffee and a doughnut on the way home from work. She quit.

Nurses' wages do not compensate for all this. Full-time senior nurses in some provinces reach the union maximum after five years. Transferring from one hospital to another often entails a 50 per cent cut in experience credits, a practice unheard of in business or other professions. Many women, now primary income earners, watch agency nurses with less responsibility earning up to 30 per cent more.

Without a good income, prestige, palatable working conditions, or even a reasonable career opportunity, why do nurses do it? The Hospital Council of Metro Toronto survey in 1988, the Alberta Hospital Association survey in 1980, and many earlier surveys say they do it for the patients.

Unfortunately, the nurses value patient contact more than the system does. Consultants conducting the pay-equity job evaluation for twenty-three Manitoba hospitals in 1987 scientifically weighted the way the facilities compensated employees for factors such as experience, education, supervision, risk of harm, exposure to the public, office procedures, paperwork, and policy development. They discovered that only 1 per cent of the variation in salary of all hospital employees could be accounted for by patient contact. In fact, patient contact, the *raison d'être* for health care, received the lowest weighted value of any other category.

The modern high-tech, low-touch hospital system doesn't give nurses enough time to establish the intimacy that is the trademark of good nursing because it doesn't value that intimacy enough. Ontario Hospital Association president Gordon Cunningham doesn't want to give "all the money" to people who are in contact with the patient. "It's important," he says, adding that the OHA and hospitals generally are "concerned about this nurse problem" and want to address it. "But I don't think we could address it by diminishing the role that other people play in the system, like the person who spends his life calibrating x-ray machines. By Golly, he's important."

Nurses aren't trying to turn back technological progress. "People say 'in the good old days,'" explains Josephine Flaherty, principal nursing officer for Health and Welfare Canada. "In the good old days, we had fifty patients; we were on alone at night. We weren't nursing patients; we were just praying that nobody died on our shift." But timing nurses to rush from one room to the other, calculating so many minutes per patient on the basis of the absolute minimum of care, is not going to recruit and retain women whose primary motivation is helping people. "You might have worked all night trying to save this person and you haven't got the time to sit down and talk to the family," explains Elizabeth Ann Stordy, a neurological intensive-care nurse at Moncton Hospital. "You say, you'll talk to them tomorrow, and when you come back in and the patient's not there, you feel like you really want to quit."

Toronto's Hospital for Sick Children, acting on a recommendation from the Dubin committee examining the facility after the baby deaths, hired a team of mental-health workers in 1984 to help nurses deal with stress. When neonatal intensive-care nurses complained about the loss of intimacy due to the high-tech machinery, the workers came up with a system of patient rotation that made sure there was at least one baby on each ward medically stable enough to hold. But nurses are so programmed into giving to others that they find it difficult to acknowledge their own needs, says mental-health worker Rick Kelly. "When you say to a nurse, 'Gee, I think you did a really good job with that patient,' the typical response you might get is a nod, if you're lucky, which to us means that they are not owning up to their own abilities and their own strengths. They are not on secure ground. There is a sort of false bottom to their professional identity."

To be happy in their work, according to the 1988 Metro Council survey, nurses want professional self-esteem, respect, recognition from their co-workers, the ability to use and develop their clinical expertise, opportunities for continuing education, career advancement, control over their profes- sional lives, and the chance to provide the best possible care for their patients. These factors outweigh considerations of pay, shift work, type of job assignment, and workload. The council's data led it to conclude that changes in the hospital *can* make an impact on nurses staying in their jobs or choos- ing to leave.

Nurses unhappy in one hospital now tend to move quickly on to another, despite the cut in pay. At Centenary Hospital in Scarborough, the turnover rate – the number of nurses who leave an organization in a given year measured as a percentage of the average number of employees during that year – was 18 per cent in 1985, up 4 per cent from 1984. The turnover rate at the Toronto General in 1985 was 20 per cent, at Mount Sinai, 15 per cent, and at the Wellesley intensive- care unit, 25 per cent. At St. Paul's in Vancouver in 1989 it was 23 per cent. That same year the 560-bed Vancouver hospital was almost completely staffed with first-year graduates who rarely last more than a year. Rosemarie Riddell still runs around all day with a beeper in case she is summoned to assist floor nurses with procedures that most of them are too inexperienced to know, and the hospital has trouble hiring, period. In downtown Toronto, the average age of registered nurses is twenty-one.

The Metro Hospital Council report recommends in-service education, job sharing, and advanced clinical training to "contribute to a sense of loyalty and reduce *needless* turnover." But now there aren't enough nurses to provide relief for staff on courses, and loyal core groups are so exhausted by the overtime, they see resigning temporarily as the only way to get a rest. Most nurses surveyed in the Newfoundland study report had been working with their current employer for less than two years, and only 15 per cent had been in their current jobs for more than ten years. This loss of the new young, unmarried nurses, the lifeblood of the future, is a discouraging sign.

The attraction of part-time work for nurses is also taking its toll. In 1986, 37 per cent of all registered nurses practising in Canada were working part-time, up from 30 per cent in 1970, and still rising. That is very high, and the Canadian average doesn't tell the whole story. In small hospitals in Ontario in 1981, part-time nurses ranged from 51 to 83 per cent of the nursing staff, and in 1990, 60 per cent of the nursing workforce in the province of Quebec was employed part-time. In 1984, the part-time figure represented 25 per cent permanent part-time and 36 per cent on call. The province's Rochon Commission, set up in June 1985, questioned "the real experience of this workforce situation and the type of short-term planning it seems to imply."

Ottawa statistician Eva Ryten believes the proportion of women working full-time in a profession is an indication of its social and economic status. The fact that only 57 per cent of the female graduate nurses in Canada worked full-time in 1985 is "the most striking figure" in her 1988 study of women in health care, she says. The much higher proportion, 75 per cent, of full-time dental hygienists, who are mostly women and include even fewer university graduates than registered nurses, may be an "instructive comparison," Ryten suggests.

A special Statistics Canada computer search conducted for this book revealed that only 56.7 per cent of the registered nurses working part-time in Canada in 1988 did so by choice; as many as 17.9 per cent of them worked part-time because they could not find full-time work. Even during the worst nursing shortage in living memory, the perceived economic advantages of the "variable" workforce prevail.

Nurses' unions, at least, have broken ranks with the traditional labour opposition to part-time employees and have negotiated benefits for regular part-time nurses, eliminating some of the inequities that have prompted employers to favour part-timers. But until all part-time employees achieve full and equal status, and until men begin to want this option in equal numbers to women, part-time work will continue to be a way of exploiting women.

Statistics released at the end of 1988 projected a need over the next year for 3,000 new registered nurses in Quebec, 2,000 more registered nurses just to meet existing budgeted allotments in British Columbia, and 1,200 to fill existing vacancies in Ontario. Although the Alberta Association of Registered Nurses, the Alberta Hospital Association, and the provincial government all refuse officially to acknowledge a shortage of nurses, a 1980 AHA report predicted that "unless action is taken immediately, the current shortage in hospitals and nursing homes will double by 1981 (down 1,591) and be six times as large by 1996 (down 4,346), with a shortfall of 7,000 in the decade between 1980 and 1990."

The extent of the problem depends on the vested interest of the organization describing it. Hospital administrators, nurses' professional associations, and nursing school educators closely tied to government funding are loathe to say anything that will further soil an already plummeting professional image. Union officials elected to raise socio-economic standards see the current shortage as an opportunity to enhance wages and benefits.

Play these competing interests against a swelling elderly population and significant upheavals in the female workforce. Add the unending ways to manipulate numbers: students who enrol in nursing schools don't necessarily graduate; nurses who register don't necessarily practise more than twenty days a year; filling hospital budgets or nursing school quotas does not necessarily mean enough positions or spaces have been allotted in the first place. Punctuate all that with political euphemisms like quote unquote shortage, coined shortage, artificial shortage, perceived shortage, actual shortage, budgeted shortage. The sitting-on-a-stick-of-dynamite metaphor used by the VGH nurse in 1979 doesn't begin to do justice to the kind of trouble the system is in; it's a volcano.

Almost every provincial government in Canada came out with at least one study in 1988. British Columbia wants immediate steps taken to train seventy-five additional critical-care nurses, including providing the appropriate incentives to undertake such training. All over the country, hospitals are falling all over each other offering perks; on-site credit courses with paid time off (if staff nurses train in areas where they are most needed), finders fees, rent allowances, relocation expenses, special hospital pins to recognize excellence, free parking, or access to a limited number of prepaid spaces at a local day-care centre. One Toronto nurse says she feels "like a pound of pork."

Recruitment efforts have not yet been redirected to women on their second careers or part-time nurses. Nor have they turned to a thirty-five-hour work week or scholarships to recruit men into nursing. Moncton Hospital extended its hospital-based diploma nursing school program for three months in 1989, expanding the time students must work free. Alberta's Premier's commission has suggested bringing back internships permanently as a way to upgrade nurses' training, reviving a concept that was a strike issue in British Columbia in the 1930s. Other strategies – a union blacklist at the Toronto General Hospital and a Toronto hospital administrators' boycott of agency nurses – are also turning up the heat in the conflict, which is looking more and more like guerrilla warfare.

But like a corset, the retrain, recruit, retain, re-enter tactics are pushing out in one place what was just taken back in another. Nurses say that once the profession is returned to nurses, nurses will return to the profession. "The way nurses are treated is the fundamental problem in the health-care system," says Gail Donner, the RNAO's outgoing executive director. "You can keep pushing them by expanding places and programs, by recruiting offshore, by training programs, by whatever the hell you want, but if you haven't got an environment in which they are going to stay for more than ten years, what the hell's the point? Something has to be done to restructure the system in which nurses work."

Nurses are leaving the Canadian hospital system; they are not leaving nursing. The Hospital Council of Metro Toronto reports that as many as 43 per cent of the nurses resigning from hospitals in 1988 were abandoning their hospital jobs rather than the profession, and only 9 per cent of the nurses who resigned quit nursing. Statistics Canada documents that only 11 per cent of Canada's 236,993 registered nurses in 1986 were employed in something other than nursing or unemployed. "Unemployed nurses do not form a large untapped pool of workers for the profession," Meltz said in his study, and he called for immediate research on the non-hospital employment of nurses. Unless action is taken soon, the hospital council warns, hospitals will go on to lose an "impressive" number of nurses.

The number of registered nurses, the largest profession in Canada, doubled in the twenty-one years between 1965 and 1986. In 1985, 3,400 nurses belonged to the New Brunswick Nurses' Union's hospital bargaining unit; in 1988 that number rose to 3,800. Registrants at the College of Nurses of Ontario are now increasing by 1 to 2 per cent a year. Each year more and more nurses work in Quebec, and almost a thousand more nurses were registered in Manitoba in 1987 than in 1983. The shortage is not a question of insufficient numbers. "There is no shortage of women with the necessary background," says Tom Mann, the executive director of the New Brunswick Nurses' Union. "There is a shortage of women willing to work."

Marney Prouse returned to hospital nursing in 1980 after a stint at a women's crisis centre in Sault Ste. Marie; she left again for two years in 1983. In 1989 she decided to give the profession one last shot by working weekends at a private Toronto neighbourhood clinic. She loved it. "It's the most satisfying nursing job I have ever had, without question. It pays peanuts, but it's an extremely collegial relationship. I love the patients. It's a very different setting than working in a hospital where people are always anxious. If the pay were better, I would do it five days a week – in a second."

Wild horses wouldn't drag Nancy Avery, a New Brunswick extra-mural nurse, back into a hospital; Dawn Prentice, a homecare nurse in Hamilton, waited for years to get on with the Victorian Order of Nurses, and Maria Goble, an *ad hoc* private-duty nurse in Moncton, would rather go on welfare than work the way her full-time colleagues do. Now able to determine her own workload, Goble is hired either by the hospital to meet a doctor's order for special nursing care or directly – for instance, by a family who did not wish their dying father, who pulls out all his intravenous tubes, to be tied down to the bed as the hospital requires.

More than 82 per cent of the 240,000 registered nurses in Canada still work in hospitals. Not all of these jobs are high-stress critical care; extended-care institutions needed three times the number of nurses in 1986 than they did in 1971. All over the country, however, history is reversing itself. Whereas the 1930s saw private-duty nurses moving into the hospitals, by the 1990s nurses were lining up five-deep to compete for the few community positions in public-health or community clinics or to make their fortunes in Saudi Arabia or the United States.

They don't stay there. They say they would rather work in a government-insured health-care system. Despite the hype about a mass exodus of nurses from Canada and from nursing, Noah Meltz reports a strong occupational commitment among nurses and a higher retention rate than many other fields.

The task of earning recognition for nurses is not going to be easy. Given the submissive nursing temperament and the increasing professional opportunities for women, many RNs are saying they'd rather quit than fight. But on the whole, most nurses love their work. They love the patients; they thrive on stress; they want to help people. Nursing is not a job, it's a perspective on the world, Gail Donner says. Nurses may have to give up their hospital role to subsidiary workers and move out into the community. They may have to offer a specialized nursing care and develop written certification for formal recognition of that specialty. They may have to turn to trade unions to teach them how to win financial recognition for their expertise. But if all this doesn't work, it is the system rather than the job that will likely destroy them.

It took Susan Mayer only a short stay in hospital as a patient to get back into the profession, teaching and nursing – nursing at a Toronto hospice, in a private practice, and one day a week at a local hospital, and teaching at Ryerson Polytechnical Institute. "I was lying there in bed. People were pushing me around like I was a piece of meat, and others were very caring. Granted I'd been out five years. I may not have the skills updated, but at least I care. At least I care. I came back. Once a nurse, always a nurse. The old nurse in you never dies."

6

Turf Wars

When Hazel Paish entered the Edmonton General Hospital's three-year nursing program at the age of nineteen in 1939, she had more to cope with than her twelve-hour nursing shifts. She also had to learn every service task in the place, including working in the kitchen and putting together the diets. Later, three months after graduation, she got a job at the fifteen-bed hospital in Empress, Alberta, the town of her birth, sixty miles north of Medicine Hat. In those days Empress boasted a population of thirty to forty people, and it's not much bigger now.

During the Second World War, after a year and a half in Empress, Paish went out on horseback as a district nurse; that's the only way the people who lived in places with no doctors could receive care. "We did bits of suturing, pulled teeth, gave the immunizations. Whatever had to be done," she says. "The health laws weren't the same then. We could prescribe medicine. We delivered babies when the doctors weren't there. We did everything except major surgery. If there was anything really bad, you took them to the doctor."

She started out at Kinuso, a little town near an Indian reserve, and then moved on to Blueberry Mountain, population six, close to the British Columbia border. "It was all the outlying areas," she says. "I took in six schools, travelling as a nurse on horseback." Despite a training she says is inferior to what nurses get nowadays, she had more responsibility as a district nurse than any nurse now does in a big-city teaching hospital.

Paish quit nursing to get married in 1944 and returned to the work twenty-five years and thirteen children later. Her marriage had ended and her youngest child was only five years old. Paish worked nights at a hospital in Grande-Prairie, 290 miles northwest from Edmonton, getting home after 7:00 a.m. to get the children off to school, sleeping until they returned, getting up to make supper, and resting again before going to work at 11:00 p.m.

She had only the youngest left at home when she moved in 1980 to the High Prairie Regional Health Complex, with seventy-five active treatment beds, fifty nursing-home beds, eight ambulatory care beds, and eight medical hostel beds. When they tried to retire her four years later, she got mad enough to take her case to court and won the right to keep working. But a transfer to the maternity ward broke her resolve, which judging from her history must have been considerable. She says she hadn't worked in a maternity ward since 1942, after she graduated. "There's a lot of monitors and incubators and things like that that we never used. I bluffed. I worked on maternity for about a year until I was having nightmares. Every time I'd see a pregnant woman go down the street, I'd think, 'Don't come in on my shift, just don't come in on my shift.' And I thought, well, this isn't worth it, so I quit."

This time she thought she'd left nursing for good. But she couldn't tolerate retirement and within a few weeks was back on call for Central Park Lodge, a nursing home in Grande-Prairie. She was also still going into Edmonton at least four times a year for board meetings of her union, the United Nurses of Alberta. Until 1988 Paish was the provincial nurses' union's regional representative for the North River district. Looking like the grandmother in the Pilsbury baking commercials, she has been a negotiator on the union's bargaining committee for three contracts. The last resulted in a highly publicized nineteen-day illegal strike of 11,000 nurses at 104 hospitals in January and February 1988.

Paish says the strike showed how many patients in the hospital didn't really have to be there. "The day before the strike, the Edmonton General tried to admit a man for constipation. Government should change the health-care policy; they should increase the health-unit workers, the VON, and let people stay in their homes. There are a lot of hospitals in Alberta. In an NDP riding up by Peace River, they [the provincial Progressive Conservative government] tore that hospital down and built one just ten miles away in a Tory riding and only fifteen miles from the Peace River Hospital. It's all politics.

"What is a profession? I don't know. I've wondered for a long time why people think they should be better than anybody else because they are a profession. Everybody has to eat and clothe themselves. I don't really know what is the difference."

The current schism between the professional nursing associations and the nurses' trade unions is historical, a split in the professional psyche that goes back to the institutionalization of health care at the turn of the century. By buying into the management principles of the new hospital hierarchy, nurses in hospital administration, descendants of Florence Nightingale's matrons, were seen by the rank and file as having chosen to align themselves with the short-term efficiency goals of the expanding health-care system. Equipped with a hundred-year "matron complex" and a two-year nursing diploma, the nurse manager was expected to represent both nurses and the institution, and she was ill prepared by her history to do either.

Nursing management was one of the weaker pillars in the team concept developed before the Second World War to organize nursing labour. Then each team member had her place: the matrons trained and supervised the registered nurses, and the RNs in turn trained and supervised the registered nursing assistants. But the matron, the only woman in hospital management, climbed to a position of responsibility without a commensurate increase in control. A generation ago, nursing supervisors at least worked on the floor. Modern nursing managers, who now call themselves nurse executives, no longer participate in hands-on patient care. Neither bedside nurses nor physicians, they have no real authority, even though they manage hospital budgets worth millions of dollars. They have only the power to govern the nurses beneath them. "Because nursing managers particularly have few organizational rewards to trade for compliance, they try to coerce the nursing staff into doing what they want done," Jenniece Larsen told a conference on nursing leadership in 1982.

When a floor nurse is overworked, it's her own nursing supervisor who has likely jiggled the staffing formula to cut costs. When a floor nurse complains about unsafe conditions, she faces her own nursing supervisor on the other side of the grievance table. When the stress of understaffing puts the floor nurse's competence in question, it is the nursing supervisor, a member of her own nursing association, who disciplines her. A nurse turning to her union is not asking for help against the hospital administration; the management nurse is the floor nurse's boss.

Nurse managers, unprotected by a union and walking a fine line between the hospital administration and the nursing department, work in a state of continuous siege. "They are caught between a rock and a hard place," says nursing dean Marian McGee. "Many of them do function as staff advocates, and they fight very long battles, but at tremendous costs. You are always alone, you vote alone, and you never win, ever."

Weakened from within, the postwar hospital hierarchy began to be barraged by a new external pressure. What Penny Erickson, dean of the University of New Brunswick's nursing school, calls "flash-and-trash, tubes-and-orifice" nursing blew apart traditional hands-on nursing care. Nurses now had to develop a relationship with machines – highly mechanized life-support systems, invasive diagnostic and monitoring procedures, Portacaths, CAT scanners, nuclear magnetic resonance, laser surgery, heparin locks, and computerized diagnostic procedures – all of which drastically changed the content and design of nursing practice. A range of other health-related workers, including respiratory technologists, occupational therapists, and rehabilitation therapists, accompanied the new technology to challenge the already ill-defined boundaries of nursing work.

Propelled by the advancement of medicine and by government health insurance, hospitals expanded, hiring more nurses. The higher concentration of employees in institutional settings made union organizing easier. And the rise in power of nursing unions and the consequent increase in registered nurses' salaries soon led hospital employers to recognize the financial advantage of beefing up their para-professional nursing staff. Governments had started to fund separate schools for these workers in the early 1940s so that registered nurses would no longer need to train them. The perceived nursing shortage at the end of the war led politicians to fund more of these programs.

It was the end of the tightly knit nursing team. The neat division of labour among registered nurses, licensed practical nurses, nursing assistants, and aides established in the 1940s by the institutionalization of health care was crumbling. The nurses' aides, nursing assistants, and practical nurses began to care for patients independently instead of merely assisting RNs, and they soon came to be seen by the public as the "real" nurses. Neither group was really doing what it had been trained to do. The non-professional nurses were now the ones at the bedside caring for patients while the registered nurses moved off to supervise and chart, still responsible for whatever the RNAs did.

The association of caring with the domestic tasks of wife and mother minimizes its importance in the public arena. Dismissing caring as beneath them, doctors give it to RNs. RNs, reluctant to revert to the non-professional mother-based caring of the untrained "professed" nurses who staffed hospitals a century ago, pass it on to RNAs. But at the same time as RNs look down on washing feet, they know care is the central focus of their work and argue that RNAs have not been trained to do it in the same professional way.

The blurring of distinction between professional and non-professional tasks is a threat to women who work in an occupation so unsure of its own boundaries. In a letter published in a 1989 issue of the Alberta Association of Registered Nurses' monthly newsletter, a group of RNs asked for a regulation that would take the word "nursing" out of the registered nursing assistant title.

Today's complex health-care technology is forcing hospitals to search for the proper mix of professional and non-professional nursing services. Various approaches have been tried and abandoned. When nursing leaders in the 1970s advanced the idea of giving one RN complete charge of a group of patients instead of working on a team, their efforts were reinforced by hospital managers who thought using RNs for the entire range of bedside care might be less expensive than paying a second person just to do the menial work. An RN can legally work alone, while an RNA cannot, and hospitals began to rely on registered nurses to fetch and carry, empty bedpans, and mop up in addition to their regular nursing duties. They rationalized the extra work by saying an RN was safer. Even the Dubin commission recommended substituting RNs for RNAs in acute-care hospitals whenever possible.

This approach brought a "major transformation," according to economist Noah Meltz in his 1988 report for the Registered Nurses' Association of Ontario. In 1971 the number of RNs in Ontario (42,740) was only slightly larger than the total (39,780) of the other three nursing categories: RNAs, aides, and orderlies. By 1986, however, the number of RNs (84,415) was two-and-one-half times the total of the other three (33,145). Meltz said the trend to making relatively less use of RNAs, aides, and orderlies was a "conscious decision" based on the "virtually unanimous view on the part of administrators that increasing the proportion of RNs was cost-effective."

Nursing leaders are predicting a flip on the subsidiary worker issue. Staff nurses told Meltz that they don't want to perform functions that "more properly belong to less highly trained staff." The disintegration of stable work groups resulting from the new twelve-hour shifts, the mounting pressure of paperwork, and financial constraints make it impossible to keep the primary RN's patient groups small enough. Rather than the intended intellectual stimulation and control, primary-care nurses are simply enduring more stress. Hospitals could be spending 40 to 93 per cent more, insists the Ontario Association of Registered Nursing Assistants, because substituting RNs for RNAs has increased the demand for RNs. Asking registered nurses to spend almost 30 per cent of their working time on non-nursing tasks could, in fact, be detracting from patient safety.

The expected return to the nursing team may force registered nurses to delineate still narrower work boundaries just to differentiate their jobs as "professional." Meltz, in his report, called for "some experimentation to determine the most effective mix of RNs, RNAs, aides, and orderlies." That plea was reiterated by then RNAO president Eleanor Ross on a TVOntario call-in show telecast in November 1988. Hospitals may think they are getting a "better bang for their buck" to get the RN to do everything from portering to breakfast trays, she said, but "we need to find a proper [staff] mix."

At a hearing of the Premier's Commission on Future Health Care for Albertans in Edmonton in November 1988, Dr. Alex McPherson, a former president of the Canadian Medical Association and provincial deputy minister of health, told his fellow commissioners: "We should not have doctors doing things that nurses are perfectly capable of doing. We should not have nurses doing things that housewives are perfectly capable of doing. We should not have housewives doing things that other people are capable of doing. We should be trying to define the particular area of competence of a particular group of individuals in the health-care system. They should be allowed to do it because they are competent and they are capable. And they should be legitimized."

   Nurses in this country have been fighting for just that legitimacy for 140 years, and they are still at a loss to define what a registered nurse does. What nurses are allowed to do is set out in terms of an accepted body of knowledge only as it is defined by male scientists. The development of medicine changed the relationship between doctors and nurses. Doctors began to expect nurses, as their assistants, to do their technical, practical, and administrative tasks. Taking blood pressure used to be a medical act performed only by a doctor, until the physicians and surgeons moved on to more complicated procedures. What has evolved is a nursing practice that derives its professional identity almost entirely from controlling medical acts. The College of Nurses of Ontario, in addition to listing basic nursing skills, also spells out exactly what acts "in the practice of medicine" the College of Physicians and Surgeons of Ontario has agreed "may be carried out by designated persons other than physicians" and under what circumstances. Each province publishes similar bulletins.

   Carol Browne, a senior supervisor at the Hospital for Sick Children during the 1981 baby death epidemic, was "always amazed that the Sick Kids had all of these other support people who came in from eight to four and from nine to five. After five, nurses were the experts in everything. It's quite okay for us to do it at eight at night but not at eight in the morning." In its 1980 brief to the Emmett Hall Special Commission (Canada's National-Provincial Health Program for the '80s) the Canadian Nurses Association called this phenomenon the "reverse Cinderella syndrome." The CNA stated, "At the stroke of the night shift, 'nursella' is deemed capable of performing tasks she is not allowed to perform with the coming of the day shift and physicians." Mr. Justice Emmett Hall was so impressed by both the brief and the sentiment he singled it out for further study. Says Browne: "I think somehow nursing hasn't stood up and said, 'This is what we offer the consumer.' "

   To help, to care, to comfort, to correct, to prevent, and then to have to fight for legitimacy? It doesn't make sense, Marian

McGee says. "RNs get angry and then they have to figure out what they are really angry at. They don't know who their enemies are." In 1960 members of the International Council of Nurses did redefine nursing, accepting a proposal by the U.S. grande dame of nursing, Virginia Henderson: "The unique function of the nurse is to assist the individual, sick or well, in the performance of those activities contributing to health or its recovery (or to a peaceful death) that he would perform unaided if he had the necessary strength, will or knowledge. And to do this in such a way as to help him gain independence as rapidly as possible." The real task of nursing, explains Lorine Besel, is to "care *about* rather than care *for*."

Canadian nurses still work under a set of systemic restrictions limiting what they can do for a patient. A hospital nurse legally can't explain a patient's medical diagnosis to that patient; she can't write orders for a patient; legally she can't tell patients they are going to die (although she is often left to do so); she can't prescribe drugs, even though she may know more about how to manage pain than a doctor does. She has been trained in health promotion but she is preoccupied with sickness. She is committed to prevention but she is plugged into medical intervention.

She lacks the legal responsibility to act according to her knowledge and training, which, in keeping with the Nightingale tradition, is much broader than disease pathology. She is the most underused worker in the health-care system. Co-opting her talents to assist doctors may be good for the doctors, U.S. educator Jo Ann Ashley wrote in 1976, but it is not good for either nurses or patients. "Medical supervision is a myth. Nurses do not practise in the presence of physicians and are not constantly supervised by them. Nursing care goes on without either the consultation or the presence of the physician, and absentee supervision by physicians is a reality in practice that ought to be recognized by law."

The alienation of rank-and-file nurses from nursing management did not begin with the 1973 Saskatchewan court decision. That ruling defined provincial nursing associations for all time as company-dominated and therefore unfit to act as bargaining agents for unionized nursing employees. The conflict among registered nurses had begun as soon as they moved back into hospitals after the Depression. The immediate result of the Saskatchewan ruling was the birth of separate all-nurse unions in every province to oversee the socio-economic welfare of working nurses, leaving the professional associations to continue to manage registration, discipline, and standards of practice. The long-term result was the erosion of nursing associations' credibility.

Nurses soon tired of having to pay double fees, one sum to the provincial professional association, in most provinces lumped in with their annual registration fee, the other, dues to the union. As unions expanded they began to be more interested in the so-called professional issues. Some unions have even insisted on calling the professional associations "licensing bodies," arguing that nursing unions can represent nurses' professional interests as well as negotiate wages and job security. Unions have also taken on matters of public interest such as pensions, welfare, taxes, health promotion, abortion, and day care. Professional associations in turn have tried to close ranks around issues such as university education, merit, specialization, recognition, pride, primary health care, ethics, long-term reform, and respectability as a way to differentiate themselves from the trade unions.

The turf wars are getting worse. In 1977 the Registered Nurses Association of British Columbia, still the official bargaining agent for nurses in the province, gave province-wide support to nurses at the Vancouver General Hospital when they rebelled against the hospital administration. At the local level, however, the committee of concerned nurses felt sold out by members of the hospital's nursing management. The RNABC in its turn is still offended by the union's initiative in establishing a professional-responsibility committee, an area the association considers its exclusive prerogative.

Union nurses in Quebec remember that the Quebec professional association, L'Ordre des Infirmières et Infirmiers du Québec, refused a request for help in organizing nurses in the early 1950s. There was a lawsuit, and the Ordre and the Fédération des Infirmières et Infirmiers du Québec now have nothing to do with each other.

The medical unit nursing staff at Halifax's Victoria General Hospital, insecure about how to treat and discharge AIDS patients, went to an annual general meeting of the Registered Nurses Association of Nova Scotia in the mid-1980s to ask for assistance. They were sent away with the admonition that each nursing unit is responsible for its own education. The staff nurses said in *The Canadian Nurse* it was part of an "ongoing lack of collegial support."

The Ontario Nurses' Association and the RNAO clashed in the spring of 1989 when Queen's Park amended the Ontario Hospitals Act, forcing all hospitals in the province to change their bylaws to ensure that nurses sit on key decision-making committees. Nurses from which camp? both organizations asked. Wellesley Hospital vice-president of nursing Virginia Sinnott supports a staff nurse "learning and observing and contributing. But to have only staff nurses sit on all three committees? That's nonsense. They can't speak on global issues. They can only speak to their little thirty-bed unit." But an ONA official in the hospital, who is afraid of repercussions if she is named, says nurse managers on the committee will be useless. "It's not going to help us in any way to have nurses on hospital boards if it's the same administrator group. I think they treat us worse than the non-nurse members of the administration."

The RNAO's November 1988 report on the nursing shortage prompted a public attack by the union in which it blasted the association for making "misleading and inaccurate statements." In a press release the Ontario Nurses' Association said, "The RNAO's document shows an abysmal lack of understanding of the dynamics of the healthcare industry." It added, "Their recommendations also demonstrate a startling lack of innovation and imagination." The RNAO had come up with innovative recommendations. But in five of them it made the mistake of suggesting improvements to the way the ONA was conducting negotiations with the Ontario Hospital Association. ONA executive director Glenna Cole Slattery was furious. "Those demands have been put up on the table every single, yes, every single bargaining round since the first day the union sat with the boss. This union was terribly angry and terribly affronted by the arrogance [of the RNAO] and the stupidity. It's offensive. If I could think of a stronger word, I would use it."

For Slattery, the RNAO is dividing the profession and letting "the marketplace conquer us." Kathleen Connors, president of the National Federation of Nurses' Unions in Ottawa, puts it more globally. "What is developing across the country is a sense that the registering body isn't doing a good job. They are not representing us. They are not listening to us."

Emotions are so high that in as many as five provinces there is a movement afoot to get provincial governments to take the licensing mandate away from the professional associations and give it to a separate college, as is now the case in Ontario. But the relationship among the three nursing organizations in Ontario is probably the worst in the country – with the possible exception of Alberta. There the Alberta Association of Registered Nurses put out a province-wide three-page diatribe against a United Nurses of Alberta plan to investigate the college option in 1989, calling it "an assault upon the integrity of the structure of the AARN." Given the history of the College of Nurses of Ontario, it is difficult to think of the union initiative as anything less than just that.

Ontario was always a bit different. Under its 1921 Nurses' Act a woman did not have to register to practise nursing, so membership in the provincial professional association was voluntary. In September 1959 the RNAO, endeavouring to bring all aspects of nursing legislation into the hands of the profession, appealed to the Ontario government for the right to approve the conduct of nursing schools. The minister of health, Dr. Matthew Dymond, responded by asking the RNAO to consider a new statutory body, called a college, comparable to the College of Physicians and Surgeons. The RNAO did as the good doctor suggested, a move widely perceived, even by the current executive director of the College of Nurses of Ontario, Margaret Risk, as "political suicide." The College of Nurses of Ontario, in addition to its jurisdiction over schools, became the licensing and regulatory body for nurses in the province, taking over this function from the professional association. A quasi-government organization that can't lobby in any partisan way on behalf of nursing as the RNAO does, the college is perceived by some as government's way of making sure it has control over the profession.

After the college was formed in 1963 with funding from Queen's Park, membership in the RNAO dropped from 28,000 to 9,000. The RNAO was, and still is, not financially sound as a result, and the current union initiatives to get colleges of nurses formed across the country can't help but be seen in that light – a death-blow tactic for a hated competitor. Bringing in a college under the wing of government will undoubtedly undermine what is left of nursing's autonomy. As Gail Donner puts it: "It would be naive of us to say other than it was mostly in government's interest to make sure we were separate."

The RNAO tried in 1965 to get special collective bargaining legislation for its nurses. It was never passed, and the Ontario union was advised to begin certifying. In 1973 the certified locals amalgamated, forming the Ontario Nurses' Association, which, at 54,000 members by 1990, has become one of the largest groups of unionized women in North America.

In 1977 the RNAO, still struggling on its reduced finances, negotiated its first deal with the ONA for block membership, giving union members a cut rate for buying into the professional association in bulk. The block membership agreement, initiated again in 1983, has been called a brave social experiment. "It was a back-door end-run on the health-care environment in terms of nursing finally getting its act together," says Gail Paech, RNAO president from 1983 to 1985. In October 1986 the ONA members became angry at being excluded from the RNAO's midwifery statement and voted to pull out again. This move led many nurses to accuse the union of acting vengefully to destroy the RNAO, of creating conflict, and of aiding and abetting government interests in keeping the nursing profession divided.

The ONA defection meant the RNAO's membership again plummeted. In a province boasting an RN population of close to a hundred thousand, 13,338 nurses belonged to the RNAO as of July 20, 1989; only 1,563 of those were also members of the union. The immediate result was a wider gulf between the groups; the long-term result, even more devastating, was that the ONA's 54,000 members were no longer part of the national nursing association. The RNAO still belongs to the CNA, an umbrella federation that signs on provincial associations rather than individuals, but the ONA members who did not join the RNAO are now disenfranchised.

The Canadian Nurses Association can no longer even pretend to claim it represents Canadian nurses on a national level. The Quebec nurses' association pulled out of the CNA in 1985, taking the 55,000 Quebec nurses with it, and the 113,000 RNs without CNA membership comprise almost half of the 240,000 registered nurses in the country.

Quebec's disenchantment with the national nursing federation had begun twenty years earlier in 1966, when the Ordre persuaded the CNA to make Quebec's per capita membership fee lower than the levy for the rest of the provinces. By the time the CNA had adopted a sliding scale unit fee in 1975, Quebec's unique Professional Code had in 1973 assigned the Ordre the primary task of protecting the public, demanding that it subordinate its mandate to represent the nursing profession to that special first mission. The extra responsibility may have given Jennine Pelland, elected president for the first time in 1980, and Thérèse Guimond, the association's executive director, the excuse they needed to claim conflict of interest with the national nursing association.

The two Ordre executives may also have been influenced by a financial setback in 1980 when one of the most militant nursing unions in the province won a lawsuit against the Ordre's own method of levying fees. The court ruled that money for the association's in-profession services had to be approved by the association's full membership rather than by the board, and the full membership began summarily to vote down every proposed fee increase. Whatever the motivation, the Quebec association had another go at the CNA fee structure in 1981, suspending its intent to withdraw only after an eleventh-hour compromise decision by the CNA to lower the ceiling for Quebec's membership fee.

The Ordre was also gathering support for making membership in the CNA voluntary, an action Ginette Rodger, the Canadian Nurses Association's executive director, saw as both professionally dangerous and politically separatist. A six-month political battle for turf followed. Rodger and Shirley Stinson, the CNA president who had helped engineer the 1981 fee compromise, began travelling around the province campaigning for the CNA, a move that according to Lorine Besel, CNA president from 1984 to 1986, just served to anger Pelland and Guimond "for parading around on their turf."

When the CNA went back on its 1981 decision to lower the fee ceiling and hiked Quebec's CNA unit fee, it must have been the final straw. In November 1984 the Ordre served its notice of intent to withdraw, listing as reasons in addition to the fees "lack of proportional representation" on the CNA board, "lack of interest" in Quebec's special situation, and "duplication of services." It refused the CNA's counteroffer for a hybrid fee formula that acknowledged Quebec's wishes for voluntary membership, and in November 1985 the Ordre acted on its required one-year notice and withdrew. "It's too much of an easy answer to say it was separatist," says Raymonde Bossé, a vice-president of the Quebec union and an anglophone. "It goes way beyond that. Whether it be in labour relations or in professional orientation, it's the feeling that wherever you are, you have a place you can influence. Any organization wants to have power."

Rodger says it's only a matter of time before the Quebec association returns to the fold. She does acknowledge, nonetheless, that the disaffiliation has had some disastrous consequences. The CNA had to stop financing the French-language version of its national journal *The Canadian Nurse*.

The CNA has not been able to represent Quebec nurses on issues like nursing manpower in a province where 60 per cent of nurses work part-time, not necessarily by choice, and wait eight or nine years for a full-time job. The CNA has not been able to support a proposal for a nursing PhD program at the University of Montreal. And the province's anglophone nurses, numbering about 10 per cent of Quebec's RNS and concentrated in Montreal, are left without an advocate.

Today's nursing leaders – Anne Gribben, Alice Baumgart (in 1990 the new CNA president), Ginette Rodger – stress that the big challenge for nursing now is to reunify. Unions, with their vested interest in nurses' socio-economic welfare, do not have the political credibility of the professional associations, they say. Ottawa nurse consultant Marie Campbell, a unionist, is also not confident the industrial-relations model can solve professional issues. There is as well a nation-wide concern among nurses that nurses' unions will abandon their commitment to nursing as a profession in favour of aligning themselves more closely with industrial trade unions.

The climate is ripe for them to do so. Management nurse Irene Goldstone predicts the time for working together is long past. In Ontario Gribben's replacement, after her retirement in 1986, by the more militant Slattery is seen by some as a significant impediment to the hope nurses will "get their act together" in that province. Others blame the RNAO for the current crisis in confidence, and Slattery herself, not a paragon of humility, says: "I'm good, but I ain't that good."

These divisions, no different from the class and language differences in other occupational groups, are the more significant for nursing. With Canadian nursing in crisis, with institutionalized health care in crisis, now more than any other time in their history nurses need a concerted strategy for change. "With the current shortage of nurses and the public's appreciation of nurses, we are in a perfect position to make demands, but we are not taking the opportunity. We are going through an identity crisis. Adolescence is the perfect image," former RNAO president Shirley Wheatley says. "We are like seething teenagers at the centre of everything moving and changing around us. We are so politically naive, we just don't know how to grab hold and run with it. Nurses are stuck."

7

Women's Work:
It Ain't Necessarily So

Quebec's 40,000 registered nurses had an answer for Premier Robert Bourassa in the fall of 1989. When he threatened them with severe financial penalties if they went on strike, they said: "You can't scare us. Women don't have to stay in nursing any more."

The nurses were right. A generation ago women had few alternatives; nursing was a career by default. Now they can choose from a variety of jobs and come home with a clear conscience. They don't have to wake up in the middle of the night in a sweat over someone's intravenous tube. In 1986 *Working Woman* magazine listed nursing as one of ten dead-end professions. "You know, you don't have to be a nurse any more," says Muriel Murray, who has been a staff nurse at Vancouver's St. Paul's Hospital ever since she trained there in 1950. "You can be a lawyer. You can go on into medicine. You can be a doctor!"

Not only are there now more career opportunities for women, but feminism has also altered the way women see themselves. Registered nurses of the older generation, says Rosemarie Riddell, "are just devoted and dedicated. These women grew up in a time when you obeyed your husband and you stayed married. It just doesn't happen any more." Women are still going into nursing. Now, however, the move is a conscious decision made from a range of options. And women are staying in nursing, if not in hospitals, despite the gruelling working conditions.

But for the women who are attracted to nursing now, it is an undertaking of an order that is beyond most of us. Although it is now out of fashion, that kind of commitment, Riddell says, remains necessary to be a good nurse.

Barbara Jane Howell, ten years out of a hospital-based nursing school in Halifax, was charged with just that kind of undertaking when she came on twelve-hour duty at 7:00 a.m., October 8, 1982. On that day she was assigned to care for one baby, Candace Taschuk, who was in an incubator on continuous intravenous. Howell had to monitor the baby's condition and keep her warm and dry, cuddling her as much as possible.

The baby's mother, Debora Taschuk, had been brought into the University of Alberta Hospital in Edmonton earlier that night as soon as she starting experiencing "pre-birth complications." Shortly after the woman arrived, at 4:30 a.m., the staff neonatologist was called. Candace Taschuk was delivered by caesarean section thirty-six minutes later. The birth was classified as a stillbirth, even though the baby lived; the baby's heart had stopped. She had asphyxiated during birth.

"Heroic measures" were begun after one minute. Four minutes later, Candace was still dead. Only after eight minutes of resuscitation was Candace revived – with a newborn vital-sign Apgar reading of one out of ten and "severe cerebral dysfunction." At 7:00 a.m. she was put on a respirator and intravenous fluids, with orders for TLC (tender loving care) plus Phenobarbital and Dopamine to prevent convulsions and undue suffering. The doctors in attendance at the delivery left the hospital at 8:00 a.m. knowing the baby was going to die. One of them testifying at the subsequent fatality inquiry said: "I do not embark on heroics if I have grave reservations, but with asphyxia, it's hard to tell. However, I guess you don't know until you try. You are committed to trying, and the problem is once you are committed to trying that means a flat-out, all-out effort."

At 10:30 a.m. the results of an EEG indicated brain activity was nil, and at 11:00 a.m. Debora and Jerry Taschuk consented to disconnecting Candace from her life-support system. They stood aside, waiting to "see if she could make it on her own." The doctors encouraged the parents and grandparents to hold the child, and prescribed Demerol, a synthetic form of morphine, so that the baby would not feel distress while she was dying. It was a standard palliative program for a baby who was basically dead at birth. In hospital jargon it's called a "no code," signifying an agreement that no more heroic measures will be taken.

Keeping a death watch on a brain-dead child has to be one of the most difficult assignments for a nurse. The doctor makes the decision, but it is the nurse who must deal with the family on a minute-by-minute basis. Family members often don't understand that their loved one's seemingly lively cries and movements are maintained artificially by drugs or machines. After the removal of these synthetic life supports, the nurse is the one left to nurse and to nourish, both the patient and the family, in the best way she can.

As October 8, 1982, progressed, Candace's convulsions and breathing got worse. Howell's subsequent testimony described the baby as gasping for breath, greyish-blue in colour, with continuing involuntary jerks of her arms and seizuring eye movements. "She was whimpering and whimpering, a bad way to describe it – but like a puppy would whimper. It's a cry but not a cry."

The medication prescribed to keep Candace comfortable did not seem to be working, and her mother and grandmother were growing more and more upset. So Howell asked Dr. Nachum Gal, the resident on duty that day, to order more drugs to help ease the pain. Science has not established that patients such as Candace *are* in pain, the inquiry was told. "Seizing and gasping for breath to me just has to be painful," Howell said, "whether it's our kind of pain or not."

Dr. Gal ordered an overdose of morphine. Howell administered it at 9:10 p.m. and forty minutes later Candace Taschuk died. She was sixteen hours old.

That would probably have been the end of the incident had a routine audit of hospital records the following February not turned up the order for fifteen milligrams of morphine (fifty times the normal infant dose) which, according to law, must be reported to the Office of Medical Examiners. The hospital suspended Howell, her immediate supervisor, assistant charge nurse Betty Schulze, and Dr. Gal, pending an investigation. Dr. Gal promptly took off to his native Israel, leaving the two nurses to face the government-ordered fatality inquiry that convened in July 1983 in Alberta Provincial Court.

Confronted before his departure by chief neonatologist Dr. David Schiff, Dr. Gal, in Edmonton on a one-year hospital training course, was reported to have shrugged and said: "You know the nurses in your unit, how emotionally charged they are." In his testimony Dr. Schiff explained to the court that nurses' requests for more sedation are not uncommon. "Nurses become very concerned and very involved with patients, and they will come to you on numerous occasions to try to get you to improve the general state of well-being."

Dr. Schiff argued that he would have warned the nurses, had he been consulted, not to give that "ridiculous" dose. Dr. John Reed, medical vice-president of the hospital, also criticized the nurses for not bringing in a senior staff doctor to overrule Dr. Gal and verify the dose. Betty Schulze said she had confronted Dr. Gal with the inappropriate order and had asked him to change it, but she had not waited to see that he had done so. Barbara Jane Howell admitted to the court she had known the order was an overdose. Her main concern had been to release the baby from suffering, she said.

Assistant chief judge Carl Rolf decided the autopsy did not definitively establish the "excessive and inappropriate" morphine dose as the cause of death. The ruling left open the possibility the baby died a natural death resulting from birth asphyxia. According to the judge, "The nurses wanted relief for the baby, her mother and grandmother." Dr. Gal "succumbed to additional requests by the nurses, [and] for some inexplicable reason, nurse Howell, despite her experience, administered the drug in the dosage ordered by the doctor."

The judge confirmed that "Nurses have a duty to question a prescribed treatment." But he also spoke of the emotional tie nurses have for patients in their role as "surrogate mothers," and recommended "a continuing-education psychological counselling program for nurses to assist them in overcoming this emotional tie. I wouldn't want them to get rid of it, just assist them in coping with it."

In other words, the women, mothers rather than health-care professionals, were overemotional, and the men, unnerved, had no choice but to give in. Would Judge Rolf have characterized a doctor or even a male nurse as a surrogate mother? Not likely.

The Canadian Nurses Association's voluntary code of ethics asks nurses to challenge any doctor's order they consider inappropriate. Provincial nursing associations in Ontario and Quebec have set out similar codes for nurses, called "ethical guidelines," which are also voluntary. They are enforceable only by disciplinary action from the professional body; the role of nurse advocate has no legal sanction. In fact, just ten years earlier in 1975 an Ontario judge had ruled that unless there was clear and obvious evidence of neglect or incompetence on the part of the family doctor, it would be unthinkable for the hospital or its agents to interfere or depart from his instructions.

The Alberta Association of Registered Nurses responded to the fatality inquiry by conducting a disciplinary hearing the following November. This time, Howell was penalized by her peers. She was suspended from practising nursing for an indefinite period, and Schulze, ruled guilty of professional misconduct for failing to recheck the unusual order, was suspended for six months. On appeal to the association, the nurses fixed Howell's suspension at one year and reduced Schulze's time to four months. Because Schulze decided to take the association to court, her sentence was stayed pending the results of that appeal.

When Schulze and her union, the Staff Nurses' Association of Alberta, took the Alberta Association of Registered Nurses to the Court of Queen's Bench in May 1984, it was the first time that the appeal procedure had been invoked since it had been established in 1916. Dr. Schiff reiterated in court that the nurse has a responsiblility to question a doctor's order. "The bottom line is that she doesn't have to give it; she can insist the doctor give it himself." Josephine Flaherty, a nursing ethics expert called in from Ottawa, explained that the code of nursing ethics holds the nurse accountable for her own behaviour. "A registered nurse can never say policy made me do it or the head nurse made me do it because a nurse is accountable before society, before herself and before God."

The court declined the opportunity to interfere with the verdict of a self-governing body like the AARN, but it did move to reduce Schulze's sentence, decreasing her suspension to one day.

The judge confirmed that the Alberta College of Physicians and Surgeons had suspended Dr. Gal's licence to practise in the province of Alberta. The Alberta attorney-general had laid nine criminal charges against him in November 1983, including one of first-degree murder. In January 1984 the federal department of justice launched extradition proceedings for his return from Israel. Howell and Schulze were granted immunity from prosecution in exchange for guaranteeing to appear as witnesses in any court proceedings. Because the government of Israel refused to extradite Dr. Gal, the case is now considered closed.

Active euthanasia is against the law in this country, although a 1990 Gallup poll says it is supported by 78 per cent of Canadians. "No codes," or passive euthanasia, is society's only medical concession to pain. "Pain management" is the current nursing euphemism. Only nurses control access to addictive or potentially lethal drugs in Canadian hospitals, and no one has given them any guidance on how much suffering is enough. Faced with painful terminal cases, some take matters into their own hands. They say they can put up a series of infinitesimal morphine doses in a slow intravenous drip, a method of "pain management" specifically designed to bring the release of death without alerting the hospital auditors.

Both the Taschuk inquiry and the Grange inquiry, occur-
ring within months of each other, delivered a similar message for nurses. When there is trouble, don't count on
doctors' support. When there is trouble, the hospital administration will protect itself. Many of the thirty or forty nurses in
the Edmonton courtroom during the inquiry felt the hospital's testimony on internal policy and procedures for han-
dling narcotics was evasive. While most nurses agree that
Howell went overboard in her decision to obey the doctor's
order and inject a lethal drug overdose, they are convinced
compassionate nursing rather than improper medical treatment was on trial.

Barbara Jane Howell's mistake was that she cared.

After a year's disciplinary suspension from the AARN, Howell went back to work at the University of Alberta Hospital
using the name she acquired during a subsequent marriage.
Betty Schulze, traumatized by the incident into changing her
name and unlisting her telephone number, was also back at
work. The shadow over her twenty-four years' experience and
immaculate record is considered one of the tragedies of the
case. The Staff Nurses' Association of Alberta feels the provincial association was incorrect in raking Schulze over the
coals for misconduct. Under the extreme stress of the
moment, Betty Schulze simply didn't keep a close enough
watch on the doctor.

Shortly after the Taschuk case hit the newspapers, the medical staff of a Calgary neonatal intensive-care unit, faced with
a dying child and apparently terrified of repercussions,
polled the nurses one by one on "heroic measures" before
choosing not to continue treatment. In the absence of clear
guidelines on where to draw the line, each nurse is forced to
develop her own. How they react depends very much on how
long they have worked in an area where death is common,
and what philosophy they develop as a consequence.

"Watching suffering is a nurse's job," says neonatal intensive-care nurse Suzanne Bowley, who was working in Calgary
when the Taschuk case became public. "The baby was going to
die anyway. She could have gone peacefully and comfortably

with a minimal or low dose. Why put yourself in that legal position? I'd never do that. It was awful. Why didn't they get that guy to give it himself?"

Because caring is emotional, society has relegated it to women. Taking care of someone, nurturing them, nursing, is assumed to be a woman's primordial role. The "womanly" qualities of caring – for children, the elderly, the sick – are the source of nurses' strength, an empowerment of the feminine principle. But these qualities have no social or monetary value. Fetching, washing, stroking, the physical manifestations of caring, are considered to be menial and unskilled acts of servility.

Susan Reverby suggests that nursing today is "a conflicted metaphor in our culture, reflecting all the ambivalences we give to the meaning of womanhood." A 1985 U.S. media study described the "Killer Nurse" phenomenon in which newspapers feed society's fear of excessive caring by sensationalizing stories of mercy killings as lethal female "mercy." One nurse in 1980 was called the Death Angel by the Boston media. Women as caregivers simply can't win. Susan Nelles didn't care enough; she didn't cry when babies died. Barbara Jane Howell cared too much. And competent nursing is put down as an unskilled outpouring of compassion.

Caring is women's work, and women's work, "put simply, is the work women do for men," nurse-sociologist Verna Lovell writes in a 1981 analysis of the Vancouver General Hospital nurses' revolt. Placing caring in the centre of the nursing ideology today is risky because society places so little value on it. A new nurse arriving to work on a hospital ward is taken for granted, if she is a woman, says Lucille Auffrey, executive director of the Nurses Association of New Brunswick. "The supervisor just says matter of factly, 'You know how to take care of a baby, don't you?' "

Only a minority of doctors considers nurses as professional colleagues, according to a 1984 report from the Royal Commission on the Status of Women. Most doctors see the nurse "as a provider of a conglomerate of insignificant services" such as "mother, child, secretary, wife, waitress, maid, machine, and psychiatrist." Studies show that this sex-role stereotyping seriously impedes nurses' ability to act. Their knowledge is downgraded in comparison with medical authority, even in areas where medicine has no demonstrable expertise. "The public image of the nurse is the underpaid, overworked assistant to the physician, with a kind heart, a tough stomach, and not too smart," says Ginette Rodger.

To be able to care for others, nurses need the power to do what they have been trained to do, to make decisions based on it, and to have their decisions respected. Nurses do not have that power, and many of them compensate for what they perceive as their vulnerable side by hiding behind technology, the ideal buffer for those who want some distance from their helplessness in the face of intense suffering. Nurses in Moncton Hospital's neurological intensive-care unit say they have to block out what's happening most of the time. They say they couldn't deal with debilitating brain injuries in any other way. Mae Reardon, an operating-room nurse in St. Anthony, can handle the raw bone, jagged flesh, deep foot-long gash, and continuous bleeding of the woman whose kidney stones are being surgically removed – but only by "turning off her emotions." Susan Mayer, who teaches at the Ryerson School of Nursing in Toronto, holds seminars and support groups for nurses in her Peterborough home. "Some of them are real tough cookies," she says. "I don't understand that phenomenon. They close right off. They can be the toughest group in the world to talk to."

Getting tough is one way for women to aspire to power. Some three hundred nursing supervisors and administrators from all across Ontario assembled in Toronto one winter afternoon in February 1989 to talk about leadership in the next century, and Jenniece Larsen, professor and director of the University of Manitoba School of Nursing in Winnipeg, stood up to give the keynote address. Introducing herself as seeing the world through a feminist lens, Larsen exhorted nursing leaders to learn to prosper in the health-care system of the future, holding out British Prime Minister Margaret Thatcher, "a leader who may be wrong but who is never in doubt," as the role model best suited to instil the required self-confidence.

Nurses are the best organized and probably the most powerful women in this country, Larsen says. Hospital nursing executives manage thousands of employees and millions and millions of dollars. "As a feminist, I don't reject Thatcher; she is probably the most significant leader in the world. She is not a feminist. She is bloody successful. She is a wonderful role model. And actually, if you look at women leaders, how many of them would you describe as feminists? I absolutely believe in feminist ideology, but for my own purposes. I also can see beyond it. You see people like me don't need it."

A few weeks earlier, Evelyn Malowany, director of nursing at the Children's Hospital in Montreal, sat in her cluttered office talking about the changes she is determined to make in the hospital's power structure. She wants equality for the department of nursing, and from all that she sees and reads, she knows feminist strategies will be useful. But she doesn't go around saying she is a feminist. "They find a category for you and they can put you into it and forget about you. Feminism is a label for any strong woman. Then you are a battle axe. I tell them I am like Margaret Thatcher. I am an Iron Maiden."

Most feminists simply want women to enjoy the same rights men do. But among nurses, feminism is a dirty word. That distrust is only logical, Larsen says. "When nurses reached out to the feminist community, they got slapped for being who they are. You'd withdraw from that and deny a relationship, wouldn't you?" It is true that many women concerned with expanding gender roles have not been interested in nurses. Instead of revering mothering and caring as invaluable, feminists have tended to encourage women to enter non-traditional jobs and to abandon the ones based on female skills. Nurses rankle visibly when women striving for power for other women ask the inevitable question: "Why aren't you a doctor?" They retaliate by characterizing feminists in negative stereotypes. For University of Toronto nursing students, women become feminists only because they are "ugly and can't get a man." But there is also the genuine and justifiable fear that if nurses attend too closely to the feminist agenda, they will lose the good things about nursing.

Nurses, however, are women; their miserable working conditions are a women's issue; and their struggle for a better deal is a feminist action. A political alliance between nurses and feminists makes sense. Low status, menial duties, minimal career potential, stagnating wages, widely varying standards of training, and rapid turnover are all classic characteristics of a woman's occupation. In 1984 the World Health Organization incorporated the goal of raising the status of nurses into its principle of universally accessible health care for all by the year 2000. The one depends on the other, the WHO said, and for the nursing image to improve, the status of women must improve. Elevating the social status of caring for the sick can be accomplished only by increasing respect for women.

Feminine qualities – insight, intuition, compassion – are a source of strength, empowering nurses, both male and female, to do what's best for the patient. Although nurses have no power to direct treatment, patients are often much more willing to talk to them than to doctors. Emotional involvement with the *patient* is not the compassion trap; the need for distance is a myth. Just let us do it, many nurses are saying. Let us nourish, let us nurse, and pay us well for it. God knows, in the era of AIDS, you're going to need us. When a *Globe and Mail* newspaper editorial in 1989 called for a concerted public-relations effort aimed at manipulating consumer attitudes to make nurses feel better, Carol Helmstadter at Toronto's Wellesley Hospital was incensed. "Image, shmimage – try paying us more."

What's happening with nursing is a larger symbol of what's happening to us as a society. We are losing our capacity to care for people. We no longer care about caring. But we are wrong. What has been dismissed as women's work is turning out to be vital to the survival of the health-care system. "Yes, I think Nightingalism is probably out of fashion," says Donald Macgregor, president of the Alberta Hospital Association. "But I still believe the typical nurse enters nursing because she's interested in caring for people. Heaven help us if that isn't true."

As a kid, Bill Grant, a stocky, big-chested man of forty with a handsome moustache and an expansive cavalier energy to match, would never have considered a nursing career. "Then, if you took typing, you were a faggot," he says directly. So Grant began working in a sawmill at the age of nineteen and stayed in the mills on and off, dabbling in university courses as he went, for sixteen years. Then he was so inspired by a woman nursing student he met that he sat up in bed one night, spending hours thinking about the attraction of nursing. "I woke thinking, what a good idea that would have been. Something clicked in me. Ding. Ding. Ding." But he hung on at the sawmills just the same, until 1984, when he lost his job.

The employment situation in Vancouver at the time was bad, and he couldn't find a thing, not even at minimum wage. Finishing his university degree was out of the question. Grant's wife, a Vancouver television journalist, would not want to support him that long. He started to think once again about becoming a nurse. When he started taking cardiopulmonary resuscitation courses just to test the waters, Grant had never been in a hospital in his life, except to look at babies through windows. Every single one of his male friends told him nurses get treated "like shit." They couldn't believe Grant would consider it, and women friends swore the reason they weren't nurses was because they couldn't deal with the inevitable abuse. Yet the women nurses he knew kept assuring him the job wasn't that bad.

The victim stereotype turned out to be false, at least for Grant. "You can stand up if you want to. I've had two major run-ins with doctors, and I've been supported by head nurses." Grant's testosterone is probably not what's making the difference, although maybe it has helped. But his is a conscious decision that any man or woman could make. Grant won't buy the Nightingale ideology. He hates the words "caring profession," and self-denial is a trait he doesn't believe in at all. "I respect human beings. Patients don't want caring. They want respect. They are humiliated enough being there as it is."

Grant's women friends think his rejection of caring will make him a much better nurse than his female colleagues. The smothering mother image is what the non-nursing women don't like. Grant has found that his male patients relate to his sixteen years in the sawmill. They enjoy his maleness; it gives them someone to talk to with a similar background. A few of his female patients have expressed reservations, especially when he must do procedures such as palpating nipples. But it's that kind of intimacy with the patient that makes nursing unique, different from doctoring or any other hospital function.

Sometimes at work he feels lonely. His male upbringing, his football, his weightlifting, don't give him a taste for talking about fashion or soap operas. "I didn't even know what soap operas were before I went into nursing school. These women know every frigging one." Although he's been living with a woman for fifteen years, he'd never worked with any women until now. So far he hasn't run across the "little women in tight little hairdos" he expected to find. The female nurses at St. Paul's hospital, however, do look at him as someone who doesn't fit their own image of what a nurse should be. "They say so many times, 'We're glad we have a real man.'"

Grant's manhood is in good shape – in such good shape he's not the least bit concerned that nursing will detract from it, despite the gay image that male nursing has. The 236 male nurses in Manitoba, sick of the gay stereotype, formed a Men In Nursing Interest Group in April 1988. Grant is also not worried about professional status. Always a member of the working class, he doesn't need to set himself apart from other wage-earners. Besides, there's no time to dwell on such issues.

Grant describes his first four months as "sheer hell." His leukemia patients had peripheral intravenous and central lines attached to them, and bags of blood and platelets hanging, and he didn't know "what hole to put anything in." There are all the various drugs to keep track of, their devastating side effects to remember, plus he often has as many as eight other patients. People "went flat" on him, "ssssssttt, no blood pressure, just like that." He went home a wreck every night. "Did I forget to add up this fluid balance? Did I forget to sign that document?" He sat up every night worrying and worrying, until finally he reached the crisis point – deal with the stress or quit. He refused to quit. Now he sees it as a matter of confidence rather than stress management. He's doing the best job he can, he says to himself, and just leaves it at that, although sometimes he still can't believe he's able to do what he does without making a mistake.

He says he's in for the duration, although he may take a leave of absence or bail out of the stress of the hospital into public health. He's working on a degree in his spare time, and in ten years he'll still be nursing in one way or another. He knows he has no status, but the image of nurses is changing, and he's more concerned about the money than he is about control. Grant is shocked by all the tax and benefit deductions from his $31,000-a-year salary. The mill wages were clear of deductions, and pensions were paid out on the top. Grant finds hospital work every bit as physically strenuous as mill work, and the stress of nursing is much higher, but they're deducting big chunks off his pay cheque, whittling it down to what he was making five or six years ago. For this he's gone to school six straight semesters, and he doesn't even get paid for lunches.

Getting dumped on to do all the leftovers, the portering, the cleaning, the carrying, the joe jobs that no one else wants, is also frustrating. But as jobs go, this one's not too bad. The patients like him. He doesn't kowtow to the doctors. What society thinks of nursing doesn't worry him too much, especially since his patients and colleagues hold him in high regard. As far as the rest, the ones who have never been in hospital, well, they are all probably thinking "what suckers we are to be nurses. I think that's what most people think."

Bill Grant maintains his *savoir faire* by keeping up a copacetic male chatter with doctors and by his private decision not to buckle under when challenged. In this way he is unlike his female colleagues. Nursing school simply reinforced what they had learned as girls, teaching them never to call doctors by their first names, to stand up when a doctor enters the nursing station, to let him on the elevator first.

In the modern hospital a nurse is expected to remain within the boundaries set by what the doctor orders. As long as a nurse fits into that mould, she can maintain the illusion of power by playing the doctor-nurse game. As soon as she asserts herself, however, she knows she'll lose her working relationship with the doctor and her credibility in the hospital. It's the same game women play with men in private life. It's what good wives and mothers do, pretending to be less informed so as not to damage their husband's self-esteem. The tactic may improve the nurse-doctor relationship but it also reinforces her subordinate role. "Look at where we are, and it's almost the twenty-first century, still at the bottom of the totem pole as far as the public is concerned," says Ros O'Reilly. "Being all women must have something to do with it. That's why we've been so slow in breaking out of this stereotype."

Canada's 240,000 registered nurses are trying to develop a new image. In 1986 the Canadian Nurses Association got a government-produced television advertisement depicting nurses in tight-fitting mini-skirts pulled. In 1989, a month after assuring the American Nurses' Association that five sexy student nurses would no longer participate in provocative locker-room aerobics, NBC had to cancel its four-month-old prime-time television series *Nightingales*. There had been a

widespread protest. Most Canadian university nursing campuses are now offering one elective course that at least aims
at incorporating feminist thinking and feminist theory. Self-
image is, after all, the place to begin. "What you think of me
is what I think of me," says Glenna Cole Slattery. "If I present
myself as knowledgeable, relatively competent, committed,
nobody's fool, I will be treated as such. You walk around with
a tin cup in your hand saying 'please,' don't be surprised if
they think you are a beggar."

The report of the Ontario Ministry of Health's Advisory
Committee on Nursing Manpower in 1988 wanted more men
to be encouraged to enter nursing. The theory is that if nursing boasted an equal proportion of men to women, it would
no longer be undervalued as women's work. Men now make
up less than 3 per cent of Canadian nurses. While more and
more women want to become doctors, the number of men
entering nursing is increasing negligibly.

But significant numbers of men are not going to enter
nursing as long as nurses earn as little as they now do. In 1889
the Montreal General Hospital paid its dog-catcher almost
twice the monthly salary it paid its nurses. A hundred years
later, in 1987 in British Columbia, general-duty nurses with six
years' experience earned $2,844 a month; a hospital plumber
earned $2,852, and a biomedical electronic technician $3,060
a month. "An entry-level nurse should earn at least as much as
a plumber," B.C. Nurses' Union activist Bernadette Stringer
told a rally during the 1989 B.C. nurses' strike.

Many nurses are now looking to pay-equity legislation as a
means of improving their wage. Pay equity is based not only
on paying people what they are worth; it also assumes that
the marketplace discriminates against women, has done so
for years, and that this systemic discrimination will not correct itself. Nurses may have more catching up to do in terms
of equal pay for equal work than any other occupational
group in the country. A nurse in an extended-care unit moves
patients in and out of bed at least four times a shift. That's
dead weight with the assistance of one other person. "Now

you find me a stevedore who does that, for that little money," says Vancouver nurse Trudy Staley.

Nurses are, however, not getting pay equity in the two provinces with pay-equity laws. And they aren't likely to get it through legislation proposed in most of the rest. The Canadian health-care system, dependent on underpaying nurses, has too much to lose.

Manitoba was supposed to have a pay-equity plan in place for health-care workers at twenty-three facilities by September 30, 1988. Consultants came up with an astronomical figure needed to close the wage gap, amounting to $2 an hour more for nurses. The employers, supported by the provincial labour relations board, balked. The Manitoba Nurses' Union accepted, in the fall of 1990, a much reduced interim wage adjustment *without prejudice* until its court challenge invoking Canada's Charter of Rights and Freedoms is heard and decided upon – a process that could take years.

By requiring female job classes to be compared with male job classes in the same establishment, the pay-equity laws in Manitoba and Ontario have effectively screened out the very group of underpaid workers they were supposed to protect. There aren't any comparable groups for nurses. In Manitoba, "house medical officer" was negotiated out as a comparable class. The laws discriminate against health-care workers because 90 per cent of health care is female. "It becomes a political issue," says Maureen Kilgour, the Manitoba government's pay-equity officer for health care. "Pay equity is a disaster. It is a well-intentioned public policy watered-down, sabotaged, ineffective. It's just not going to work for nurses."

At the Mississauga Hospital, pay equity put nurses on the same level as pastry cooks. Mortified, the nurses wore measuring spoons and cups on their uniforms in protest. A November 1989 Supreme Court of Ontario ruling, upheld in September 1990 by the Ontario Court of Appeal, has paved the way for fifty-two public-health and nursing-home nurses working for the Haldimand-Norfolk regional government to negotiate pay equity by comparing their jobs to the regional police. However, at the time of writing, it remains unknown if the police and the region will continue their appeal of the precedent-setting case. One tiny group of nurses working as researchers for the University of Toronto received a 47 per cent pay increase under the law. A non-union group working for one employer, they were able to establish male engineering technicians as a comparable group.

But the Ontario Nurses' Association had to give up trying for a pay-equity plan at ninety nursing-home locals: no comparable groups, no pay equity. Hospital nurses in Ontario are having an extremely hard time. The ONA has appealed pay-equity plans at 220 hospital agencies. The Pay Equity Tribunal is listening to nurses' concerns, says Noelle Andrews, in charge of pay equity for the union. Nurses' jobs are at least getting evaluated for the first time in history. But after spending $500,000 in 1989 and an estimated $1,000,000 in 1990 to pay for the appeals, consultations, and other paperwork, the ONA had not posted one pay-equity plan as of June 1990, six months after the legal deadline. The union also had to open for the first time ever its emergency security fund (not called a strike fund because Ontario hospital nurses are not legally permitted to strike).

Ontario Premier Bob Rae has promised to change the Liberal government's pay-equity law to include women, such as nurses, who work in female-dominated job classes. But such an action will be very expensive for Canadian taxpayers. The truly astronomical cost is one reason why the precise consultants' figures are being kept secret in Manitoba. An American judge dismissing a pay-equity application by Colorado nurses in 1978 raised the spectre of "economic chaos," adding that implementing pay equity "is pregnant with the possibility of disrupting the entire economic system" of the U.S.

Nurses' pay ambitions are unrealistic, says McGill University's Dr. Walter Spitzer. "I don't agree that nurses assuming more responsibility should be paid more. Equal pay for equal acts does not account for training and experience. The kind of training we give them doesn't put them in a position of

accepting the kind of responsibility a physician would have."
The Manitoba and Ontario pay-equity laws do account for
training and experience. They also assess effort, responsibility, and working conditions like dirt, noise, risk, and mental
stress. Although these are not the traditional values of the
marketplace, the availability of quality care may depend on
giving nursing the recognition it deserves.

"Before you do the studies on satisfaction, why don't you
give nurses $50 an hour and then see if you still have a
problem?" says Margaret Ethier, outgoing president of the
United Nurses of Alberta. "But that would upset the whole
economic system, paying a bunch of women more money." A
world view such as feminism, by requiring the recognition of
systemic injustice based on gender, challenges the fundamental structure of society. "Why is upward mobility an honest activity for other professions but a dirty word when
applied to nurses?" Monique Bégin asked the Alberta Association of Registered Nurses in the spring of 1987. "Only a
feminist analysis will explain that contradiction."

Pay equity, according to Diana Dick, a nurse now working
for Ontario's Pay Equity Commission, "is the key to everything, the number one top-priority issue for nurses." But they
aren't going to get it, at least not through legislation. Canadian provincial governments are understandably reluctant to
set precedents for a job classification that employs more than
200,000 women. The challenge of getting justice for nurses –
recognition, respect, and money commensurate with the
importance of the work they do – may have to come from
outside the law. Nurses' unions all around the country are
coming to terms with that.

8

The Highest Respect for the Law

The nurses on the morning shift at the Edmonton General Hospital start work at seven o'clock, almost two hours before the February sun gets up. Once over the hospital threshold, they are in a place that is never dark. Today, Monday, February 8, 1988, nothing much disturbs the artificial light. No staff nurses, their white uniforms covered by heavy parkas, are hurrying down the hall to their stations. Today, fifteen minutes before the morning shift begins, only the heels of the nursing supervisors click-clack across the hard bare floor.

Outside in the dark the hospital's floor nurses are doing their morning shift on the picket line. They have crossed a different threshold, the one that divides law-abiding citizens from criminals. It is day sixteen of the United Nurses of Alberta's nineteen-day illegal strike, and Alberta hospitals have already sued over a hundred of them for civil contempt. The province has secured its first conviction for criminal contempt against the union, forcing it to pay a $250,000 fine. Another criminal contempt charge is pending.

At $28,500 to $32,900 a year, Alberta nurses are the third-highest paid in the country after Ontario and British Columbia. They are seeking an increase of $1.50 an hour across the board over fifteen months, which would raise their yearly salaries to a range of $31,858 to $36,349. More important than money, however, are improved working conditions. They want the professional-responsibility committee in their contract to give them more control over patient safety. They want wards redefined to give them more control over their own safety when they work alone at night. They want to prove to the provincial government, once and for all, that they are not just "going to lay down and die."

The United Nurses of Alberta has struck three times before in the union's eleven-year history, but this is the first illegal walkout. This is the first time that Alberta hospital nurses have dared walk the pavement since 1983, the year a new anti-strike law ended their third strike.

The 11,000 nurses from 104 hospitals are out on a long limb. The illegal picket line cancels the protection provided by the union contract, and none of them knows for sure if she will have a job to return to when the strike ends. For the first time their colleagues from Alberta's seven provincially owned hospitals are out on the line with them. But their rival union representing 2,300 nurses at Edmonton's University of Alberta Hospital is not on strike. In fact, the members of the Staff Nurses' Association of Alberta are exhausting themselves trying to take care of nursing emergencies. They vote tomorrow on a wage package identical to an offer rejected over the weekend by the UNA.

The women on the line this dark and frigid February morning are putting up a brave show. "Patients need nurses, not another machine that goes 'ping'," one sign reads. "A subservient nurse is a poor model of health," another states. They whisper in hushed tones about the rally the previous day, about the meeting tomorrow night, about the strategy of lawbreaking, slapping their hands against the bitter –30°C cold and cheering themselves by recalling those who came before them – other heroic lawbreakers like the suffragettes and Martin Luther King Jr.

They've printed up a bright yellow leaflet bearing the words of the murdered civil rights activist. "In no sense do I advocate evading or defying the law," it says. "That would lead to anarchy. But an individual who breaks a law that conscience tells him is unjust, and who willingly accepts the penalty of imprisonment in order to arouse the conscience of the community over its injustice, is in reality expressing the highest respect for the law." The signature, Martin Luther King Jr., stands out in bold black letters to inspire the house-wives, single mothers, students fresh out of school, and wid-ows brewing coffee in the basement room of Local 79's strike headquarters across the street.

In that office some of the women sweeping the floor and unstacking chairs are old enough to remember nursing's domestic roots. "Just call me Hazel the Maid," is the way one nurse introduces herself, and she is only half joking. A nurse for forty-three years, Hazel, an orphan, went into nursing because it was the only way to put a roof over her head. Now a widow, Hazel scabbed during the strike in 1982; support for her seven children was the reason she gave herself then. But today she says: "I understand the issues now. We have no other recourse than to stand up and be counted. How did women get the vote? How many women then had to get out there and fight and got put in jail and still walked out there with their pickets and said, 'We deserve the vote'?"

Helen Rebalkin, a fifty-eight-year-old psychiatric nurse, is more than angry. They served her with the contempt charge right in her apartment, she says. She had been "fingered" by one of the Edmonton General's human resources people who said he saw her picketing. "I didn't know it was against the law to picket," she says. "Anybody can picket. It's not con-tempt of court to picket." The humiliation of being charged like a common criminal is only half of it. Rebalkin says she's been manipulated; she's been patronized; she's been infan-talized. The nurses now working around the clock at the University of Alberta Hospital "are the good girls," she says. "We are the bad girls. And the government says, just like a patronizing parent, 'Now then, why don't you be like your sisters?'"

The hospital is pressing charges against the UNA nurses to make an example of them, as a deterrent for other "bad girls," she says. But they have underestimated Helen Rebal-kin. She is not as afraid as some of the younger ones who have been charged. "I've lived quite a while and I know life

can be tough." A nurse for thirty-three years, Rebalkin views
the court appearances as just one in a long series of challenges. She has a lot of responsibility in her department, she
says. Her patients may not be acutely ill, but they take overdoses. They are unpredictable. They have medical problems
like heart conditions. They have attacks and seizures. She
and the other nurses in her group are asked to work alone
and are sometimes assaulted.

During the last strike, in 1982, more people voted to strike
than not to strike. That's why the union went out, Rebalkin
recalls. But every time the Alberta Hospital Association made
a threat, "We ran back." This time they can threaten all they
want, she vows. "The first thing we got offered was a rollback.
That's not an offer. It's a slap in the face. We felt enough is
enough. It's not just money. It's self-esteem. If you are essential and you are earning money below the wages of other
people, how essential can you be?"

Margaret Ethier, in her seventh-floor office in Edmonton's
Principal Plaza (later, after the Principal investment scandal,
renamed Metropolitan Place) calls the nurses' new awareness
of how little they are valued "a loss of innocence." Ethier
says, "This is what the government and their employers really
think of nurses. It's like the mother in the home. 'You know
we love you. You're doing the most important job in the world.
But you don't want to demean that by dirtying it with money.
So you don't get any.' "

"Loss of innocence" – Ontario nursing leaders had used
the same phrase to assess the national impact of the Grange
inquiry four years earlier. Nurses are supposed to be naive
enough to continue to put the needs of others before their
own.

"Nurses believe all that hype," says Ethier, a member of the
union's executive since its first annual general meeting in
1978. Although she was not elected president until 1980, just
after the union's second hospital strike, Ethier is credited
with commandeering this group of women through three of
their four hospital strikes, despite what she calls Florence
Nightingale hype. "Nurses wouldn't be on strike as ordinary

people would be on strike, the same way that a woman wouldn't leave her children just for herself," is how Ethier describes what she's up against.

To say that walking out on patients, even in a legal strike, goes against the grain of nursing is more than an understatement. For a nurse, abandoning a sick and suffering person is nothing short of sacrilege. From 1965 to 1972 the Canadian Nurses Association said no nurse should withdraw her services from patients – no matter what. That ban was lifted in 1972, when the CNA recognized that without a strike mandate, nurses had no bargaining tools.

But although the national organization may recognize the value of the strike threat as leverage, it does not want nurses out on the street. In 1980 the CNA board tried to get the withdrawal of nursing services identified as unethical behaviour in its code of ethics. Delegates to the biennial meeting rejected that blanket condemnation and the CNA board had to modify its position. Now it says patients are entitled to emergency nursing services during any job action by nurses and, "The safety of clients should be the first concern in planning and implementing any job action." The UNA and other nurses' unions, not placated by the compromise, view this section of the 1985 code as simply a continuation of the CNA's anti-strike policy.

Provincial laws give hospital nurses the unfettered right to strike in only three provinces: Manitoba, Saskatchewan, and Nova Scotia. In Ontario, Newfoundland, Prince Edward Island, and finally Alberta, unresolved disputes go to binding arbitration. (Public-health nurses in Ontario are allowed to strike.) In British Columbia, New Brunswick, and Quebec, nurses' strikes are restricted by a requirement to keep a certain percentage of nurses on the job as an essential service for an emergency. The joke among unionists in Quebec is that the essential-service level of 90 per cent legislated by the province requires more nurses to work during a strike than are ever called in to work on normal days.

In 1983, the same year the Progressive Conservatives in Alberta passed the first version (Bill 11) of their now infamous law outlawing nurses' strikes, the Parti Québécois passed a similar law (Bill 37) prohibiting public-sector strikes over the new contracts it had imposed on teachers, nurses, and government workers. The sanctions provided under that law were declared unconstitutional by the Supreme Court of Canada in March 1990, although the law itself still stands. In 1986, Liberal Premier Robert Bourassa came down with Bill 160 "to re-establish the balance between the state and the unions." It imposes crippling fines and penalties on any illegal strikes carried out in the essential-services sector.

Whatever the legal restriction, the decision to exercise any limited or unlimited right to strike remains an agonizing dilemma for nurses. Ann, when she is not on the picket line, works with stroke patients on the neuromuscular unit of the 253-bed Glenrose Rehabilitation Hospital in Edmonton's north end. Glenrose is located in the hub of four busy Edmonton cross streets, and many of the rush-hour cars this Monday morning honk in support as they pass the women walking the bitter-cold mile around its perimeter. One elderly gentleman has brought a bag of candy for the nurses. It's all he could think of to do to help, he says. The Glenrose is a provincially owned hospital governed by public-service legislation that does not permit strikes. But because the UNA strike is illegal, there is no incentive to play the game according to the Labour Relations Act; all the regular hospital locals are out, not just the ones who voted in favour of striking, and the union this time has polled Ann and her colleagues at Glenrose, and they too have voted to walk.

Ann always wanted to be a nurse. But she got married when she was seventeen, in the early 1940s, and she didn't have the money to go to nursing school. She worked in a bank at first and looked after her three children; the oldest one is now married. She has been nursing for twenty-two years and considers herself devoted. "I didn't go into it for the money, that's for sure. I wanted to give something of myself." Ann wept as the nurses at Glenrose walked out at 7:30 a.m. on January 25. "We all did. Our patients are long-term patients, not acute care. I work with head injuries. They are there for a long time, sometimes for a year or a year and a half, and you become very attached. It was very, very difficult for me to walk out. I had tears in my eyes."

Deserting a post of compassion by participating in a legal strike would have been bad enough, but in this illegal one Ann and her colleagues have had to face a public hostile to lawbreakers and schooled for centuries to put its trust in the devotion of Nightingales. Dr. Roy Le Riche, registrar of the Alberta College of Physicians and Surgeons, called the strike "no different from terrorism. I did not believe that nurses ... could sink to such depths of degradation. I am sure Florence Nightingale is rotating at great speed in her grave."

Donald Macgregor defended the Alberta Hospital Association's decision to take the nurses to court as necessary to establish a legal precedent that the Alberta Labour Relations ruling is enforceable. "What happens when a government can't enforce its own laws? That's called anarchy." A *Globe and Mail* editorial sounded a national appeal for "no more acts of anarchy" such as the nurses' strike in Alberta, which "should not have happened ... the United Nurses of Alberta brought no honor on themselves or their profession by rejecting mediation and, if necessary, binding arbitration under Alberta's labor legislation."

The media seized on stories of medical emergencies. "Man blames Alberta nurses' strike as wife flown to B.C. for operation," one headline screamed. Other stories described desperately sick babies being airlifted to Saskatchewan. The president of the Alberta Medical Association, Dr. Ruth Collins-Nakai, was quoted in the *Edmonton Journal* on February 10 as pleading with the striking union. "Nurses can't use patients' lives or health as bargaining tools," she told a news conference. "Why should patients have to put their lives on the line?"

The Alberta Association of Registered Nurses, which had been sued for libel by the UNA after the 1982 strike, was cautious. "We support nurses' right to free collective bargaining but we can't support breaking the law," said president Sharon Snell. The AARN, charged by government to discipline nurses, put out bulletins warning nurses of their liability in terms of professional misconduct. But as the strike wore on, AARN bulletins talked more about nurses getting a fair shake and less about lawbreaking.

Management nurse Dorothy Falk, assistant director of nursing at the Royal Alexandra's women's hospital, was glad she didn't have to make the decision to picket. "It doesn't seem professional for them to walk the picket line," she said, "but just the same, I have a lot of support for these nurses." The members of the Staff Nurses' Association at the University of Alberta Hospital were in an even more difficult position. By the time the tentative agreement their executive had accepted in principle came to a vote on February 9, their hospital was packed full with every conceivable medical crisis. On Saturday, February 6, their emergency reported 298 visits, up 33 per cent over the normal daily average of 178. Hundreds of athletes and journalists from all over the world were pouring into the province for the Winter Olympic Games opening in Calgary on February 13.

The defiant picket lines became not only a focal point for other Albertans, other trade unions, other nurses, politicians, and women's groups but also a source of inspiration for Canadian women in all walks of life. Donations during the strike reached $130,000 and were still trickling in eighteen months later. The contributions finally totalled more than $500,000, as supporters sent money to pay for $427,750 in fines. A second criminal conviction five days after the nurses returned to work on February 13 had increased the total of the fines to $400,000, as the judge made the union pay another $150,000 for bringing "the administration of justice into scorn." The individual nurses charged with civil contempt had accumulated $27,250 in fines. On appeal, the Court of Queen's Bench in Alberta overturned the civil convictions in March 1990, but upheld the criminal convictions, and the union then took the matter to the Supreme Court of Canada.

During the strike, nurses' unions, afraid to send cash, established lines of credit worth hundreds of thousands of dollars. The UNA mailed $1.1 million out of the province in an attempt to guard against the threatened seizure of its assets. Meanwhile, telegrams to Alberta Premier Don Getty and to Alberta Health Minister Marvin Moore, letters, phone calls, and money poured into the union's provincial headquarters in Edmonton.

"Bad labour laws only change when workers fight back," nationally known feminist unionist Madeleine Parent wrote from Montreal. Betty Shifflert, a sixty-five-year-old retired diploma RN, wrote from Gossano, Alberta, sending in $400 from her husband and herself: "Nurses today, (unlike us in the '40s) are better than ever educated, have a strong self worth, and I'm so proud they are not going to let an arrogant, overconfident government push them around." In addition to support from industrial trade unions, there were messages from women's groups of all descriptions in every part of the country. Audrey McLaughlin, New Democratic Party MP for the Yukon and later leader of the party, stood up in the House of Commons to condemn the Alberta government for "scape-goating the traditionally female profession of nursing."

The UNA nurses on the picket line had dismissed suggestions that their actions were a step forward for women. Many of them insisted nursing was not a women's issue. But they were out there just the same; Gloria Steinem didn't have anything on the middle-class middle-aged women walking that picket line in Alberta in the winter of 1988.

The strike is credited for getting a special report on nursing concerns included in the Premier's Commission on Future Health Care for Albertans; the nurses finally had the ear of the government. But it failed to win better working conditions or to correct the funding cutbacks nurses say are contributing to a deteriorating health-care system. The union did not win protection against contracting out; and it had to reduce its monetary demands. Many nurses were so unhappy with the tentative agreement that the UNA's secretary-treasurer Heather Malloy predicted they would reject it. Vancouver nurse Bill Grant was devastated. "I mean they got nothing.

I was stunned that they'd risk the illegality and all for what they got."

But the strike was a public-relations victory. In the winter of 1989 the Fraser Institute, an ultra-conservative think-tank, released the results of its study of the coverage of health care the previous year. "The big story in health care last year was not a new advance in disease treatment, nor was it innovative care. It was the illegal strike by Alberta nurses." The illegal strike in Alberta put the utter dissatisfaction of Canadian nurses on the national map. In 1988 the United Nurses of Alberta became the undisputed vanguard of a new militancy in Canadian nurses' unions.

The Alberta union had started out in a different direction from other provincial nurses' unions. Kathleen Connors, president of the National Federation of Nurses' Unions in Ottawa, says: "They [the union's nurses] were more militant; they were more trade unionist; they were not hung up on all these professional issues. That's the only way they have been able to survive in that province."

The union's separation from the Alberta Association of Registered Nurses in 1977 was a battle royal. The collective bargaining arm of the professional association was not getting nurses anywhere. But it took guts for the unionists to march out of AARN headquarters on June 14, 1977. One staff member, Bob Donahue, was described later as a Pied Piper leading the nurses to a dangerous new freedom. Splitting off from the education, registration, and licensing body for bargaining purposes certainly upped the ante considerably in terms of how they were going to approach the bargaining table, says Donald Macgregor. "They said publicly, 'We are a union.' Now nurses never said that before. They categorically said, 'You betcha, we're a union.'"

Three weeks later, on July 4, the fledgling union, not yet on Rand formula checkoff and collecting dues by passing the hat among its members, launched the first hospital strike in the province's history – smack in the middle of Ottawa's new high-profile wage-and-price-control policy. The only way the province could end the six-day strike was to order the nurses back to work. It did so, setting up a tribunal to effect a settlement. But when the tribunal gave nurses a 9 per cent across-the-board increase over one year, granting them special status to exceed Ottawa's 6 per cent price control guideline, the federal Anti-Inflation Board stepped in and threatened to quash the provincial ruling. The new union took Ottawa to court and won. "The United Nurses of Alberta succeeded where all other unions had failed, namely to compromise the federal government's anti-inflation program," Judith Hibberd, an associate nursing professor at the University of Alberta, points out in a recent nursing textbook.

The victory was not immediately reflected at the bargaining table. The union negotiated a settlement in 1978, winning the Rand formula checkoff for dues deductions that had been denied the year before, but losing its bid for a professional-responsibility committee. The monetary settlement of 6 per cent, leaving nurses with a wage lower than the average wage for supermarket packers, infuriated the nurses. By the time the union struck again in April 1980 it was ready to defy the back-to-work order that arrived three days later.

Ethier had just been elected president by a small majority at the annual meeting. A feminist and a militant unionist, she was willing to take an aggressive and public stand against anyone who presumed to tell nurses what they could or could not do, Hibberd says. The 1980 strike was hugely successful. The union challenged the back-to-work order in court, and nurses at eighty-one hospitals stayed out for another seven days. They won a 39.8 per cent increase over two years, a staggering feat during a time of wage and price controls. They also won the much-coveted professional-responsibility committee. The lesson: defiance beats conciliation as a strategy by a mile.

But the third UNA strike, with nine thousand nurses at sixty hospitals out on the street from February 16, 1982, to March

11, 1982, was a bitter comedown. Picket lines stayed up until March 10 when the government passed Bill 11, banning all strikes in the health-care system and ordering nurses to solve their problems through compulsory arbitration, with severe penalties if they refused. "If Canada's constitution doesn't prevent this outrageous authoritarian invasion of union pre-rogative by the state, it should," a March 12 *Edmonton Journal* editorial blasted. "How could a Tory government even con-template this?"

Capitalizing on public hatred for a repressive government, Ethier, flushed and angry, told reporters that Alberta's strik-ing nurses would obey but never forgive the provincial gov-ernment for forcing them back to work. As the downcast nurses returned to their jobs to await the decision of the government-ordered Public Arbitration Tribunal, Ethier and Simon Renouf, the union's executive director, "paraded their nurses in front of this tribunal with their horror stories," recalls Heather Smith, then president of the union local at Edmonton General Hospital.

It was a battle of wits, and the union, exhausted by a host of problems, lost it. On July 17 the tribunal ended the bitter seven-month dispute by announcing a wage increase less than the one the nurses had rejected in March.

The following spring, when the government rolled Bill 11 into Bill 44, an even harsher anti-strike policy, Ethier and Renouf appeared before the legislature during the public debates on the proposed law. "What was the real reason for dreaming up new legislation for the nurses?" Ethier asked the packed galleries. "I believe it was pure and simple revenge. After all, [Premier Peter] Lougheed's boys don't take kindly to being outsmarted by a bunch of women. Let's not pretend it has anything to do with concern for the public."

The day Bill 44 was introduced was the day Wendy Danson was hired as an UNA employment-relations officer. Danson says she doesn't know another union with such an effective communications network. "They had ten thousand members on the phone within hours – one person calls two people calls two people. It's incredible when you think of the power that has." Reaction to Bill 44 was swift; the UNA immediately adopted a policy of refusing to participate in arbitration.

But the union had to go into hibernation after 1982. "We couldn't afford education, we couldn't afford to do anything," says Smith, Ethier's successor as UNA president, "and it took us several years to rebuild within our membership a confidence that the strike could be a potential measure of force. It took us until 1988 to do that." By the end of the 1982 strike, the union had acquired a reputation as pugilistic and strike-happy. As Louise Rogers, executive director of the Staff Nurses' Association, says: "It's not normal for a union to go out on strike always. There are times when you have to take a tough stand, but it still isn't normal to have all these rounds of bargaining when you go on strike."

The UNA's own members reflected this lack of confidence; in the years between 1982 and 1988 they twice turned down a recommendation for an illegal strike by their negotiating committee. But secretary-treasurer Heather Malloy says the illegal strike in 1988 paid off. The next bargaining round in 1990 brought a negotiated settlement of 19 per cent over two years, redefinition of a ward, and a forty-five-day fast track to the board of directors for patient safety complaints. As union negotiator Hazel Paish puts it, "A lot of administrations realize that us girls out there striking is the only way we can get this government to make any changes."

Some eight months after the 1988 strike in Alberta, 5,750 Saskatchewan nurses walked off the job at ninety-three hospitals. The key issue in the Saskatchewan Union of Nurses seven-day strike was the right to blow the whistle publicly on unsafe staffing levels and patient care. They won an 11.5 per cent pay increase in a thirty-nine-month contract (the initial offer was between 11 and 14 per cent over four years), a settlement estimated to cost the province $19 million. The final deal included a contract clause establishing an independent, public committee of nurses to hear complaints from any of their colleagues dissatisfied with their hospitals' response to their concerns about health care.

The following spring, in April 1989, the 17,500-member British Columbia Nurses' Union, then in contract negotiations, refused to continue performing any non-nursing services. Nurses wanted a 33 per cent wage hike over one year. After twenty-two days of mediation, on June 14 the union embarked on a phased-in strike, which at its peak included picket lines at sixty-nine hospitals (with 70 per cent of the nursing staff working inside to provide essential services); no picket lines but maintaining only essential-service levels at eleven hospitals; and bans on overtime and non-nursing duties at sixty-four other facilities. The last strike action taken by hospital nurses in British Columbia had been in 1976, six years before the birth of the BCNU. Before that, the only nurses to strike in the province had been those at St. Joseph's Hospital in Comox in 1939.

The seventeen-day strike, however, will not be remembered for the union's initiative, but for the mutiny. When it was learned that the union executive had accepted a tentative offer of 29.5 per cent over three years, a militant group of Vancouver General Hospital nurses forced the executive to withdraw its recommendation at a raucous meeting of 700 Vancouver-area nurses. Another 150 nurses stormed the union's Burnaby office demanding a ratification vote. VGH nurses staged a ninety-minute walkout in the VGH operating room and 65 per cent of the 77 per cent who turned out for a ratification meeting formally rejected the offer. Nurses continued working to rule. Finally the B.C. labour minister had to ask Victoria to get involved. But the dispute continued, even after an ultimatum from B.C. Premier Bill Vander Zalm, until a government-appointed mediator, on August 16, 1989, *imposed* a two-year contract with a wage increase of 20.9 per cent.

The final contract was not considered a substantial improvement over the one the union had rejected a few weeks earlier. It did, however, include a new professional-responsibility clause, a benefit sought by B.C. nurses in every round of bargaining since the 1977 Vancouver General Hospital revolt. B.C. employers now had to establish professional-responsibility committees allowing nurses to take unresolved concerns directly to the board if necessary. A dispute about the format of report forms was sent to binding arbitration, a process that, according to the union, again resulted in an *imposed* decision "mainly in the employers' favour." After six weeks of turmoil, everyone was unhappy. And there was still the threat of a permanent rift in what *Maclean's* on July 17, 1989 called "one of the country's strongest and most militant nurses' unions."

The union "quite simply lost touch with its members," then BCNU president Pat Savage stated in the November 1989 union newsletter. "We missed how far nurses' expectations might run beyond the capacity of the negotiation process and how years of anger at the terrible effects of the nursing shortage might focus on the union instead of the government and the employers. The BCNU has failed to educate its members about some hard realities of collective bargaining. You can't get everything you want and need, even if your cause is just."

Probably no nurses' union in the country knows that better than the Fédération des Infirmières et Infirmiers du Québec. Its 40,000 members began shaking their fists at the provincial government, despite its harsh anti-strike legislation, even before the B.C. job action. They publicized their demands by demonstrating outside the National Assembly wearing black arm bands on International Nurses Day in May and by launching a province-wide work-to-rule campaign boycotting overtime. The campaign began on April 21 and by the end of its nine-week run, 2,100 of the province's hospital beds had to close.

Quebec nurses cope with the worst working conditions in the country. More than 60 per cent of them work either part-time or on call. It takes Quebec nurses twelve years to reach the top of the pay scale compared with eight in Ontario, and their wages are at the bottom end of the national average. "Our jobs were done by nuns for a long time in Quebec and nursing was a vocation to them," CEGEP nursing program co-ordinator Helen Boissoneault told the *Montreal Gazette* in May 1989. "And decades later, the old attitudes that say nurses should be passive, uncomplaining caregivers still linger."

With the provincial election scheduled for September 25, 1989, and the FIIQ bargaining for the first time as a single union, expectations were high. The FIIQ was going to improve things for Quebec nurses – their salaries, their working conditions for the night shift, and their credit for extra training. The union began by asking for an initial 11.5 per cent pay hike and a 6.5 per cent increase over the following two years; the offer was 4 per cent. But after nurses rejected the government's final offer in June, the Quebec government brought out its heavy guns, asking its Essential Services Council to conduct hearings.

On June 23 the FIIQ negotiators agreed to a tentative contract granting nurses an escalating pay increase of 16 to 21 per cent over three years (at a cost of $630 million). As many as 77.8 per cent of the nurses who voted rejected the deal, causing fourteen of the fifteen union negotiators to quit. A July 21 editorial in the *Montreal Gazette* described the FIIQ delegates coming out of their meeting as "sadly divided and demoralized." They had not been able to come to any decision about calling a general strike against the collective agreement accepted by their negotiating committee. They had not even been able to decide how to instruct negotiators to continue to bargain for them – on the salary clause alone, on non-salary clauses alone, or on everything all at once.

Two weeks later the delegates voted by a narrow margin to accept new pressure tactics, renewing a ban on overtime, but a motion asking the FIIQ to seek a strike mandate on August 24 was overwhelmingly approved. The Quebec Treasury Board countered by threatening to use Bill 160, the law passed in 1986 "to redress the balance between state and unions." Under its terms, any nurse out on an illegal strike could be fined up to $100 a day, be docked two days' salary for each day off work, and lose a year of seniority for each day out. Union leaders in an illegal strike left themselves open to fines of up to $25,000 a day, and the union itself could be fined from $20,000 to $100,000 a day. Under the law, hospitals were allowed to hire non-union nurses to replace the strikers and to stop the deduction of union dues by the employer for twelve weeks for every day of an illegal strike.

On August 24 the nurses voted to strike, and despite a subsequent Essential Services Council restraining order the nurses walked out at 8:00 a.m. on September 5. Hospitals, forced to close 5,000 beds, were paralysed. The Quebec Hospitals Association instructed its members to start penalizing the striking nurses, making the allowed two days for one salary deduction. Premier Robert Bourassa, denouncing the strike as a "threat to the legitimacy of the state," served notice he was not going to budge from the $630-million offer already accepted by the union bargaining committee. The democratic system was at stake, Bourassa said. He refused to set "an extremely dangerous precedent for ourselves and for those who follow us" by rewarding "civil disobedience in a matter involving public health and sick people."

But Jack Todd, a columnist for the *Montreal Gazette*, said Bourassa's government was in fact the party endangering the safety of sick people, calling the Treasury Board position a "war on health care in Quebec." The nurses, nonetheless, called a twenty-four-hour truce on September 12. Two days later, FIIQ members accepted, by an 85 per cent margin, the same three-year agreement they had rejected two months earlier, sweetened only a bit with a lump-sum bonus of 2.5 to 4.5 per cent ($605 to $1,500 for each nurse).

Most striking nurses had lost much more than the bonus. Off work an average of four out of the seven days, because the FIIQ had to maintain the 90 per cent staffing levels required by the province's essential-service legislation, they each lost about $1,000 in deductions and salary. Seniority losses were even more expensive; one part-time nurse reported a drop from more than four years' seniority to just twenty-five days, from the second highest on the recall list to the second lowest. Union leaders were charged, convicted, and fined for contempt, and the union forced to collect its own dues for ninety-six weeks. The FIIQ fought back, instruct-

ing its nurses to deluge their employers with paperwork, filing grievances, boycotting employers' fundraising cam-
paigns, harassing politicians, and applying to the Quebec
Superior Court to suspend sanctions and declare Bill 160
unconstitutional.

The FIIQ, however, was now in dire financial straits. Other
unions, representing the 95,000 public-sector health-care
workers who had joined in the illegal walkout for one day,
also faced penalties, but they had had years to build up strike-
defence funds. The FIIQ, only two years old, had no war chest.
It appealed to its own members for funds. By December 1989,
almost 35,000 members were paying dues, voluntarily. But it
was a "very demanding, very tiring" process, and the union
depended heavily on $200,000 in donations and almost $1
million in interest-free loans, says Raymonde Bossé, FIIQ
vice-president.

On December 6, Quebec Superior Court Justice Jacques
Dufour agreed the nurses were "suffering irreparable damage" from the law but refused to grant an injunction that
would suspend its sanctions. An identical ruling greeted the
union's March 1990 appeal against sanctions. The results of
the FIIQ's longstanding challenge of Bill 160, originally expected in September 1990, may not be known for years.

In the 1980s nurses, accustomed to seeing and being silent,
turned to their union to repudiate their years of unquestion-
ing service. "We're not Florence Nightingales," mutiny
spokesperson Debra McPherson announced during the B.C.
strike. Unenlightened observers were again outraged at
nurses using Florence Nightingale's name in vain. *Financial
Post* Western editor John Scheiner wrote: "She has come to
symbolize for nursing what Hippocrates symbolizes for doctors, dedication and integrity. So why are some B.C. nurses
snarling that they've had it with being nice Nightingales?"
Because for nurses today, the image of Florence Nightingale
is a regressive and archaic leftover from a time when nursing
was simply an extension of womanly virtue.

"That's where the guilt trip comes from," says Vancouver nurse Jackie Barnett, who was working in Alberta during the unpopular 1982 UNA strike. It was freezing, recalls Toronto nurse Suzanne Bowley, also in Alberta during the "unforgettable" dark days of January 1983. "Everyone had just been through it a few years before, and the public said, 'These greedy nurses, what are they after?' Everybody was against them. They looked real bad in the press. Those cruel nurses, walking out when all those people are dying." A 1985 assessment of news coverage of U.S. nursing events over five years reported that striking nurses were consistently portrayed as uncaring, callous, and greedy women who had abandoned their commitment to nurture for their own personal gain, and whose selfish actions created an unjustifiable strain on ambulance and other health-care workers.

Public perception is changing. A national poll conducted by Canada West Foundations just after the UNA's legal strike in 1982 turned up only 23 per cent of Canadians in favour of nurses having the right to strike. Six years later a national poll done by Angus Reid Associates just as Alberta nurses were returning to work revealed that Canadians were almost evenly divided, with 48 per cent opposed to a right to strike for nurses and 44 per cent in favour.

The United Nurses of Alberta's illegal strike was a barometer for that change. The lawbreaking was not the significant factor; there have been many illegal strikes in Canadian labour history. It was the fact that these "criminals" were all women that stunned the nation. Not only were they all women but they were also all caregivers. Militant unionism among nurses shattered the professional women-in-white stereotype.

The strike also made a lasting imprint on nurses' image of themselves. Until the beginning of the 1980s, nurses equivocated between professional association and alignment with industrial trade unions. Professional associations, by promoting nursing as a profession, tend to reinforce nurses' natural disposition to put others' needs above their own. Unions, on the other hand, see nursing as a job. If staffing, scheduling, and the general conditions of the working environment become unbearable, patient care is the responsibility of the employer, unions say, not the nurse.

All-nurses' unions have accentuated this polarity between altruism and economic self-interest. As labour organizations, nurses' trade unions are an anomaly. None of them is affiliated with a provincial federation of labour or with the Canadian Labour Congress, and there is a longstanding reluctance to mimic what many nurses see as the hard-hat we/them mentality of industrial trade unions. Nurse practitioners working in Winnipeg health clinics say their membership in a public-sector trade union has distinct disadvantages; the Canadian Union of Public Employees has many other things on its mind besides nurses, they say. And because the entire membership of nurses' unions are nurses and 97 per cent are women, the focus is homogeneous and largely professional.

Yet nurses' unions are not a professional white-collar group, despite a growing tendency to avoid concentrating on wages in favour of negotiating the very context of the nurse-patient relationship. "My concern is with nurses," Margaret Ethier says. "If their biggest concern is being able to give proper patient care, then that will be my concern. But patient care or the advancement of nursing, generally, is not my concern. My concern is the nurses themselves. I represent nurses as opposed to nursing."

The next decade is likely to see the end of nurses' equivocation. The series of four strikes in 1988 and 1989 may have rerouted the carefully plotted middle-of-the road course among Canadian nurses' unions. "It's the nurses who have been militant who are gaining respect and recognition," says NFNU president Kathleen Connors. "The nurses in Alberta, Saskatchewan, British Columbia, and Quebec have said they can hold their heads high because they stood for what they believe in, and had the courage and the guts to do it."

Ontario nurses, especially in Toronto, were incensed by their 1988 contract; in times of short supply, a three-year term just made no sense. "We are sitting on a powder keg," says Glenna Cole Slattery. "We've been in a pitch of rage here for three years. I have nurses in hospitals so angry with that settlement, if there was anything they could do about it, they would."

Slattery, a native of Nepean, Ontario, has spent years with unions in the United States. Brought in after Anne Gribben's retirement to play political hardball, she is already a household word among nurses. The Ontario Nurses' Association at 54,000 members "pushes around" $15 million a year, she says. "This building cost $10 million and we paid for it in cash. We have got a big business here and the women did it themselves. Nurses are good, smart business women. Once you can get them past that 'but I'm just a nurse,' they are tigers."

Although the election in September 1990 of an NDP provincial government has "her smiling, just smiling," one has no reason not to believe Slattery when she predicts "a bumpy ride ahead" for Ontario, "a ride that will make what happened in B.C. look like a little sleigh ride."

Five years ago Gail Paech, former president of the professional association in Ontario and now a consultant with Coopers & Lybrand, would never have considered nurses in Ontario to be trade unionists. Hospital nurses in the province have been forbidden from striking since 1965. They took their first and last-ever strike vote in 1975, winning a huge 50 per cent arbitration award. "When I talked with people, they would say, 'We would never go out on strike. Okay, we joined our union but if we ever went on strike, we would not be members,'" Paech says. "But I think now we're at a point you will see that we will have a strike next time out."

The last decade saw the extent to which provincial governments are prepared to interfere with nurses' collective bargaining. Nurses' services are essential, and politicians can't afford to let patients die while women walk the streets. Alberta passed a new labour code in 1989 enabling the government to decertify a union overnight. In the fall of 1989, an editorial in *Le Devoir* predicted "carnage as the only forseeable outcome of the dispute between Quebec and its striking nurses. One cannot but condemn the general strike by the nurses as they try to cash in on the current provincial election campaign . . . . the nurses are wrong to want to re-dress in one contract all the wrongs they believe they have been dealt over the years."

Nurses' unions emerged from the four strikes of the late 1980s fragmented and demoralized, but angrier than ever. Connors at the NFNU calls the inner turmoil a symptom "of health and growth. Nurses are telling unions they want things cleaned up and they want them cleaned up now. 'That's what we elected you people to do. That's what we pay our union dues for.' And the union leadership is going to have to deal with very high expectations that may be some-what unrealistic at times." Although the largest nurses' unions – in Alberta, Quebec, British Columbia, and Ontario – do not belong to the National Federation of Nurses' Unions in Ottawa, they do meet with the members from Manitoba, Saskatchewan, and New Brunswick to co-ordinate a national strategy.

Nurses' unions are still young and inexperienced. The FIIQ was accused of irresponsible naivety in allowing its nurses to return to work without negotiating an amnesty; such ingenu-ous behaviour may have precipitated a provincial labour dis-aster, observers said. Connors defends the union. The entire Common Front of Quebec tried to fight Bill 160 from 1984 to 1986 and couldn't, she says. But with the kind of legislative interference now on the books in at least two provinces in Canada, their strike weapon is only a symbol, and nurses may have no choice. Now nurses are getting pushed into develop-ing a closer identity with industrial unions, and no one knows how militant they will be prepared to grow over the next decade.

Government after government study dangles rewards in front of nurses to substitute for money and the outdated ethic of social virtue. Supported by nursing professional associa-tions, the studies are suggesting specialties and various nursing titles to promote nurses *and* keep them at the bedside. Mar-garet Ethier says nurses don't want that kind of advancement. She says none of that professional identity business is going to change the fact that nursing is a hard, dirty job, which must be adequately compensated.

"Nursing is bad smells," she says. "You work with people who are not very nice to you because they're sick – or their families aren't very nice. You could have all the advancement you want; you could have all the input into nursing, but that's not going to change the fact that you're a nurse, and you are going to have to go in there, and maybe take this whole dressing off where cancer has eaten away so it's just rotten tissue here.

"It's going to be very smelly, and you're not going to want to do it. That's nursing."

9

Education by Degrees

At the age of forty, Nikki Rankin was already a nursing administrator at one of Canada's most renowned institutions. As director of nursing for critical care at Toronto's Hospital for Sick Children, she was responsible for nursing services in the neonatal intensive-care unit, in the pediatric intensive-care unit, in the recovery room, and in the operating rooms. She also had responsibility for nurses on the transport teams keeping patients alive as they were flown in from all over the world.

She has worked in recruitment, in human resources, and in organizational development. She has served as national president of the Canadian Association of Critical Care Nurses. During the administrative shake-up following the Grange inquiry, she was one of four women selected to rotate through the hospital's director of nursing position.

Rankin's formal training for this high-level nursing career was outside a university; she graduated in 1971 from the Kingston General Hospital's three-year diploma program. The Hospital for Sick Children was her first nursing job. Hired as a general-duty nurse twenty years ago, she has been employed there ever since, working her way up the ladder. To do what she did requires more than competence, she says, although she did demonstrate that and excellent communication and personal skills as well. To do what she did requires expertise.

Judy Grabham is also forty. When she works at the bedside, she can do anything from changing diapers to giving bed baths to helping a resident shave. When she works in the dining room Grabham butters toast, mixes laxatives, or coaxes an old woman to take her vitamins by accepting a kiss on the cheek.

One of only four registered nurses on day duty at Victoria's Mount Tolmie Hospital, Graham supervises long-term-care aides who help her nurse the elderly residents in this extended-care institution. She has power; she can send a lab technologist around to the bedside to take blood or perform other expensive tests. She has responsibility. No doctors are on staff at the hospital; they usually visit only once a week. There are no interns or residents or registered nursing assistants.

Grabham started out, like Rankin, doing her training outside a university and working in acute care. Graduating from a community college diploma course in Ontario, she began, at the age of twenty-two, in obstetrics. Then she came out to British Columbia to work at a burn unit. She didn't like the pace, she says; she didn't have time to get to know her patients. So she moved on to nursing the elderly, working for seven years in an intermediate-care facility where residents are able to take care of themselves better than the residents here.

By then she'd decided geriatric nursing was her niche. She liked the people; she liked the responsibility. Because she was going to make this her specialty, she opted for more training. Grabham, buttering pieces of toast in assembly-line fashion in the Mount Tolmie dining room, has a university degree.

It's an old story. Nursing has been trying, and failing, to define itself as a profession since the turn of the century. No single quality sets apart a profession more than the level of training and education necessary to gain access. Training for nurses started out as indenture, and even today diploma students in hospital-based schools whose "education" is administered by hospital trustees tend to be treated as staff apprentices.

In the first third of this century, the campaign to free nurses from this service-based model of education focused on getting them out of hospital schools and into community colleges. After the Weir report of 1932, the strategy was to give nurses a liberal university education. But in most provinces in the 1990s nursing training is still divided among the three tiers – hospital schools, community colleges, and universities – with no integration of curricula and no method of moving from one to the other without losing credit. Consolidating nursing education to prepare for the demands that will be placed on nurses in this next decade is now imperative.

How to go about that task, however, is the most controversial issue in nursing today. Nursing associations, committed since 1946 to the re-professionalization of nursing, are counting on legislation for mandatory university education to pave the way to full professional status. Public-health departments in most provinces have required nurses to have degrees, or at least one or two years of post-RN training in a university, for fifty years. Shifting nursing education to a university setting was the associations' key goal for the 1980s; in 1982 the Canadian Nurses Association announced that every nurse *entering* practice in or after the year 2000 would have to have a university degree. The policy now is known as the "entry-to-practice" position.

The move to universities was going to provide a new context for learning that would ground registered nursing as a science and an art distinct from medicine. In this environment, the curricula could be controlled and nurses would be taught non-medical nursing theories and the more holistic concepts of health care. The University of Toronto Faculty of Nursing 1988/89 calendar describes the goals of the four-year BN university degree as designed to produce nursing leaders with the "ability to *go beyond* the application of principles in familiar situations to *higher order* problem-solving ... [which] must be accompanied by a capacity for decision-making ... [and] must be underscored by a spirit of inquiry and comprehensive knowledge of a scientific and humanistic nature." (My italics.) In addition to courses in nursing, chemistry, medical microbiology, pathology, physiology, statistics, research, nutritional sciences, community health, and epidemiology, students are also required to round out their education by qualifying in social science and other electives.

"You can teach someone the techniques of anything," says the University of Victoria's Jessie Mantle, a diploma graduate who is now a clinical nurse specialist with a masters degree in gerontology. "But then, what you have is a technician. I made a thousand beds when I was in training. It never stopped for three years. I had mastered bedmaking at the end of a month." Evelyn Malowany, director of nursing at the Children's Hospital in Montreal, puts it another way: "If you have the theory and you understand the importance, you will question a doctor's decision. A diploma nurse won't do that."

University-educated independence is not a surprising aim for a professional nurse in the 1990s, especially given the history of the professional associations' attempts to limit access to nursing. But although the nursing associations have absolutely no power to implement this position without the help of every provincial government in the country, for nurses' unions the CNA's 1982 entry-to-practice agenda is a source of both fear and hate.

More than 80 per cent of registered nurses working in Canada today have graduated with diplomas, either from a hospital-based school or a community college, despite the fact that the percentage of nurses with university degrees almost doubled, from 7 per cent to 13 per cent, between 1971 and 1986. Trade unions have a duty to protect the job security of their members. They are likely to resist any move that compromises workers' jobs or promotions over the short term. The CNA policy, if it ever is legislated into being, theoretically affects only potential nurse recruits now in elementary school. Nevertheless, Canadian nurses with diplomas – 160,000 of them – no longer feel secure.

Hiring practices have already been influenced by the national lobby for "entry to practice." After 1982, hospitals, despite union contracts, started to hire and promote degree nurses first. The Dubin report in 1983 recommended that hiring preference be given to those with nursing degrees, a suggestion supported by the Registered Nurses' Association of Ontario. The diploma nurses began to realize that many of them were going to be excluded from future leadership positions. In fact, the diploma nurse now faced a dead end in a job already characterized for a century as a dead end.

Given the huge discrepancy in the way nurses are being trained, nursing education for all nurses must be improved; unions do acknowledge that fact. But nurses' unions want paid recognition and improved working conditions for all nurses as they now are, first. Unions are fighting for more increments on the pay grid, more money and time to pay for on-the-job training, more time and money for night upgrading courses (credit towards a degree notwithstanding), and a salary schedule that truly reflects a nurse's skill and experience.

Glenna Cole Slattery has nursed for thirty-five years; she has a BA in health-care administration and an MA in public administration. But if she wanted a BN right now, she'd have to start again in first-year university at square one. "I have nothing against a BN for nursing, absolutely nothing," she says. "As a consumer, you'd better go to school, honey; I don't want you to be giving me no hypo if you don't know what you're doing. But I live in the world of reality and I deal with the marketplace, and we do not want total disenfranchisement. If they [professional associations] would have been the least bit reasonable; if they would have been the least bit sensitive to the 2,200,000 RNs in North America, they could have had this sucker twenty years ago." She is speaking of an education developed from the bottom up for all practising nurses, aided by special programs and encouraged by administrative changes.

The professional associations have not had much marketing success. The American Nurses Association had begun lobbying in 1965 to get states to allow only graduates of a Bachelor of Science in Nursing to be permitted to register as nurses, siphoning off the nurses trained in colleges or hospitals as task-oriented technicians. After twenty-three years, in 1988, nurses in only two states had managed to get the plan beyond the proposal stage. The Alberta Association of Registered Nurses was the first in Canada to adopt an entry-to-practice position in 1979, and over the next eight years, every provincial nursing association in the country, except one, followed suit. But the Manitoba association was the first, in 1984, to suggest that the training required to enter nursing may not need to be a degree but could be a "university-based" program "meeting the criteria for the granting of the degree" and enabling "the graduate to demonstrate competencies."

The professional associations did little to reassure bedside nurses. There wasn't much said at first about arranging part-time courses for diploma nurses now working shifts and overtime in Canadian hospitals, or about arranging transfer credits for prior learning or experience, or about fashioning a challenge examination or any other method of helping a practising diploma RN become a degree BN or BSCN. Hospital nurses find it financially impossible to arrange relief staff, leaves of absence, and flexible scheduling to make room for further study. The Saskatchewan association took pains in 1984 to clarify that any nurse registering before December 31, 1999, would not be required to have a university degree. But nurses must have some way to ensure that experience will count towards a degree without having to go back to school, says Margaret Risk, executive director of the College of Nurses of Ontario.

The manner in which the CNA policy was developed, without clarification or consultation, offended the unions and their members. The professional associations are correct in saying that degree nurses are more likely to challenge lack of respect from doctors, says Lisa McCaskell, a night supervisor at Toronto's Wellesley Hospital. "The problem is nurses' condescension to other nurses. The BN nurses with their noses up in the air don't want to get their hands dirty."

The issue is more complicated than deciding where a nurse should be trained. Liberal education can take place in a community college, and community colleges or polytechnical institutions can, with the appropriate legislation, be allowed to grant degrees. The crux of the conflict is what a registered nurse should know. "If nurses need more knowledge or a different kind of knowledge, why not just teach it to them?" Newfoundland nursing director Dianne Simms asks.

There is no research to support the contention that the Bachelor of Nursing degree actually does a better job of preparing nurses for independent primary care. There is also no evidence a university degree turns out a better hospital nurse. "These are the kinds of studies that the CNA should have been doing," says Ottawa statistician Eva Ryten, director of the office of research and information services for the Association of Canadian Medical Colleges. "Where are they? I want them to go back and do their homework. In a sense, really what they ought to be looking at is *what* does one need to be able to do and to know to be a registered nurse, not *where*. It's nonsense to say a degree teaches you how to think; if you can't think before a degree, you won't think after one."

In fact, Shari Cooper, a twenty-one-year-old first-year diploma graduate working at the neonatal intensive-care unit at Toronto's Mount Sinai Hospital, went into community college training precisely because she thought it would provide better training than a university degree. "I went into a college because I knew college was clinical. I saw the nurses from U. of T. coming into a hospital. They were in their last year, and they couldn't do half the things we could do." A degree is just a status symbol, Cooper says. Besides, the kind of advancement a degree would get for her is sitting behind a desk, she says, "and I love the nursing part of it."

Degree nurses do take longer to get the hang of hospital work. The period of adjustment they experience when they start work in hospitals was a syndrome named "reality shock" by researchers in the 1970s. Yet nursing academics argue that degree education is a better investment over the long term. A

1979 London, Ontario, study reported that degree nurses make better use of their time. British Columbia's 1988 nurse "manpower" report says that degree nurses are more flexible and adaptable, adding that university education will be essential to help nurses cope with the future changes in service demands.

Recent studies, however, also show the value of experience in making decisions rather than simply knowledge of theory, and the premise that intuitive judgement is an essential part of clinical judgement is gaining new ground. Education does not occupy a big place in the criteria for rating job classes in Ontario's new pay-equity law; it is only one of three factors contributing to skill (along with experience and special abilities), and skill in turn is only one of three other bases of comparison; effort, responsibility, and working conditions.

Rank-and-file nurses have begun to see the proposal for a degree requirement as elitist. Nursing has traditionally been an occupation that working-class women could rely on, they say, and imposing university education will exclude many women with a real potential for nursing.

No one would ever use that argument for medicine, nursing leaders counter; keeping nurses in community colleges so that working-class women will have a place to be trained, as Alice Baumgart puts it, is just another way for governments to make sure nurses stay "barefoot, pregnant, and on the farm." Governments should be ensuring that working-class women have as many opportunities for education as anyone else, says Gail Donner, now the director of nursing education at the Hospital for Sick Children. "Tell me, do you think it's just a coincidence that nurses who are women have been told it is good enough to get educated at college? It's not good enough for the male-dominated professions."

But rank-and-file nurses, already stressed to the breaking point by chronic understaffing and underrecognition, are railing against the extra burden of an expensive "higher education" they perceive they will never be allowed to use and will never get paid for.

What's the point of "higher order problem-solving" when university graduates, hospital school graduates, and community college graduates all write the same national RN exams to qualify for a licence? Why bother to get a degree when RNs from all three tiers are sucked into a hospital system where "a nurse is a nurse is a nurse"? A university-trained RN is paid at the same union wage-scale as a diploma-trained RN. Doctors, social workers, respiratory therapists, and other members of the RN's professional team rarely know how a nurse has been educated. In fact, Canadian hospitals are staffed on the premise that an RN can function adeptly in any setting, and many are hired as "floats" specifically for that purpose.

Nurses are already overeducated, learning to do more than the law permits them to do, says Diana Dick. This is illogical. It's frustrating; they learn all these wonderful things and never get a chance to use them. The hospital organization doesn't support higher education for nurses; they may give lip service to it but they don't support it, nurses say. And educators are caught in the dilemma of training inquiring minds to question and argue at the same time as preparing graduate nurses for working in a doctor-driven system. They may personally disagree with the doctor-nurse game, but they know they must teach nurses how to play it just the same.

"A professional historically is someone who is self-employed like a lawyer or a doctor," says Vancouver nurse Bill Grant. "What you have [here] is people with little power or no power calling themselves professionals." University-educated nurses experience a higher degree of job dissatisfaction than the other two streams, the "reality shock" research documented. "It's one thing to have a professional right and a professional responsibility," says Phyllis Giovannetti, new president of the Alberta Association of Registered Nurses. "It's another to be in a work environment where no one will listen to it."

The energy to fight the proposed entrance requirement on hospital floors around the country is palpable. Dianne Simms

is studying for a degree but it's in philosophy. Jeannette Gallant, a thirteen-year nurse now at Moncton's Dr. Georges L.
Dumont Hospital, warns that if she is forced to get a degree,
she'll "forget nursing. I'm going to be an interior decorator."
Scary words at a time of a crisis in nursing supply.

A Victoria, B.C., geriatric nurses' aide takes one look
around her and says: "If I am going to go to be an RN, I
would spend all this money to get my degree plus all the work
and then my time, for what? To come back and be a care co-
ordinator? Here? After spending that much money?" The
woman is shouting now, right in the corridor. No other issue
among nurses is so sure to generate this kind of passion. "It's
a gruelling four years, getting a degree," says Grace Barfoot,
a diploma nurse working at a private doctors' clinic in
Toronto. "You are pushed to get 97 per cent. And then, after
all that, who in their right mind wants to work shifts and
nights for $32,000 a year and be treated like garbage? Young
women today have so many better things to do."

Gail Donner finds it incomparably sad that women like
Barfoot and the geriatric nurses' aide have such a low perception of their work. "What those women are really saying is
'My God, to do the kind of crappy job I do, you don't need to
have a degree.' And yes, they are yelling. But they are yelling
at the wrong things. Their yell is really a cry for power."

Degree-prepared nurses don't feel inferior in the same
way, Jessie Mantle says. But right now, the CNA's entry-to-
practice position is precisely what is making diploma nurses
feel inferior, creating turmoil in a profession already
plagued by insecurity and stress. Until the entry-to-practice
position materialized in 1982, RNs had no motivation to
enrol in the more expensive degree-granting institutions.
Now, despite government opposition to creating 10,000 new
university spaces a year for undergraduate nursing students,
RNs, terrified of being left in the lurch in the year 2000, are
enrolling in post-RN programs in droves, at great emotional,
physical, and financial expense. "Yeah," says Barfoot, "we're
all going to have to get a degree. We sure feel sold out
though."

Jessie Gaudet, the patient classification officer at Moncton Hospital, started to take extra courses "because this BN entry to practice was a very big issue. My reaction was to go with the flow and see what I can do. I went through five years of taking extension courses which just about did me in because I was also working full time. I was trying to study and take care of my family. It was very stressful." Gaudet says any nurse will corroborate her experience. What with working, taking call, studying, looking after their families, and attending classes on their own time, all during the worst nursing shortage in living memory, RNs are burning out.

A survey conducted by the Newfoundland and Labrador Nurses' Union in 1987 found that 88.6 per cent of nurses believe a BN is needed for advancement in nursing, but only 19.7 per cent were financially able to study for one. Distance education and educational teleconferencing for nurses working in remote areas is now a must for faculties of nursing at most Canadian universities.

Funds to pay for nursing education have never been secure. Until the early 1960s education – such as it was – was financed by the donations from private business, supplemented during the war years by the Canadian Red Cross Society and sweetened by the incentive of free labour. As late as 1958, Saskatchewan hospitals with teaching programs reported a direct profit to the hospital from the free labour of the students. But ever since the unlimited free labour of nurses-in-training became morally and politically indefensible, nurses have had to pay for 99 per cent of their own education, and despite the technological pressure for specialized training and orientation programs, money is still tight. Financial support for training is haphazard, often political, waxing and waning as special groups of nurses are needed in times of shortages. Ottawa used to divert transfer payments into hospitals to upgrade nursing skills in fields the country needed, like critical care. But in 1986 Finance Minister Michael Wilson announced new federal financing priorities, bringing the expected annual increases in the established program funding to an abrupt halt.

System support for advanced education is also lacking. Hospital administrators are worried about the long-term effects of higher education on the cost and supply of nurses. How will they redistribute the work among nursing personnel? And exactly what role are they educating nurses for – a co-ordinating manager or a floor nurse at the bedside? The Ontario Hospital Association response to the RNAO's support of entry to practice in 1980 was cautious: "There must be input from employers, educators, and professional associations [not just nursing associations] as well as long-range planning and research before any major program change is embarked upon." Doctors, threatened by the prospect of competition from a more educated nurse force, warn that nurses with more training will not want to work in the trenches. Dr. Hedy Fry, a Vancouver general practitioner for eighteen years, opposes primary-care training for nurses; the more nurses opting for higher education and knowledge, the fewer there will be who want to stay at the bedside, she says.

It is extremely unlikely that the professional associations are going to get the kind of political and financial support they need. At present, the Ontario government funds 400 university seats for degree-prepared nurses, at $40,000 a seat. In 1989 only 13 per cent of Ontario's 100,000 RNs had university degrees. The estimated price of training the rest is making governments balk. The CNA says that assumptions that the cost will be exorbitant are "unclear, unfounded, unwise and unwarranted," uncorroborated by a single well-designed study. The November 1989 decision by the government of Prince Edward Island, where the nursing degree did not even exist until 1988, to phase out all diploma nursing schools in favour of a degree program was touted in the CNA journal as "leading the way nationally."

But Ontario has already said it will not support an amendment to the Health Disciplines Act that would establish a university degree as the minimum educational requirement for entry to nursing practice. It cited lack of evidence to prove diploma-prepared nurses are not adequately prepared to care for patients and, of course, the lack of differentiation in employment function between the diploma and degree RNs. The College of Nurses of Ontario got into such hot water from its members (many of whom belong to the union) for including the degree in its revised standards of practice that it had to back down in August 1989. At the moment, most provincial governments in Canada are not in a position to give the legislative support that nursing associations need to put their idea into practice.

All nurses' unions now oppose the CNA's position, "as it is currently structured." Heather Smith says the United Nurses of Alberta figured it out during the 1988 round of bargaining. "For a nurse to go back to school for two years to get her degree, including the wages she gives up even if she's working (we calculated it out on the basis of her working summers and working holidays), it takes her forty-five years to gain back what's she's lost. It's ghettoizing the poor. And I don't see forty-five years' worth of improved knowledge there just to come back and work in the same environment."

The one nursing association holdout was the province of New Brunswick, for seven years a bellwether of the conflict in the rest of the country. The Nurses Association of New Brunswick had scheduled an unprecedented vote on the matter at its May 1987 annual general meeting, even though, as the licensing body for the province, it had the power to take a stance on entry to practice without consulting its 8,000 members, most of whom also belong to the New Brunswick Nurses' Union. But then, the union, worried about mobility, about promotion, about job security, decided to challenge the association on the issue. Union president Madeleine Steeves sent out a series of communiqués across the province urging each and every member to attend the annual general meeting to vote the position down, and Moncton nurses describe being so concerned about the future of their livelihood that they booked off work in busloads. Only two degree-granting institutions exist in the province, one anglophone and one francophone, and many diploma nurses were exhausted by the sometimes seventy-five-mile commute to a class conducted in their own language.

At the annual meeting the CNA's entry-to-practice position was defeated by sixty-seven votes. The next day the union was accused of vote-buying. "It was quite a mess," says Norma Poirier, a community college nursing instructor in Moncton. "We couldn't even finish the meeting. We all left." Lawyers were consulted; constitutional experts were interviewed; private hearings were held; and in August the executive committee of the association declared the 'no' vote null and void. All hell broke loose. A committee of concerned nurses formed in October in protest, accusing the association of acting in an undemocratic manner and of washing dirty linen in public; there was even talk of taking the dispute to court.

A new vote, nonetheless, was scheduled for May 1989. Some changes were incorporated into the entry-to-practice resolution to reassure the union, and it passed. Union executives feel it was a lot of work for nothing. Marlene Mercer, a diploma nurse, has been forced to look "long and hard" at the issue. "I'm in favour of education but not in favour of entry to practice," she says. "We have to have standards in terms of a degree. I see nothing wrong in that, but not if we are throwing the baby out with the bath water."

In a time of shortage it is unlikely that governments are going to throw out the diploma nurses. Many observers say legislating the degree requirement will only make the shortage worse. Between 1970 and 1986 the number of Bachelor of Nursing graduates grew, but only to the level of 1,249 per year. Even 10,000 new BN graduates a year will barely meet the future demand, Ryten says. And it cannot be assumed that students who would be willing to enrol in a two-year or three-year community college or hospital school program will automatically switch to a four-year university program.

The RN just beginning practice still has a large part of her training left to do. Pressed by the increasing demands of technology, 31 per cent of all registered nurses enrolled in a post-RN program in 1987. Upgrading or specialty courses for RNs, called post-basic or post-RN, have existed since the outpost nursing program was created in the 1970s to prepare nurses to fill the gap left by doctors. Since that time there have been other innovative projects aimed at providing hospital nurses with specialized skills, and hence more status. Primary nursing, implemented in the 1970s, was designed to encourage more autonomy for the bedside nurse; a model of nursing taught at McGill University and used primarily in anglophone hospitals in Montreal allows nursing practice to expand beyond task-oriented intervention. Canadian hospitals are also toying with the U.S. idea of "clinical laddering," a way to recognize clinical expertise without making a nurse go the administrative route, giving her an elevated position such as team leader or preceptor based on experience rather than education.

Nurses have been clamouring for long-term system support for continuing education, but government funds are scarce and there is no concerted plan, leaving each facility to initiate fragmented and isolated approaches to ongoing education as the need arises. Juan de Fuca Hospitals provide a $1,000 scholarship for any nurse returning to school for a degree. Toronto's St. Joseph's Health Centre reimburses any employee enrolling in Ryerson's new part-time Bachelor of Applied Arts in Nursing program or in Ryerson's part-time seven-week critical-care program on site. The Canadian Nurses Foundation gives out about $20,000 a year in scholarships for university study for nurses at the undergraduate and graduate levels.

McMaster University began training neonatal clinical-nurse specialists as soon as it became clear that Ontario's critical-care units for newborns were dangerously short of doctors. The sixteen-month masters course empowers nurses to write orders at the bedside as medical residents do. But continuing education for nurses is haphazard at best. Anne Beaufoy, the infection-control nurse at St. Paul's Hospital in Vancouver, enrolled in a similar post-graduate program at the University of British Columbia but it ran out of money after three years; the only infection-control program now, in a time of mushrooming AIDS cases, is in Hamilton, Ontario, or Atlanta, Georgia. And although some hospital nurses wear "clinical nurse specialist" or "nurse clinician" credentials on their identity buttons, few really understand what the term means, and the very idea of specialty nursing, as the Grange inquiry illustrated, is often still an anathema to other professionals. There is a tremendous amount of wasted effort, as Sharon Snell of the Alberta Association of Registered Nurses told the Premier's Commission on Future Health Care for Albertans in October 1988. "We don't know how to get our educators in the hospital working together," Snell, then president of the association, said. "All we are doing is putting out fires and dealing with the urgency of how we are going to staff the next shift."

Formal recognition for the extra training needed by nurses taking on an expanded role is also a problem, with the predictable conflict between professional associations and unions; nurses' unions oppose specialty pay. "Okay, you tell me who's not special," Slattery challenges. "A nurse up in Sudbury keeps the patient alive until they can get him to a big special unit in Toronto. It's harder for her, because she has no house staff, no residents or interns. She has to do things like blood gases that a nurse in the intensive-care unit can ask a resident to do." Slattery is in a rage about a document put out by the RNAO blaming the nursing shortage partly on the lack of financial enticement for specialty nurses. The union has no quarrel with paying nurses for education, basing the extra pay on extra steps on the union grid, available to all nurses. But the union does not favour wooing an unprepared nurse into a large urban intensive-care unit with a bigger pay cheque that isn't based on seniority. "Our membership has always said they want provincial rates with no specialty pay," Slattery says.

Nurses, however, are practising in highly specialized areas: intravenous therapy, intensive care, oncology, emergency, palliative care. About 120 special-interest groups now registered with the Canadian Nurses Association wish to gain recognition and would like to develop a standard for their advanced knowledge and skill. Some way must be found to integrate the practice with the concept of specialization, professional associations say.

Because neither the university nor the community college setting is adequately training nurses in a specialty, many Canadian campuses are experimenting with trying to collaborate between the two. The University of British Columbia has started to integrate the Vancouver General Hospital nursing school. The RNAO has put some money into a research project in Sudbury to study ways to integrate Cambrian Community College and Laurentian University nursing programs. Students enrolling at Red Deer Community College can graduate with a degree granted by the University of Alberta. The diploma school at the University of Alberta Hospital is now integrated into the Faculty of Nursing as a joint hospital-faculty department, and soon it will be possible for students from all collaborating diploma programs to apply for transfer to the university at third year.

"I think the attitude we have demonstrated is that we are going to try to use everything we have," says Yvonne Chapman, the former Alberta Association of Registered Nurses' executive director. But the University of Alberta's Judith Hibberd admits the collaborative model is an interim strategy to get provincial governments onside in the ultimate goal – funding university education as a minimal requirement for all nurses. In some parts of the country, the strategy isn't working; the former Liberal Ontario government, for example, did not support collaboration between colleges and universities.

Scrapping its earlier wait-and-see attitude, the CNA is now developing standards of competence and national examinations for nursing specialties that may expand the potential for formal (but not legal or paid) recognition of expanded-duty nurses. But even the first phase of the new CNA strategy, certifying ten groups in the next ten years, will cost, by conservative estimates, $5 million. Only two groups, occupational-health nurses and neuroscience nurses, have succeeded in getting formal recognition as a nursing specialty.

"This is a movement we aren't going to be stopping," Sharon Snell warns. "It is essential that we address problems. It's an expensive task; we are going to have to find money from somewhere." Competency has to be tested and retested, she says; it is the only way the profession will be able to retain nurses.

When professional associations in the 1970s suggested making an MA a requirement for certification, the report of the Joint Ministerial Task Force on Nursing Education in Manitoba predicted in December 1977 that such a move would "be doomed to failure." It is important that specialist certification should be "realistic," the report went on to say, "and that, at least in the early stages of the process, certification should not be limited to graduates of academic programs but should be open to nurses with equivalent practice and experience."

Up to now, post-graduate work for nurses has been carried out in other disciplines such as health administration or business management. Too many nurses have gone into business administration, as far as the University of Ottawa's Marian McGee is concerned. The University of Alberta and McGill University are trying to launch nursing PhD programs. But getting university recognition for a curriculum or program is not under the control of professional associations in every province. Adequate funding has not been secured, and the idea of nurses advancing their knowledge is not universally acceptable.

Nowhere in the country can the women who now practise as expanded-duty nurses receive formal credentials for what they do. As a result, they simply have to take on the extra responsibilities without getting paid for them. Denise Boggs manages 80 to 90 per cent of a busy Toronto doctor's infertility practice; she makes $28,000 a year; he probably bills $300,000 a year at that location alone. Boggs, a diploma RN, has no objections to going back to school at night but she doesn't want to start all over again by enrolling in the "generic" BN, and there are no specialty post-RN programs that meet her needs. As a member of the Nurse Practitioners' Association of Ontario, Boggs is actively canvassing universities to find one willing to revive the nurse-practitioner program.

The fate of the nurse-practitioner program, an expanded-duty training developed in the 1970s to groom nurses to provide health care to Canada's northern communities, is the extreme example of the political exploitation of nursing education. A short-term and temporary one-year university-based program financed at a time of tremendous doctor shortages, it was withdrawn as soon as sufficient doctors were again being trained.

Nursing leaders of the time also helped in its suppression. They knew the country could not afford to educate nurse practitioners (most of whom started out in diploma programs at hospitals or community colleges) for a post-RN session at university, as well as fund enough university spaces for degrees for every nurse practising in Canada by the year 2000. Although the professional associations had no power to suppress the nurse-practitioner program, they did urge universities to include training for an independent nurse practitioner in the BN program instead. The original nurse-practitioner program was too dependent on the medical model, they said, and although there is no research to support their contention, they thought the primary-care nursing skills (to do the assessment and diagnostic tasks now performed by doctors in non-isolated areas) needed by the nurses of the future would be better taught in a more universal setting.

The end of the special program, however, now leaves such diploma graduate RNs as Boggs, who want more training, in limbo. It also turned the graduates of the nurse-practitioner programs into dinosaurs. "We took the risk to pioneer the concept, and now we are sacrificial lambs," says Lynn Crocker. She is a graduate of the now defunct McMaster University nurse-practitioner program who works at the Women's Health Centre in Winnipeg. She says that the degree nurses "have one course; we had a whole year. There is not enough time to provide enough clinical hands-on experience."

Without a policy commitment from government, however, both Crocker and Boggs are likely to stay out of luck; the independent nurse practitioner has no professional or legislative support.

10

~

Back to the Future

In the dead of winter Black Tickle, Labrador, is one of the most desolate places on earth. A string of asymmetrical wood bungalows built on a slab of rock in Canada's subarctic, the community looks as if it's been put to sleep. Winter has drifted in from the sea, blurring the borders of the frigid bay and burying the lonely road around the perimeter of the settlement. The snow looks like a white plastic oxygen mask. The chimneys' soft curls of grey smoke are the only vital sign that the population of 237 is still breathing.

Black Tickle residents say their numbers swell to over a thousand during the summer, when the men from Spotted Island, Punch Bowl, and other satellite communities come in to fish. A cluster of buildings – the schoolhouse, a one-room store, a Roman Catholic church, and a community hall where the government sets up make-work projects in winter – stands at the midpoint of a line of bungalows: to the south is the two-storey brick nursing clinic and the airstrip; to the north, the sea.

A pack of black and brown husky dogs guards the door to one of the bungalows. Inside the air is warm and hazy; the mingled smoke from the wood stove, sizzling bacon, and tobacco shudders for a moment at the threshold before flying out into the cold. A woman washes socks in a basin of water she has carried in from outside; most of the houses are without plumbing and sewage. A man smokes silently in front of

175

the TV set. A gun rack and fox furs hung on the wall testify to busier times – at least for him.

The grandmother is in bed when the nurse greets her. She rises slowly; her old joints, cramped by arthritis, are so sensitive to the cold that she is housebound all winter. Delrose Gordon has walked down from the clinic to check the pills she has prescribed, for arthritis, for hypertension. The grandmother has also been given blood thinner for the clot in her head. The old woman, a stroke victim with only one arm, opens the pill bottle with difficulty. "When it is warmer, come into the clinic for a bath," says the nurse, putting on the boots she has left at the door. The Grenfell nursing station is the only building in town with running water and central heating.

Founded as a mission in 1892 by an English doctor shocked at the sorry state of medical care on the coast, Grenfell Regional Health Services, now run by the provincial government, manages three six-nurse health centres and eighteen nursing stations. There were also clinics in Charlottetown and Paradise River but they've been closed because no nurses can be found to staff them, and in the winter of 1988 they must be serviced by remote control. Grenfell's health-care workers come in by snowmobile or plane once a week to help the local clinic aide.

Here in Canada's Third World, the gravel air strip is the centre of the universe. Gordon is busy trying to fly Maria Theresa "out"; the woman fell off her snowmobile last weekend and has been in pain ever since. A seventeen-year-old who sprained his shoulder lugging wood may need the services of a physiotherapist, which means an hour's plane ride to the Grenfell hospital in Goose Bay. Arrangements must be made soon for a woman who is pregnant. Although Gordon was trained as a midwife in Britain, Grenfell wants all the pregnant women flown out at thirty-eight weeks. The women and their older children must board out with friends or relatives in Goose Bay until they deliver, alone.

Pauline deVette, Grenfell's assistant community nursing supervisor, based in Goose Bay, says she has spent countless hours on the telephone calming nurses stranded for weeks by the weather. During her afternoon clinics, Gordon has one hand on the patient and the other on the telephone, either conferring with the doctor in Goose Bay about results, diagnoses, and treatments, or ordering supplies and monitoring sleeping accommodation for patients' families.

Originally from Jamaica, Gordon trained in England and was working as a nurse in London when Grenfell recruited her about ten years ago. Grenfell's outpost nursing stations are almost entirely dependent on non-Canadians, and importing nurses into Canada isn't easy. Most employers have to hire sight unseen, and then there is the hassle of language tests and provincially regulated registration requirements. In Canada on a two-year work permit valid only for one specified employer-sponsor, immigrant nurses have much the same status as the foreign domestics Canada imports. Nurses and domestics both gain entry by doing jobs no Canadian will do. The short-lived family-practice nursing program at Memorial University in St. John's was supposed to turn out locally trained nurses to staff the stations, but Canadian women are not fighting for the chance. Most of Grenfell's nurses come from Britain or Ireland on three months' probation. They stay for an average of a year or a year and a half, and go home. Gordon, forty-two, is an exception.

She likes the quiet. She likes the people, and she likes clinic work better than the deadlines, the hellish pace, and the routines of acute care. She enjoys her own company, spending her evenings listening to the BBC or Radio Moscow on her high-frequency radio (the clinic's television set doesn't work) or going down to the clinic to spin blood or work on charts. She lives in a four-bedroom furnished apartment over the main-floor clinic for only $183 a month, including board. Other perks include an annual isolation pay of about $1,200, a northern-residence tax deduction, and four weeks' paid vacation a year. She gets a weekend "out" once a month, with Grenfell paying for two out of the twelve trips. Gordon's $31,164 annual salary (almost $3,000 more a year than Grenfell's hospital staff nurses) is a lot higher than most other salaries in Newfoundland, and she can save a good part of it. What's more, because she is the only nurse at the station, she is classified as management. No one looks over her shoulder here; Delrose Gordon is her own boss.

Many of the health problems, apart from snowmobile accidents, are chronic; diabetes, tuberculosis, chest and respiratory problems. Nell, who has had TB, is coughing up blood. Gordon checks her blood pressure and collects a sputum sample to be sent out to the Goose Bay lab. Pearl and Pauline, both with diabetes, are here to have their blood sugar checked. They'll be back for a second test after lunch. Doris and Ann, both obese, have come in to be weighed.

Janice, a pale girl of about eight, is not eating; she has diarrhea; her thin blonde hair is falling out; her ears are full of wax. Her mother is worried. Gordon tries to take a blood sample. "It's going to hurt a little bit." Janice starts to cry. "I'm more nervous than you are," Gordon laughs. When the blood doesn't draw up, Gordon doesn't push it; the blood sample will have to wait for the doctor's next clinic. She does, however, obtain a urine sample to send out to the lab. As she hands the mother some ear drops, "one in the morning in each ear and one at night," she talks gently about nutrition. Does she have Kraft dinner at home? Is the child drinking regularly? Does she eat cereal for breakfast? She strokes the child, cajoling her: "You have to drink for Nurse." No judgements. No hurry. But after mother and child have zipped up their snowsuits and left, Gordon writes in the chart: "Watch this one closely."

Gordon decides what drugs to prescribe, dispensing the pills, ointments, and eye drops from a double-locked pharmacy and collecting money from the patients herself. In hospitals, clinics, and offices in the rest of the country, a nurse gives out drugs only on the written order of a physician. Gordon and the other nurses on Canada's frontier perform this medical function with special permission. The Association of Registered Nurses of Newfoundland, in co-operation with the provincial medical regulatory body, has delegated it to them.

She writes the prescriptions, in between the doctor's visits once every six weeks, and does routine check-ups, taking temperatures and blood pressures, sending blood and urine samples out to the laboratory in Goose Bay. In fact, the moment she opens the clinic doors after lunch, Delrose Gordon becomes the first point of entry into the regional health-care system for everyone in Black Tickle, Labrador. For medical insurance and statistical purposes, she is classified as family practice; up here the nurses are the general practitioners and the doctors are the specialist consultants.

The clinic's doors are never really closed. The phone could ring at any moment, severe chest pain in the dead of night or an appendix on the way to rupturing, either one a potential catastrophe for which Gordon bears total responsibility, twenty-four hours a day, seven days a week. Her only relief is a nurse at a neighbouring station who covers for her one weekend a month. For moral and professional support there is a monthly "grand rounds" by teleconference on the satellite hookup among the eighteen nursing stations, deVette in Goose Bay, and the head supervisor, Joan Gibbons, in St. Anthony.

Briget McGrath, the nurse in Cartwright, an hour's snowmobile ride north, has been up all night. A seventeen-year-old girl went on a rampage, tearing up her books, breaking chairs, and spilling blood on the bed. She just saw a film on child abuse at school and says she wants to kill herself. Her babysitter sexually abused her, she says, and she can't bear the memory. She came into the clinic at about 11:00 p.m., just as McGrath was going to bed, saying she'd swallowed thirty Tylenol. McGrath, also trained in Britain, has decided not to pump the girl's stomach. The teenager wasn't showing symptoms of overdose. So the nurse has sat up all night talking with her instead.

It goes without saying that no fee-for-service worker could possibly take the time to do what McGrath or Gordon do; only a salaried person can afford to give this kind of care. John Vivian, business agent for the Newfoundland and Labrador Nurses' Union in St. John's, calls the inevitable unpaid overtime and the lack of privacy "nineteenth-century bull-shit." Only an organization "stuck in the last century" could plan on getting "good little nice girls to work whenever they are called and to be totally dedicated; that's why they have to change their entire staff every two to four years."

Religious or secular charity is a longstanding tradition in outpost nursing; many of the stations dotting the map of Canada's frontier were begun by non-government community service organizations like the International Grenfell Association and the Canadian Red Cross. The legacy of this missionary heritage is frequently a somewhat patronizing attitude. Grenfell nurses are instructed not to fraternize with the "townies," and social life for women isolated in tiny northern communities is further constricted by the self-imposed stricture to appear as a professional at all times. Although Gordon puts on none of these airs, she doesn't have that much in common with Black Tickle residents.

Including outpost nursing stations in the public provincial health-care networks was one step towards bringing outpost nursing into the twentieth century. The International Grenfell Association, which used to have offices in Montreal and Ottawa, was turned over to Newfoundland/Labrador in 1981; the federal government gave the Northwest Territories full responsibility for its own health care on April 1, 1988, and while the Red Cross still administers six outpost clinics in British Columbia, they are all funded by the province. Another step will be to change the way outpost nurses are required to live. Pauline deVette is the first to admit that lingering Victorian values will eventually have to give way.

Health care in Canada's remote north has always been characterized by chronic nursing shortages and excessive turnover rates. Isolated communities in the Northwest Territories report a 70 per cent turnover rate; in 1988 there were so many unfilled vacancies that staff nurses had to be flown out to rest from overexhaustion. DeVette has many times been forced to fly in and take over responsibility for nursing stations in her region for months at a time in addition to doing her own job; at thirty-one, she has an ulcer. As the shortage escalates in the rest of Canada, the north is finding it harder to recruit nurses. The consequence for its people, already disadvantaged by poverty, poorly insulated homes, contaminated water, and inadequate sewage, is that their health is jeopardized. "Are you here to stay?" asks a timid middle-aged woman perplexed by a recurring vaginal yeast infection: "There are so many new faces."

Unlike in the urban south, the shortage of nurses in Canada's Third World cannot be blamed on lack of job satisfaction; most nurses who go up north love it, despite the difficult working conditions. The surroundings, however, are usually so incompatible it is hard for them to stay. Local women with ambition don't seem to take to the idea of nursing their own communities. It's equally hard for the urban women who have been up north to find anything in nursing to keep them, once they're back down south. The result is that a lot of these specially trained highly skilled nurses are lost, either to the profession or to the country.

Susan Lévesque nursed in Ontario's Sioux Lookout area on and off for three years in the mid-1970s. She and three others had been trained at a special University of Toronto community-nursing program. There she learned how to deliver babies, take histories, and exercise clinical judgement in treating and assessing health problems. When Lévesque got off the plane at Big Trout Lake in 1972, the entire community came out to meet her; they had never before seen a Canadian nurse. Despite being chronically overworked she was entranced with the adventure, the variety, the independence, the thrill of using her own judgement, and above all, the profound satisfaction of constant contact with the same patients.

Fourteen years later she has to pause a long time before she can explain why she came south again. "It's a real addiction," she says. "The north gets in your blood in such a heavy way. I had to make a decision either to go cold turkey or marry the north." It took her a "whole solid year" to readjust to the south.

Lévesque's first job out of the north was in research at the University of Toronto's Faculty of Medicine, and it fit in well with her nurse-practitioner skills. Later, Lévesque moved on to work in occupational health, involving herself on the front lines of the Nurse Practitioners' Association of Ontario. But she could never really bring herself to go into hospital nursing. "When you've had such independence, I think it's impossible for any individual who's worked up north and had the mind-set and ability to problem-solve so much on your own; I don't think too many of those people make the step back to a hospital." She is now a Toronto stockbroker, although she keeps her registration with the College of Nurses of Ontario.

Most of what Lévesque enjoyed doing up north is illegal in the south, unless a doctor covers for her – and very few doctors choose to spend the money to do so. They can't bill government medical insurance for what a hired nurse practitioner does in the office. The alternative for nurse practitioners – setting up a private practice and billing patients directly for only nursing acts – carries more legal liability than the job is probably worth. Lévesque knew in 1980 that finding a Toronto job that would allow her to use her nurse-practitioner skills was hopeless. She would have needed to take on the whole system in a battle she had little chance of winning; all the legal and financial barriers were not going to come down that fast. "I think it's sad that we constantly have to be covered by somebody," Lévesque says. "It's difficult for anyone who is a professional to have the sense of always having to be covered. If the nurses sat back and said, 'We are not going to cover for the doctors,' we'd have a lot of dead patients out there."

Lévesque misses nursing, at least "the nurse-practitioner stuff." She says, "When you saw a [new] mother, you would talk to her about her baby, and then you would be feeling her stomach or doing a blood pressure. Or you'd be talking to someone with hypertension, and you thought they were anxious, and you could lean across and hold their hand." She doesn't get to touch people in her present career; she is not "needed" in as open a way, and "once a nurse, always a nurse," she says.

Nurses are allowed to take on expanded functions in the north because few if any doctors will go there. They are, however, still constantly "covered." Although Dr. Ann Cobourg, one of Grenfell's district physicians based in St. Anthony, calls the outpost health network "very much a team approach," the telephone line at the nursing station is a one-way conduit from the doctor to the nurse, tuning one into the other's non-stop remote-control medical supervision. Delaying treatment or advice until the doctor is consulted seems to be the rule rather than the exception, especially when newly arrived nurses like McGrath are uncertain about how their training compares with the educational preparation of northern nurses in Canada.

Training is an issue. After national health insurance enshrined universally accessible health care in 1966, Health and Welfare Canada began setting aside funds for university programs designed to prepare Canadian nurses to go where doctors were loathe to tread. As it turned out, the country's local nurses weren't anxious to tread there either, and by the time the nurse-practitioner concept went into decline a decade later, most of the Canadian outpost nursing programs went with it.

During the intervening ten years, nurses trained to function beyond the usual scope of practice rode the wave of the future. Nurse practitioners were used almost exclusively in the north until 1972, when a federally appointed committee chaired by Sherbrooke university professor Thomas Boudreau threw out the narrow geographical focus by predicting a nation-wide shortage of doctors. The committee of three doctors and three nurses examining the role of the nurse practitioner suggested bringing her farther south by developing *short-term* programs in selected Canadian universities.

A joint statement by the Canadian Medical Association and the Canadian Nurses Association endorsed the notion of the nurse practitioner in 1973, and doctors, so bogged down with common complaints in general practice they were unable to attend to more serious illnesses, welcomed her assistance. The Family Practice Nurse Program at the schools of nursing and medicine at McMaster University in Hamilton was just getting started, and soon universities in Montreal, Vancouver, Toronto, and St. John's all had special programs designed to train nurses to *assist* doctors in "underserviced" family practices and clinics in both urban and rural communities.

While the programs taught nurses to make decisions and exercise clinical judgement rather than simply to learn procedures, the emphasis was on assisting doctors, not on substituting for them. Although the nurse, called a "co-practitioner," could decide on her own whether to treat or to reassure the patient, she had to be "covered" at all times. The expanded-duty family nurses were even more dependent on medical supervision than nurses practising in the north.

The idea took off, nonetheless, in a flurry of pioneering studies and demonstration projects. Random trials were conducted in southern Ontario by the McMaster people, and in Newfoundland; five nurses entered a provincially funded demonstration training program in Saskatchewan from 1974 to 1976; and "physician extenders" in rural clinics and urban offices across the country were evaluated and re-evaluated.

The results were favourable. By 1975, the trial in Burlington, Ontario, had demonstrated that "a nurse practitioner can provide first-contact primary clinical care as safely and effectively, with as much satisfaction to patients, as a family physician." The need for acute care in hospital decreased by 5 per cent in Newfoundland as a result of primary health care by nurses, while the hospital admittance rate increased by 39 per cent in a group receiving traditional, physician-based care.

Other studies, some in the United States, variously reported that between "40 to 90 per cent of primary physician visits can safely be delegated to nurse practitioners," targeting their greatest promise in helping children, the elderly, and pregnant women. As the late Dorothy Kergin,

a prime mover in the Canadian nurse-practitioner movement, stated in 1978, nurse practitioners come out of their
training "high on independence, flexibility and self-accept-
ance and low on nurturance, deference and order." Scientists
conducting the tests heralded the enormous potential of
nurse practitioners in opening up hitherto unexplored fron-
tiers in environmental medicine, occupational health, and in
reaching the old, the infirm, the disabled, and the poor.

The province of Quebec, encouraged by a separate provincial commission of inquiry, reorganized the delivery of
health care on a community-based model by establishing a
network of local community service centres (CLSCs) designed
to administer health and social services regionally in each
neighbourhood. In other provinces, urban nurse practitioners who had been trained in crash courses to work alongside
overtaxed doctors in their offices found an increasing market
for their special skills in community clinics. Doctors employed on salary rather than billing on fee-for-service made
these health centres especially suitable for nurses to take on
expanded roles.

By the end of the 1970s, moving health-care delivery into
the community had become the international slogan for universal access to health, and it was nurses who were charged
with carrying its banner. After the Thirtieth World Health
Assembly in 1977 adopted the goal of "Health for All by the
Year 2000," the World Health Organization/UNICEF International Conference on Primary Health Care in Alma Ata,
U.S.S.R., in 1978 exhorted nurses to take the initiative by
pressing for an increasing role in health education and promotion, maternal and child care, immunization, prevention
of local endemic diseases, appropriate treatment of common
diseases and injuries, promotion of mental health, and provision of essential drugs.

To achieve health for all, nurses had to have direct access
to patients, and it seemed as if the newly urbanized nurse
practitioner could be the one to lead them to it. By 1978, 93 of
the 109 graduates of the new provincial post-RN university
programs had found positions in Ontario in community

health centres, family-practice units, and hospital specialty units, almost a third of them in doctors' offices; only three worked in northern nursing stations. After decades of promoting a consumer-based approach to health care, nurses looked to the nurse practitioner to bring the nursing profession into its own.

The first problem was numerical. By the end of the decade, immigration and government-funded expansion of medical schools had turned the doctor shortage into a glut. Now the doctors who had welcomed the nurse practitioner a few years earlier began to look at her with suspicion. In urban centres, family-practice doctors began to fall over each other to take on the prevention-oriented functions previously performed by nurses.

Medical associations put out signals that the need for nurse practitioners had diminished. But it could be said that it was the need for doctors that was diminishing. A research report put out by McMaster University health-policy experts in 1982 said nurse practitioners could have safely replaced 20 to 30 per cent of the general medical practitioners practising in Ontario in 1980 had they been fully introduced at that time.

But the powerful doctors' organizations won out. The new nurse-practitioner courses began to disappear, one by one. Basing society's primary-care needs on the supply of doctors, "while it may be a reasonable position to take in the short-term, has dangerous implications," according to the McMaster report. "If, as has been the case, future plans are made on the basis of current physician complements, then there is never likely to be a situation in which the introduction of the nurse practitioners to primary care is a supportable option." In other words, the first problem is numerical, and most likely always will be.

The second problem was, and still is, legal. Although the year-long Burlington trial conducted in the primary-care practice of two family physicians proved that nurses are competent to act *alone* in 67 per cent of patient visits, they have never had the opportunity to do so. The question of supervision Lévesque described has not been resolved.

The self-regulating professional associations in each province decide who is allowed to do what where. Any crossing of prescribed professional boundaries must have the appropriate association's written authority. For nurses, the official sanction is a "delegated medical act" published on a list periodically by nursing licensing bodies in collaboration with their medical counterparts. The person delegating the act, the doctor, retains the legal responsibility for its execution.

Provincial associations of doctors and nurses in Canada have never given the nurse practitioner permission to act in an expanded role without a doctor's supervision. In Manitoba the medical and nursing associations came to an informal agreement in 1983, which nurse practitioners interpret as a guarantee that when acting in an expanded role they will not be charged by the Manitoba Association of Registered Nurses for practising without a licence. The 1984 Manitoba Nursing Review Committee warned that such agreements were "likely to be seen as a recognition by nurses of the limitations under which they practise" and "present a serious threat to the profession." Licensing bodies in Saskatchewan, the only province to extend its Nurses' Act to provide for an expanded nursing practice, have not followed through. Any nurse in Canada can call herself a nurse practitioner.

Lynn Crocker was a diploma-trained RN only three years out of high school when she left Winnipeg to take the nurse-practitioner course at McMaster. When she returned to the Health Sciences Centre's outpatient clinic in Winnipeg, she encountered resistance from the staff doctors. "They weren't ready for nurses in an expanded role. I was expected to keep my place. We were used as helpmates, drawing blood. It was a very busy clinic, but I was sent in and out by the doctors to put on Band-Aids."

The limits on a nurse practitioner's practice in doctors' offices are just as haphazardly defined. It is up to her individual doctor-employer, who has also had to sponsor her training, to decide how much of his practice he is willing to delegate and what he can afford to relinquish. Medical insurance plans cannot be billed for her work. Because her function has no legal status, the doctor is not required to pay her more for the expanded duties and responsibility. As well, medical liability insurers are interpreting the legal ambiguity to mean that doctors must supervise her entire patient workload.

Denise Boggs earns $28,000 a year to manage a busy Toronto infertility practice entirely on her own three days a week while her employer is off at one of his other clinics or attending to his in-hospital practice. Many of his patients go months without seeing the doctor. The doctor "covers" for Boggs by being readily accessible by telephone. Even though she has no special training, Boggs feels confident she could run her own infertility practice, referring out what she knows she can't do, if the law would allow it.

Linda Metcalfe, one of the original five nurses in Saskatchewan's short-lived nurse-practitioner course, spent several years as a nurse practitioner in charge of out-patient care for a surgical team in Thailand. Metcalfe is sure she did things in Thailand no Canadian doctor has ever done. "Part of the nurse practitioner's learning is to know our limitations," explains Metcalfe.

Allowing nurses to treat vaginitis, urinary tract infections, sore throats, ear infections, and other minor problems on their own was the norm in Ontario until a doctor was called to account. A complaint about the bill was sent to the Ontario Health Insurance Plan from the parent of a child examined only by the McMaster-trained nurse practitioner. The nurse was fired, and doctors were more wary about taking time to "cover" after the incident. But their caution is a response to insurance regulations rather than to non-existent legal standards.

"There was nothing wrong; the nurse practitioners were giving absolutely outstanding care," says Mary Buzzell, a former director of the McMaster program called as a witness in the disciplinary hearing. "So I knew at the bottom of it all was a money issue. The double standard is so upsetting. If the nurse practised in a government-run clinic, the child wouldn't have had to see any doctor. OHIP was just awful. All they did was argue money."

The third problem was, and still is, financial. The doctors who hired registered nurses in the 1970s, sponsored them for the nurse-practitioner course, and then brought them back to help out in the office, lost money. The income of the Burlington family practice that was used for the nurse-practitioner trial dropped 5 per cent despite a growth in volume of services that would ordinarily have produced a 9 per cent increase. The loss was a direct consequence of a national, public health-insurance policy that does not cover *unsupervised* nursing services. The doctors had to review each and every case personally to be reimbursed, encouraging them to oversupervise and negating much of the time saved. The complementary working relationship had no chance to thrive when doctors were obliged to delegate only low-level tasks in order to keep afloat financially.

Ironically, these restrictions on nursing practice are a direct consequence of a national health-insurance policy designed to make health care accessible to all. The health-insurance billing policy did not allow for a nurse practitioner's work to be billed on the same fee-for-service basis as a doctor's work. The doctors, who were paying a nurse wages to do work they could bill for if they did it themselves, felt penalized. A 1976 survey, however, showed that a third of them would not employ nurse practitioners regardless of insurance policies: doctors in solo practice did not have enough work to keep a nurse busy, and the rest in group practices or clinics needed financial incentives to overcome their resistance.

Professional regulations and economic restrictions have suppressed the widespread use of the nurse practitioner, and governments have refused to remove the structural barriers. Except for the northern outpost stations and those working in what Greg Stoddard and Jonathan Lomas called in 1982 "a handful of pioneering group practices," the nurse practitioner in Canada "now works with physician supervision over every encounter and performs services which are largely spin-offs from everyday physician functions." What's good enough for immigrant nurses in Canada's Third World is not good enough for Canadian nurses in Toronto. The standards of accessibility are not being equally applied.

The fourth problem was, and is still, philosophical. Canadian nurses didn't, and still don't, want to be doctors' assistants. Picking up the pieces doctors discarded for lack of time or interest insulted the nurse practitioner. It asked her to abandon her focus on the patient and adopt the doctor's focus on the illness. It was an easy leap from there to the conclusion that nurses performing delegated medical acts were contaminating the sacred calling of nursing to a point that came close to heresy; "nurse practitioner" became a dirty word among Canadian nurses.

So, when provincial medical associations and provincial governments withdrew their support for the short-term nurse-practitioner programs, that suited the nursing academics just fine. Primary health care would be promoted better by expanding the role of all nurses rather than splintering off one little group to assist doctors temporarily, the deans of nursing felt, and they promised to ensure that certain nurse-practitioner skills were incorporated into the curricula of all Canadian nursing degree programs. The idea was that every BN-prepared nurse would be a nurse practitioner.

The last of the nurse-practitioner courses begun in 1972 vanished in 1983, and the nurse practitioner became an endangered species, dispatched to the north in a state of disarray. Until the nursing associations get provincial legislation passed, the status of nurses who function outside the normal scope of practice will continue to depend on an arbitrarily supervised patchwork of special certificates, special courses, special programs, and a benign tolerance that could be withdrawn at any time.

Nancy Avery's first patient this morning needs a lot of babying. A sweet seventy-one-year-old man, Dennis has been in and out of hospital for a triple coronary bypass operation, a pacemaker, and most recently a bowel obstruction. His wife has just died of a brain tumour, and by his own admission, "If it weren't for these girls, I just wouldn't be around."

"These girls" are the nurses employed by the Extra-Mural Hospital of Moncton, New Brunswick, "a hospital without walls," which started as a pilot project in 1981 and in 1988 was expanding as fast as the provincial government's restricted budget will allow. A hospital at home is an idea whose time has likely come.

Dennis's doctor had discharged him early from the Moncton Hospital where he had surgery and admitted him to the Extra-Mural. As in a regular hospital, Dennis's doctor writes the orders. But unlike in the regular hospital, here Nancy Avery is his only bedside nurse, his bedside being the lounge chair in the corner of his living room. Avery is now on her knees beside it, placing gauze in the hole in Dennis's stomach.

She is not a visiting homecare nurse. Homecare nurses such as the ones sent from the Red Cross or the Victorian Order of Nurses or from the municipal homecare program are not on duty twenty-four hours a day. They do not provide short-term acute care as Avery does, checking stomach tubes, intravenous antibiotics on heparin locks, Portacath IVs implanted under the skin for continuous morphine, ventilators, and even giving blood transfusions. Avery is a hospital nurse working with patients in hospital at home.

Avery's hospital employs respiratory technologists, dieticians, and occupational therapists who may come to her patient's bedside from time to time. The patient's doctor may make the occasional visit as well. But Avery as the primary caregiver is the co-ordinator of his hospital treatment. She works alone. Using the same finely tuned assessment and teaching skills that nurse practitioners such as Delrose Gordon use in the north, Avery decides what services Dennis needs, by whom, and when.

When Dennis no longer needs acute hospital care, his doctor will discharge him, as in any regular hospital. Then he may require a homemaker or a visit from a homecare nurse. But right now, he must have hospital care. If it weren't for the "hospital without walls," that care would cost $350 a day. This way it costs only $35 a day. While regular hospitals measure non-physican costs in terms of the number of beds, this hospital can measure them in terms of the number of visits.

The Extra-Mural Hospital does not handle patients who are medically unstable. It cannot provide continuous around-the-clock monitoring. But a patient with Crohn's disease, for example, who might spend many hours in a regular hospital bed waiting for the medication to take effect and waiting again between doses, can, as a patient in the hospital without walls, attend school during those periods. Avery visits the patients on her caseload once a day or two or three times a week.

The nursing is organized according to the primary nursing model, with one nurse responsible for a group of patients, following them right through from admittance to discharge. If any one of Avery's patients needs a second visit that day, the nurse on the afternoon shift will be assigned. And should any emergency arise, one of the nurses in her unit is on call from midnight to the morning. But Dennis isn't likely to be one of those emergencies. In fact, although Avery enjoys the time she spends with him, she knows she is going to have to pull back; Dennis has a tendency to become dependent, and the Extra-Mural Hospital is a health-care institution, not a social services agency.

Brian, on the other hand, may deserve some babying. Brian is missing half of his face. He has no tongue and gets his nourishment from an elaborate feeding tube pushed through one of his nostrils into his stomach. Avery has had to teach his wife how to feed him through it, how to clean it, how to put him on gravity feed at night, and how to suck the mucous out of his infected eye socket. Avery is at his home now to treat the eye.

The role that Brian's wife plays may also be an idea whose time has come. She's a lay helper, trained to do specific, minor nursing tasks. Training Brian's wife fits in well with the new definition of nursing – caring about instead of caring for. Brian's wife is now adept at many procedures that a nursing assistant in hospital is not allowed to do. The ideal would be to get Brian to care for himself more. His condition, once the infection heals, is permanent. But Brian is depressed. He's an alcoholic. Those two factors are what prompted him to blow away half his face with a gun in the first place.

Teaching is a major part of what the Extra-Mural Hospital is all about. Avery and the other extra-mural nurses spend a good part of their time teaching – teaching diabetic teen-agers how to inject themselves with insulin, teaching families to give needles, teaching somebody how to hook themselves up to a continuous bladder irrigator, teaching spouses how to cope with death and grief. The nurses aren't required to have medical supervision. In fact, doctors don't have the time or often the patience to engage in this kind of instruction.

Avery's third patient this February morning has needed more than teaching. It's taken Avery months of coaxing to get the woman to look into a cancer patients' self-help group. Brenda's bedside is her living room couch; the room is full of the trappings of longtime family ties. No trinkets brought to a hospital room could substitute for this emotional history.

Avery is here to help Brenda manage pain; she comes twice a week. Today they discuss the woman's constipation; her diet; the self-help group. Brenda's husband laughs at his new-found expertise in the kitchen. They talk about their family. Is that her daughter's photograph on the mantle-piece? No, it is Brenda in a photo taken just last year. "Don't kid yourself," Avery explains after she is out of the couple's earshot. "She is in the very end stages."

Palliative care is a major component of extra-mural nurses' practice. Avery's fourth patient is also dying of cancer. His wife has moved him to the room right by the kitchen, which now smells of fresh-baked bread. The man's wife is a very good "nurse," Avery says. She really doesn't want any help "nursing" her husband. But Avery notices the man's fingers are "bluish." Gently, diplomatically, she inquires about the electric oxygen pump on the floor next to the man's bed.

Perhaps he needs a bit more oxygen? They discuss his medication. Avery cannot prescribe drugs, nor does she carry any
drugs with her. But she checks the dose and helps the woman
solve a problem with the local pharmacist.

The extra-mural nurses on shift this Saturday morning
meet for lunch at the regular place. Because they work alone,
they need the daily contact. Personal safety is a primary concern for these women, who drive in marked cars, often at
night on long country roads. They enter the houses of sick,
irritable people, many of whom live alone. They don't have to
go in when they feel unsafe. One nurse, Pat Lewis, remembers making the excuse that she forgot her glucose and calling her husband to drive by and wait in front of the door.
They can always call an ambulance. But it is lonely work with
great responsibility. Their patients are acutely ill people who
would, if not for them, be in hospital.

"I feel that some of what we do is almost like a nurse
practitioner," says Glenys Olts, a care co-ordinator of the
Extra-Mural Hospital's Moncton unit; "I think that nurses will
gradually evolve into practitioners but in a subtle, soft way.
The way we can practise best is with preventative medicine.
The doctors try that too but sometimes they're so busy and
the follow-up is what is important."

The nurse practitioner, however, is not sanctioned in the
province of New Brunswick. Extra-mural nurses are not the
first point of entry as Delrose Gordon is, and unlike the
homecare nurse, they cannot admit or discharge patients
from care. "We haven't sold physicians on letting us do what
we consider nursing care yet, let alone anything more independently oriented," says Penny Erickson, the University of
New Brunswick's dean of nursing. The hospital without walls
has succeeded only by playing a cautious political game.
Careful in its original proposals not to threaten hospital
administrators, the budget it draws from the government is in
addition to New Brunswick's hospital budget. "We took the
approach at the beginning that Extra-Mural would be an
additional expenditure," says executive director Dr. Gordon
Ferguson, a former civil servant. "We were not used as a

threat to hospitals. Otherwise, we wouldn't have received much support from hospitals."

Hospitals were initially suspicious of the new program; they feared it would be used as an excuse for cutting funds or closing beds, Ferguson says. Doctors, who have to apply to the board of the Extra-Mural Hospital for admitting privileges like any other hospital, were also placated. The Extra-Mural medicare codes allow doctors to bill for what the nurses do, for mileage, one-way above the initial five kilometres, and for telephone consultations. Mileage and telephone charges are not usually permissible, but the Extra-Mural wanted to give doctors an added incentive to discharge early and to refer patients to the hospital without walls, and the extra incentive, for people in private business, has to be financial.

Nurses working in hospitals in Moncton have an increased workload, however, now that the Extra-Mural exists. They are now always under pressure to discharge early, and earlier discharge means sicker patients to look after in hospital. Getting patients out of hospital quickly does not reduce cost when doctors simply fill the bed with someone sicker.

Nurses working for the Victorian Order of Nurses or other homecare programs in New Brunswick were also not placated. The VON, in fact, was pre-empted by the Extra-Mural. There is, by Ferguson's own admission, a lot of overlap between what the extra-mural nurses do and what a good provincial homecare program might do, and once the government can afford to expand the Extra-Mural Hospital's budget, the plan is to extend its services into more long-term care at home for the elderly.

At that point, Ferguson says, the Extra-Mural and the homecare programs are going to have some negotiating to do. The jump from hospital to homecare is at present extremely confusing for patients. It is not good care, Ferguson claims, to discharge patients from an active treatment hospital into a short-term program from which, after the expiry of a predetermined number of days, *regardless of condition*, they must be passed on to a long-term service, and finally perhaps to a fourth agency.

Extra-mural nurses, however, seem happier in their work than any other nurses in the country. They are serving patients, not doctors or hospital administrators; they have the power to make decisions; they have time to do what they do best. "Nurses could make such a difference in so many places," says Avery, "but people don't recognize that."

Dawn Prentice is a visiting nurse with the Victorian Order of Nurses in Hamilton-Wentworth in Ontario. A diploma RN trained at a hospital-based nursing school in Niagara Falls, New York, she does a lot of bathing, a lot of babying, and a little bit of rolling her eyes to the ceiling.

A man whose second-degree burns from cooking french fries are almost healed is a first-time visit for Prentice. His regular nurse is off sick today. Prentice would have discharged him had he been on her patient roster; homecare nurses have that degree of autonomy. But as the other nurse did not choose to do so, Prentice is gently applying gauze soaked in sterile water to the thin new skin on the man's hand. She uses the tongs the families of her patients are trained to have boiling on the stove before she arrives. Leaning against the wall in the narrow hall, the man's wife apologizes for the "bad times" she knows her husband's pain has caused his nurses. "Thank you very much, Nurse," she says, dwelling on the title with awe.

"Is there something else I can do for you?" Prentice is packing the supplies that have been kept there the past few months in boxes to carry to the car.

"Yes, put this on." He hands her the little ball of gauze, hand held out, palm up, like a child waiting to have it kissed better. That's when Prentice rolls her eyeballs to the ceiling slightly, smiles, and begins to wrap the gauze around his wrist. "You have to have a sense of humour," she explains later, walking to the car. "A sense of humour, a love of people and a strong back. That's what it takes to be a nurse."

The VON has saved Prentice for the nursing profession. Two years earlier she was so disgusted about working in hospitals that she had seriously considered becoming a bank teller. "Did they tell you about having to make all the beds before breakfast? I felt like one of the machines." Prentice is happy now that she stayed in nursing. She considers herself fortunate to have landed this job; competition for places in the community is fierce, and the VON gives nurses with university degrees preference. Prentice is working on a university degree in her spare time. But she won't stay in homecare. She doesn't find giving baths all day as stimulating as she would like.

The VON, a non-profit voluntary organization administered by a lay board and financed largely by charitable donations, is paid on contract to administer the official government homecare program in Hamilton-Wentworth. The area is one of only four communities left in Ontario where that is still the case – although VON nurses, employed by the other official government-contracted homecare agencies, carry out 80 per cent of the homecare visits in the province. Most of the other thirty-four homecare programs are now managed by municipal departments of public health, squeezing the VON, the founders of homecare, back into adult day care, Meals on Wheels, and other "paraprofessional" nursing activities.

When the VON was first established in Canada in 1897, their schools were the only place hospital-trained nurses could develop the skills they needed to provide care in the community. Pioneering cottage hospitals in remote areas, VON nurses worked on a fee-for-service basis, providing charitable service free for anyone who could not afford to pay, until Metropolitan Life incorporated VON visits into its private health-insurance policies in 1903. Provincial insurance of homecare, beginning in the 1950s, conflicted with the VON's mission – giving care to all who need it – by introducing pre-set criteria to determine the frequency and scheduling of visits.

Now the VON, first-contact primary health-care providers to this country for ninety years, and the delivery of government-financed homecare are on a collision course. That collision, when it comes, is going to be very costly for consumers of Canadian health care. Soon more babies are going to have to be born at home, and more people are going to have to die at home, and more care will have to be provided at home for all the years in between.

In 1991, only a small percentage of admissions to hospitals is elective. Urban hospitals are fast evolving into intensive-care units, pushing less intensive care into the community. When that happens, doctors are not going to be able to manage. We are not all going to be indigent; we are not all going to be stricken by environmental illness; we are not all going to get AIDS, contract cancer, give birth, or get hit by a car. We are all, however, each and every one of us, going to get old.

11

~

The End of the Rainbow

With the guard rails up, the bed looks like a crib. A diaper stack leans against the side table, and a mischievous black cloth monkey dangles his legs over the window sill behind. But this is not a nursery, and the fully clothed woman lying flat on her back in the crib-bed is no child; she is simply too old and too frail to sit up. The unbending persistence of her outstretched arms betrays the raw strength of the spirit still burning inside her. That and the volume of her moan. While the sound is unintelligible, the desperation behind it rings loud and clear; she wants to be up and out of this safely segregated wing at the far end of the hospital corridor.

"Lovey, what can we do to help you? How can we make you feel better?" Jessie Mantle is an internationally known clinical nurse specialist in gerontology; the Juan de Fuca Hospitals' facility in Victoria, British Columbia, is the best of its kind in the country, and the wing at the far end of the corridor is the Rainbow Room, a refuge for residents with behavioural disturbances. "The only thing that will calm her is her monkey. Give her her monkey," explains the nurses' aide, a man with a long pony tail tied at the back of his neck. He is spooning food into another Rainbow Room resident. They all must be washed and fed, toileted, read to, cuddled and, since none is wearing restraints, watched lest they wander off the edge of the world.

If this is the end of the rainbow, one questions the point of continuing to search for it. The suicide rate for people aged sixty-five and over is higher than for any other population group: in the United States it's 21.6 per 100,000 compared to 12.8 per 100,000 in the general population. Between 1981 and 1986 the rate rose by 25 per cent.

Wheelchairs, more than Mantle would like, line the brightly lit corridor leading to the dining rooms. In each chair is a resident with a grey head, hunched shoulders, flowered dress (85 per cent of the residents in this institution are women) with hidden buttons down the back for easy diaper changes, and a multi-coloured hand-knitted afghan. "Nanee nanee nanee na nee," one woman drones, swaying. Another wearing headphones hums quietly, and a handsome man with a grey moustache sleeps in a leather reclining chair that prevents him from sliding down. Of the 475 "residents," as Juan de Fuca mentor Vera McIvor insisted on calling them, 40 per cent are aged ninety or over; 60 per cent are incontinent all or most of the time; and 40 per cent are confused all or most of the time.

They live here at Mount Tolmie Hospital, or at one of the other three Juan de Fuca Hospital sites, because the rest of the health-care system doesn't have the space for them. Each province has its own jargon for the stages in its long-term-care network. In British Columbia, for the most dependent, it is "extended care" administered by the Ministry of Health in an institution such as this one, and two levels of "continuing care" managed by the social service ministry – "intermediate care" in lodges for those people who can go for walks and take day trips, and "personal care" in group retirement housing with extra services for those the provincial government would now prefer to see living outside institutions. The disintegration of the family and the influx of women into the workforce, however, is making that goal difficult.

Juan de Fuca provides extended care. Although it has none of the high-tech trappings of an acute-care facility, it is a hospital funded by the Ministry of Health, not a home for the aged administered by the Ministry of Social Services. In some other provinces these services overlap; in Quebec and New Brunswick, the health and social service ministries are combined. Across the country provincial governments are grappling with the problem of what is the most appropriate mix of professional and non-professional care that will be needed by the nation's rapidly growing elderly population, either in institutions or at home. Care for the elderly has little to do with traditional medicine, pathology, or disease. It has a lot to do with health, nutrition, diet, and exercise, and even more to do with psycho-social factors like dignity, self-sufficiency, loss, and isolation. It is a sector that needs more skills than it attracts: the fastest growing segment of Canadian health care is still minimally funded and encumbered with the low status that results from prejudice against the aged.

Juan de Fuca's Mount Tolmie isn't just a hospital; most of the seventy-three men and women here have come to live out the rest of their lives. Those with only their pensions live in public four-bed wards; others have expensive private and semi-private rooms. Rich and poor are here together, sharing feebleness, disorientation, disability, boredom, and loss – loss of memory, loss of loved ones, loss of the status that comes with earning a livelihood, loss of hearing, sight, bowel control, limb, loss of dignity and choice, and the one common leveller, loss of youth and all the health and vigour that goes with it. There is a quiet sunroom, an inner courtyard where residents can walk outside even if they forget where they are, and red, blue, green, and yellow stripes on the walls in the corridor to show them the way back to bed.

At a counter in the corner of the larger dining room, Judy Grabham is popping bread slices into three six-piece toasters, assembly-line style: in with one hand, out with the other, and butter. In the smaller dining room the residents can feed themselves, but the ones in the larger room need to be fed; only the very sick eat in bed. Most facilities would use the kitchen staff to do this work, but not here. Grabham is not only a registered nurse, but a registered nurse with a university degree. "It's not underutilization. No, not really. I incorporate it. It's part of my job. It depends on how you make use of it."

Grabham is in charge of planning the care for twenty residents and for supervising how the nurses' aides carry out her plans. Her work in the dining room gives her a chance to keep an eye on both groups. When the nurses' aide in charge of making toast is finished getting the others washed and dressed, she'll take over from Grabham. It is not that the hierarchy of the acute-care bureaucracy has no relevance here but, as in Labrador, every one has moved up a few notches: the RNs supervise, co-ordinate, and direct the aides in the hands-on care. While acute-care hospitals are phasing out nurses' aides and nursing assistants, the geriatric sector of the Canadian health-care system uses them on the front line.

One aide feeding one resident would be the ideal staff-patient ratio. One woman has a privately hired "special" to feed her. Another's husband comes in to get her up every morning before going on to help with the others. The rest, however, are being fed in groups, with the aide turning to one, watching her swallow, and then turning to the second. The aides try to chat as they work, but there is almost no conversation among the old folk, even though they sit in the same groups of four to six every meal. Hard of hearing and insular, they eat in slow motion, absorbed in each separate action, as Grabham and the other three RNs give out medication. A lot of the interaction is non-verbal. Finally Grabham speaks. "Can you swallow a couple of pills? It's down here. There's one more in your hand. That's to make you feel better." Voice raised only slightly, Grabham has her face right up next to the woman in the wheelchair at the table.

"I think I do feel better, because I like that face of yours. Can I have a kiss? I like your face. Oh, that's nice." The woman enjoying Grabham's kiss has a cockney accent.

"Are you going to take that pill for me?"

"What, dear?"

"Can you swallow that pill for me?" The pace of Grabham's voice has changed, not the volume or the intonation. Impatience or imperiousness has no effect here.

"I'm letting it get soft."

"What about this one here?" the nurse asks, enunciating each word slowly.

"My tongue goes against it."

"Well, have another drink. There you go. Maybe I'll hold this one for a while." That's about as far as Grabham is going to get.

The pill at breakfast is a vitamin; the spooned medicine is Colace, a laxative. Nothing life-threatening; nothing life-saving; nothing that won't wait for tomorrow. The day-to-day treatment is reactivation and recreation conducted by "therapists" trained in a community college course; bowel-care and skin-care programs designed by Mantle, the clinical nurse specialist and University of Victoria nursing professor who is consulting here; and a regimen of washing, dressing, and toileting performed by health-care aides or relatives and supervised by registered nurses. Something new called "reminiscence therapy" is being added as funds permit.

Geriatric care epitomizes the nursing goal of caring about rather than caring for; the idea is to empower the men and women living here to do things for themselves. A photograph above each bed and a life history of the "resident of the week" in the central corridor are testimonials to the older people. But they also remind their caregivers that any comparison of their mental condition to childhood is much too superficial. These people, child-like, not childish, have eighty or ninety years of the fullness of life behind them that must not be ignored. Each nursing care plan is geared to adding life to those years, a radical change from the years-to-life focus of the medical model. Geriatric nursing has broken with its acute-care prototypes.

Although Mount Tolmie is more than a hospital, it *is* a hospital; all the residents have been sent here by their private doctors, who are required to drop in every three months to reassess any prescription drugs they have ordered. Every facility must have a staff doctor on call to meet the legal criteria of the province. But the house doctor is rarely used, except in the periodic review of each resident conducted by the health-care team – doctor, registered nurse, health-care aide, social worker, physiotherapist, chaplain, pastoral volunteer, and care co-ordinator – many of whom work part-time. There is no doctor on the floor; if there is an emergency, the nurses deal with it themselves.

That challenge is why Grabham chose this setting, that and the opportunity to use her more basic nursing skills. "Acute care is so fast-paced, you don't often get time to know your patient. And the doctor is in every day. You use your assessment skills but it's different. Here I have much more responsibility. A lot of times the doctor is not able to come in. So he has to diagnose over the phone and give you an order." Does doctor by telephone have a familiar sort of ring? It raises the question of whether it would be more effective to introduce geriatric nurse practitioners into Canadian long-term-care facilities, as Mantle has written in a recently published nursing textbook.

In 2001, 3.4 million Canadians, 11 per cent of our population, will be over sixty-five. That figure was only 2 million, or 8 per cent, in 1971. By 2001, the number of people aged seventy-five to eighty-four in Canada will have doubled. The number of people over age eighty-five will have tripled, two-thirds of them women. The elderly accounted for nearly half of all insured doctors' services in Quebec in 1972 and for 42 per cent of all insured hospital services in Saskatchewan in 1976. In 2025, when 7 million Canadians or 25 per cent of our population will be over the age of sixty-five, it will cost 2.5 times more to support a senior on all government programs than it now costs for one child. That could bankrupt provincial governments.

Treatment and therapy for the elderly are not being developed fast enough. The world-wide nursing shortage has forced geriatric facilities to fill nursing positions with what one nurse calls "a warm body of some kind." A number of B.C. facilities use unregistered nurses, graduates of other countries who do not qualify in Canada. But increasingly RNs, burned out by general hospitals, are moving to geriatric care, where at least they have the satisfaction of ongoing patient relationships and greater responsibility. Noah Meltz reported in 1988 that the proportion of RNs filling the 22,500 new jobs in Ontario's nursing homes and homes for the aged tripled between 1971 and 1986.

The same technology that permits people to live longer is also making the care the elderly now require more complex. The traditional methods of dying, using slow-release morphine and allowing nature to take its course, are being replaced by high-tech heroics to maintain life. Doctors may decide to use "heroic measures" and to get the family's permission, but the nurse at the bedside is the one to whom relatives turn for advice and guidance.

One of the Mount Tolmie residents not in the dining room takes her "meals" in bed, through a naso-gastric intestinal tube. When the woman was having trouble swallowing after a stroke two years ago, the night nurse encouraged the doctor and supported the family in deciding that she should be fed artificially. The woman, in her mid-eighties, wasn't talking; in the very late stage of Alzheimer's disease, many patients don't communicate. Now the woman remains utterly non-responsive, and Grabham has reservations about the decision.

Grabham removes the empty plastic bag hanging from the intravenous pole by the woman's bed and replaces it with the full one, flushing a little of the milky formula through the tube as she works. "She had really lost touch with reality anyway. To me, that's just prolonging the inevitable. She was not swallowing. Was she not telling us she didn't want to live any more?"

The woman's eyes are open, staring at the ceiling. An electric suction machine near the bed is standing by in case she chokes again. This is how things have been for the entire two years. The family felt that not to act when their mother was choking would have been signing her death warrant. But it's hard on them now, Grabham says. She can't help wondering if they should have just stuck with tradition, keeping the woman comfortable, feeding her what she could eat, and letting nature take its course. Once in, the naso-gastric tube can't be taken out without going through the rigorous protocol for withdrawing life supports.

Nurses at another B.C. facility take pride in the fact that they dared buck "heroic measures" when they removed three tubes from a sixty-seven-year-old woman transferred from an acute-care hospital. After talking with the family and picking up the woman's silent "cues," the long-term-care nurses took out her permanent naso-gastric tube and her urinary catheter, putting the woman on a program of pureed food and motion and balance exercise. She did fine.

Making a resident more comfortable is palliative care; high-tech heroics are the *modus operandi* of acute care. It is the difference between suctioning someone who can't breathe and putting someone on a ventilator or total parenteral nutrition. It is generally understood in extended-care facilities such as Mount Tolmie, although there is nothing in writing, that even cardiopulmonary resuscitation is unnecessarily heroic. "Anything that keeps them comfortable and pain free, that's what we do," says Grabham. "If antibiotics help them to be more comfortable, then yes, but if they are already comfortable, we don't like to intervene in the inevitable."

As the increasing number of elderly people living out their longer lives puts more pressure on the traditional health-care system, establishing what kind of care will be necessary, where, and by whom is an urgent priority. Something will have to be done about the shortage of doctors who choose geriatrics as a specialty. Hospitals and nursing homes need to prepare now for the fact that the elderly will be staying home longer and, thus, entering institutions in a more fragile condition than ever before. June Nakamoto has noticed a tremendous difference even in the four years she has been administrator of the geriatric division at the University of British Columbia's Health Sciences Centre. "They are going to need a higher ratio of RNs," Nakamoto predicts, "not just nurses' aides."

In twenty years every existing hospital bed could be occupied by someone over sixty-five, and in fifty years the present national hospital system will have to clone another exactly the same size just to meet the needs of the aged. These figures give new meaning to the word crisis. Provincial governments caught between not servicing these people or getting the money from somewhere else are turning to privatization as a way out, abandoning the financial headaches of managing geriatric facilities to for-profit agencies.

Canada's rate of putting the elderly into institutions, 8.9 per cent in 1987, is one of the highest in the Western world, almost double the rate of the United States and Britain. Institutional care not only costs the government more but is also linked to seniors' mental and physical deterioration, as the Canadian Nurses Association's 1980 brief to the Health Services Review pointed out. The brief stated that one-third of nursing home patients were inappropriately placed. Health dollars will need to be moved away from acute-care treatment hospitals and institutions for the aged, and into community-based programs that look after the elderly in their own homes. The elderly are already ten times more likely to use homecare programs than the rest of the population.

Other types of care, different ways to come into contact with the system, and more health-care personnel must be found for the care of the aged, and the Canadian Nurses Association's 1980 brief went on record as saying that nurses in Canada are able and willing to establish these innovative alternatives, "if governments will only alter legislation, financially and administratively, to allow them to do so."

New Brunswick is planning to extend its hospital without walls to serve older people living at home where, according to Dr. Gordon Ferguson, there isn't the temptation to use the life-prolonging high-tech paraphernalia. "Aging in place" at home is a more attractive option for provincial governments, now that the low-income elderly have, according to Statistics Canada, four times more disposable income on hand to pay for services than they did in 1971. But home health care is not a standard medical service insured in all provinces. Where it is, insurance payments depend on meeting bureaucratically determined conditions. The type and length of service that qualifies for public insurance are not being interpreted consistently by doctors. This explains why 80 per cent of the homecare in Canada is provided by family and friends.

If the frail elderly are going to be asked to "age in place," they are going to need health-care support, not just social services, and safe health care at home is far beyond the scope of what is done today. According to the 1989 Final Report of the Ministry of Health Operational Review of the Ontario Home Care Program, the homecare sector, neglected since the end of the Second World War, is in disarray. Many different service providers exhibit little co-operation, minimal co-ordination, and an administrative inconsistency that encourages physician manipulation to increase patient volume. Operating without a long-term plan and about to go bankrupt from chronic underfunding, homecare does not have the clout to wrest money away from hospitals.

Yet the increase in the demand for homecare is simply staggering. Between 1978 and 1986, homecare visits climbed by 144 per cent in Ontario, and by a further 27 per cent between 1986 and 1989. Ontario's 1989 report, conducted by Price Waterhouse, called homecare programs the community's "deepest pocket," filling in the gaps between other service areas, especially those for the elderly. Hospitals, their beds clogged with chronic "placement problems," are stepping up the pressure for community support; family members have come to expect access to higher-quality care for their ailing relatives; and family doctors with no admitting privileges to highly specialized hospitals are plugging into homecare as a back-up.

Provincial governments initially looked to homecare as a way to save money; a day in hospital costs between $200 and $400; one day in homecare costs only $40. Each family, however, pays more to keep an ailing relative at home than they pay a hospital to keep them, since hospital services are unequivocally insured. But although the growth of homecare (from twenty-one to thirty-eight programs in Ontario alone from 1981 to 1985) is likely to bring in substantial savings in capital construction costs for governments, there is no research to confirm that care at the same level of intensity at home would cost taxpayers less.

Statistics from hospital emergency rooms over the past decade show that relying on a medical diagnosis to determine access to service does not always meet community needs. People who use emergency rooms often have more trust in that highly technological environment than they do in their family doctor's office, and doctors, in fact, often refer their patients to emergency rooms at night.

Health-care consumers turn to hospital emergency facilities as a safety valve for reassurance when they have no other alternatives. "If I am a young single mother, and my two-year-old starts to cry, I may know he's not [seriously] ill but I also know I have to go to work tomorrow and leave him with a sitter. So I go to the emergency room tonight to get a medical opinion rather than miss two or three hours' pay the next day," explains Lois Scott, the nurse in charge in Moncton Hospital's emergency room. Built to accommodate 30,000 visits a year, the room now deals with 83,000. Scott has difficulty defining the mother's non-urgent emergency room visit as inappropriate. It is a problem with the health-care system, she says, simply confirming that the community support network is failing.

Toronto nurse Dilin Baker's clients used the emergency rooms of neighbouring hospitals on a regular basis before she helped set up Toronto Street Health in 1986. Serving the city's homeless on streetcorners, in churches, and in various shelters at night, Baker's "nursing station" is a portable accordion file folder, two plastic buckets, a dish pan, a handful of tea towels, a plastic bag of clean socks, and an assortment of Band-Aids, ointments, antiseptic creams, Kleenex, soaps, and gauze packages she calls "Becker's drugs."

Her "patients" don't have a medical insurance number and wouldn't know what to do with one if they did. Part of her "nursing practice" is helping them fill out forms, making their phone calls, writing their letters, and driving them to doctors' appointments. A lot of her hands-on nursing is comprised of cutting toenails and washing feet, an act of caring since the time of Christ.

One man "attending" an afternoon nursing clinic at the All Saints Church has maggots living in his ulcerated shins. An alcoholic with congestive heart failure, the man has been discharged from the hospital still too ill to walk, and Baker has had to cajole him into the church. He won't answer to any of the other nurses, and booking him a doctor's appointment would be an exercise in futility. Bed rest is all that's needed to cure his ulcers, but Baker has not been able to find a permanent home for him to rest in. When he's finished here, he'll hobble over to wait five hours in front of another shelter until it opens.

Another man's sock is growing right into his leg. He won't allow anyone to clean it up; he wants only a bandage. And a third, a big man whose eyes are full of tears, has an ingrown toenail. "You are going to need to see somebody. I can do some of it," Baker says, gently trying to fit some cotton batting under the nail. Baker isn't allowed to inject antibiotics here as she used to when she nursed in Labrador; she has to make do with teaching the man to coax cotton under the nail. She knows he won't go to a doctor.

Toronto Street Health's two-hour afternoon and evening clinics are located at several shelters throughout the city. They form the kind of "non-traditional" setting that has the potential to make health care truly accessible for all. The Ontario Ministry of Health, in a highly touted initiative to move medical services away from hospitals, has made millions of dollars available for communities to set up innovative health-service centres. But Baker hasn't been able to get her hands on any of it. "The system is physician-based; they have no funding mechanism for nurses. And they are worried about setting a precedent by funding nurses," she says.

She doesn't want a physician on staff; the only doctor around is the one who now volunteers to nurse, cutting toenails as everyone else does. Without a house doctor, the clinic can't qualify for government funding as a health-care facility, nor does it satisfy ministry criteria for a homecare program. So Baker has made do with bits of short-term money from the City of Toronto and a one-time grant from the provincial housing ministry during the Year of the Homeless. A news conference and a community petition jolted $156,000 loose from the health ministry in the fall of 1989, but the money, from the ministry's mental-health budget, did not pave the way for future funding, and what's more, it has reinforced the stereotype of the homeless as mentally ill.

Baker, who picks up extra money doing acute-care shifts for a private nursing agency, doesn't mind relying on volunteers, as long as they reject any Lady Bountiful image. If health care is going to meet the needs of the future, the rigid lines of demarcation between institutional expertise and local community resources will have to be redrawn.

Ottawa nurse Valerie Judd models part of her practice on Baker's. Carrying a little green bag, Judd and her colleague venture out twice a week into housing complexes where people who have absolutely nowhere else to go "live." It is a pilot project of the Sandy Hill Community Centre and designed to reach the disadvantaged.

One of four RNs, two nurse practitioners, a handful of doctors, and four social workers employed on salary, Judd had trouble coping at first. Hospital rules are so clear that here she found herself constantly asking for reassurance; she's had to wean herself from her dependence on doctors' orders. "The role is very foggy and we don't have clear distinctions right now. I'm not doing social work. It is a holistic approach." During the current move towards deinstitutionalization, one woman, discharged onto the street after four years in a psychiatric hospital, caused such a ruckus she was barred from shelter after shelter until a church took her in. A chronic schizophrenic, she is never going to get any better. "I have never seen such sick people, sicker than any I have seen in hospital," Judd says. "They're not sicker in terms of their illness; they're sicker because they're not being treated. Or they're not complying with their treatment plans. It's unbelievable."

When neither volunteer nurses like Baker (who now can pay herself a bit) nor salaried nurses like Judd can guarantee access to health care, even the outside-the-system system is failing. Because medical insurance does not pay for community-based nursing care, only the people who can afford to pay private nurses are getting it. "It's a real issue," says Toronto nurse consultant Mary Vachon, a research scientist at Toronto's Clarke Institute of Psychiatry and an associate professor at the University of Toronto. Vachon's government salary enables her to see people who come in off the street. The chronic staff shortages in acute care limit the expansion of prevention services in the community. Nurses who leave hospitals to work for agencies are essentially setting up their own private practices, Vachon says.

Nursing care in the community cannot expand unless governments finance a community-based delivery system, and the current underfunding of existing acute-care and chronic-care services makes that notion increasingly remote. "We are still waiting to see that happen in real terms," says Molly Anderson, director of the government homecare services administered by the Victorian Order of Nurses in Hamilton-Wentworth. "There is not a lot of turnaround in terms of money from the institution to the community, and that's going to be needed [to make health care accessible to all]. And it's the government who is going to have to do it." What about hospitals and doctors? Anderson's answer is only to laugh. "That's when the cows come home. It's a lot easier for doctors to keep their patients in hospital. They aren't being compensated appropriately for making home visits."

The network of local community service centres established in Quebec during the mid-1970s broke ground in this country by showing what kind of community and preventative health was possible within a decentralized framework. A Montreal school program had nurses teaching primary age children muscle-relaxing exercises to deal with stress, a move with tremendous long-term, cost-saving potential given the high probability of their developing a stress-related illness – colitis, gastric ulcers, or heart disease – in later life. The nurses were taken out of the classroom in 1988. "CLSCs [local community service centres] were told to concentrate on everything to keep people out of emergency rooms," says Montreal nurse Martine Éloy, a mother of children in the innovative school program.

Public health, which is what the CLSCs represent in Quebec, is the country's best weapon in the war against sickness. Disease patterns are also increasing the need for community-based health care. The health-care personnel of the future will be treating chronic illnesses rather than infections. They will have to adapt to the rising incidence of long-term disabilities, the devastation of the AIDS epidemic, and the adverse side-effects of new toxins in the workplace. A large part of the new agenda will be preventing stress-related illness, promoting lifestyle alternatives to alcohol and cigarette consumption, drug abuse, overeating, and traffic accidents, and devising strategies to bring the disadvantaged and the disenchanted into the health-care system sooner. The agenda will have to capitalize on the exercise and nutrition fads of the 1980s by encouraging people to take responsibility for their own health in their own environment at their own pace. All that, according to the International Council of Nurses' 1960 definition, is "the unique function of the nurse."

AIDS is probably the best single example of both the challenge nursing is facing and the kind of legislative support it is going to need to rise to the occasion. The cost of looking after people with AIDS in Canada, either at home or in hospital, will quadruple to at least $508 million by 1992; the number of cases is doubling yearly, and drugs, homecare, and visits in and out of hospital for *one* person with AIDS can cost more than $82,000 over the course of the disease. The eight beds dedicated to AIDS at Toronto's Wellesley Hospital cost $900,000 in 1988. Vancouver's St. Paul's Hospital, which handles 75 per cent of the AIDS cases in British Columbia, estimates that each AIDS patient needs 9.8 hours of nursing care every twenty-four hours; the hospital budget allows for

5.2 hours. "If all six of the patients assigned to us were AIDS patients, it would be unbearable," St. Paul's nurse Jane Wray says. "About two is all you can handle."

St. Paul's nurses describe having to put on gown and gloves six or seven times a day. Sores need new dressings every four hours, and nutrition must be maintained under difficult, if not impossible, conditions with patients wasting away from rapid loss of fluids. Pain control, an aspect of treatment that most hospitals hadn't expected, is also time-consuming; nurses are having to experiment with massage, whirlpools, acupuncture, and other relaxation techniques borrowed from a more holistic and less high-tech approach to health care.

"Taking care of somebody, attending to their comfort, attending to their well-being, working with them on what they want, this is what everybody here calls 'real nursing,'" says Cathleen Dunphy, a nurse at the twelve-bed Casey House, Toronto's hospice for AIDS patients. Dunphy graduated from a two-year diploma course in nursing five years ago at the age of fifty. Caring for AIDS patients is the essence of nursing, and AIDS nursing is caring at its highest level of commitment. The tasks to be done, however, are sometimes at the lowest level.

AIDS will revolutionize homecare in this country, predicts Irene Goldstone, director of medical nursing at St. Paul's. A new Unemployment Insurance mechanism will have to be developed to help families take over the care. There are no full-time women waiting at home to do it any more. Managing somebody with end-stage AIDS at home takes two healthy adults with a lot of homecare support, Goldstone says, plus a general practitioner willing to do home visits, an out-patient clinic, and a bed in a hospital if things fall apart.

The gaunt man staring out the window into the Vancouver rain came to St. Paul's only when his mother wore out; she couldn't manage his wandering at home. Like 60 per cent of the other AIDS patients at St. Paul's, who number about fifteen out of every hundred medical patients admitted, this man has dementia. Caring for a thirty-five-year-old man with AIDS dementia is not much different from caring for an eighty-nine-year-old woman with Alzheimer's disease. To avoid using either physical or chemical restraints the hospital has had to hire a "sitter" sent by an agency to watch the man twenty-four hours a day.

They want to promote the quality of his life; they don't want to wipe him out so that he vegetates in bed. "Custodial care is warehousing," says Goldstone, a member of the National Advisory Committee on AIDS: "We need a program that would have recreation therapy and music therapy. A structured day. We usually have one or two patients at a time [integrated into the various medical wards]. But as the numbers grow, there will be a critical mass at some point. This is just an example of what is to come."

Medically stable but confused and disoriented, the man has no active infection; he is simply growing thinner, paler, and more feeble every day, despite the fact that he eats like a horse. The attention he requires is demanding, sophisticated, and labour-intensive, but like the elderly, he is relegated to the lowest-status caregiver in nursing and health care – a babysitter.

Dementia is a blessing for some AIDS patients; they aren't tormented any more by what is happening to them. Their befuddlement protects them from the stigma still surrounding the disease. Dunphy has heard horror stories about AIDS patients in hospitals being ostracized like criminals, their food shoved through the door. A Toronto nurse was fired when it was learned he tested positive to the HIV virus, and he had to fight for the right to return to work in his profession. In April 1988 a VON Canada survey of 2,794 visiting nurses revealed homophobia and unjustifiable concern about risk of infection with AIDS; some went as far as to say they'd do anything rather than work with AIDS patients. Nurses reported extreme levels of anxiety expressed by their sexual partners, and some of the nurses participating in the survey said they would rather quit than continue to nurse AIDS patients. The level of knowledge about the disease among the surveyed VON nurses was, according to chief investigator Dorothy Pringle, "at best, modest and at worst, dangerous."

A 1988 survey of sixty-five nurses in Lethbridge, Alberta, showed a third of them believed AIDS could be transmitted passively in saliva and nearly a quarter believed in transmission by unsanitary conditions. Both beliefs are wrong. Nurses are experiencing similar difficulties in Moncton, New Brunswick, where there is a large gay population and where AIDS cases are increasing every year. Norma Poirier organized a special workshop for nurses specifically on AIDS. In 1984, nurses staffing the medical unit at Halifax's Victoria General Hospital were so insecure about how to deal with AIDS patients they asked for assistance in learning about the new disease. Never before had the nurses had to confront their own beliefs to be able to provide patient care, head nurse and co-author Yvonne Lynch wrote in the CNA journal.

Hospital education programs are not always effective in situations where there is a constant influx of new, inexperienced nurses, says Ann Beaufoy, who is in charge of infection control at St. Paul's. The virus is easily killed with soapy water, but "if someone is homophobic, they aren't going to believe you." New techniques are being developed to augment the "blood and body fluids" safety-precaution guidelines put out and updated at regular intervals in Ottawa. Monojets, new safety gadgets developed in response to AIDS, allow nurses to recap used needles with one hand to reduce the risk of piercing their own skin. But Beaufoy's talks with nurses on her regular hospital rounds over the past few years have led her to conclude that it takes "seven times around with this disease" before nurses are informed enough to manage without giving in to their own fear and anxiety. Nurses reluctant to take on AIDS patients simply resign from St. Paul's and go to the Vancouver General Hospital, which does not admit many AIDS cases. Half of the four full-time and one part-time intensive-care unit nursing teams surveyed in 1988 in Saskatoon believed AIDS would have a negative influence on their continuing to nurse in that type of unit.

Treating AIDS is different from anything nurses have ever had to do before. Women enter nursing fully expecting to cope with terminal illness and exposure to infection.

Although death is never pleasant, two St. Paul's nurses describe the gruesome last days of a man in the end stages of leukemia as satisfying. It fulfilled for them a primal professional commitment to be present and to care. AIDS-related deaths are not as easy. People with AIDS die lingering deaths when they are still very young (the average age at death at St. Paul's is thirty-seven). Because they die within nine months to two years from diagnosis, they require palliative care almost immediately. They can't wait for a prolonged course of treatment before making decisions about their future care.

Nurses called upon to deal with the patient's inevitable intensity of feeling are often in conflict themselves. When a blind man with open lesions from Karposi's sarcoma looked at St. Paul's nurse Mattie Wiens "with great big blue eyes in such an accusing way that sort of shrivelled you up," she was overcome with guilt. She should be there dying instead, she felt. Forced to watch intelligent, smart, witty, creative people in the prime of life waste away, nurses feel powerless, helpless, and angry. "It goes on and on, and nobody is ever going to get any better," says Dunphy, who chose to nurse in palliative care. Nursing AIDS patients is affecting Dunphy personally in a way she hadn't expected. "Do you give them anything they want because they are dying or do you try to push them to get up?" Dunphy says there are times when she finds herself doing irrational things: "Like denial. I remember one was dying and his feet were cold just before he died and here I was putting blankets on his feet. And all of a sudden, I said, 'What am I doing?' You want to make people better."

Some of her patients are angry and hostile; others are needy, and Dunphy finds herself wondering why they are calling for her every five minutes. Tense and lonely, they require a great deal of social support and often get very little. Communication is the big challenge, and although nurses have training in counselling skills, they now rarely have the time to use it; one can't just march in and say, "Now I'm going to talk to you about death and dying."

Dunphy says, observing the gay partners of dying AIDS

patients, "These are real ties, real devotion, real commit-ment." In Casey House, these are men caring for men.

The two men in the St. Paul's hospital room, however, are not family, not even friends. Barry Griffin, a B.C. fisherman with time on his hands during the winter months, just cares. An AIDS Vancouver volunteer who comes in every day during his off-season to help, Griffin never stops talking to the thirty-two-year-old man in Attends diapers he is washing. "There you go. Does that feel a bit cleaner? I'm going to move you up a fraction, kiddo. Here we go. I want to get a gown on you before you catch cold."

Griffin gives the man's back and shoulders an extra rub as he passes the warm wet cloth over them. Then he dips the cloth back into the stainless steel basin. "Are you getting a bit tired of it all? You probably want to slip away quietly, you know what I mean?"

Without volunteers from AIDS Vancouver and the Persons With AIDS Coalition, nurses say they wouldn't be able to man-age. The man in the St. Paul's hospital bed with end-stage AIDS is a "no code." He's had spinal meningitis and rarely speaks, and even when he does, he never makes much sense. But his eyes are open; they flicker in recognition every once in a while, and Griffin knows he enjoys watching television.

"I'm going to get these little ones down you, okay? Try the little ones first. First open your mouth, kiddo. Here's some milk. Not on your nose. Now swallow it in one lump." Griffin strokes the man's face down each bearded cheek as he offers the vitamin pills. The tenderness from one adult man to another, from a perfect stranger, moves one to tears. Nursing is not women's work; the fact that only women do it is an historical accident that a skewed value system has perpetu-ated.

Cindy Carson is also in the room. She has to change the tubing on the Portacath, which pumps pain-killers and other drugs directly into the man's jugular vein. Her paid profes-sional knowledge is crucial at this point; it is vital that this kind of intravenous never be allowed to go dry. Carson is wearing gloves to handle the tubing. She recaps the needle she has just used in the small tubular monojet that sits on the bedside table, and shoves it through a small hole in a red double-plastic bucket marked "SHARPS" in big capital letters. The man's bedlinen is tossed into special double-bagged plastic, red instead of the usual dark green.

This is Cindy Carson's first year as a nurse, and it's been trying. There are many deaths – four or five in one forty-eight-hour period this fall – and six weeks ago a friend who was like a brother to her also died, of AIDS. At first she'd nursed him at home, taking care of him early every morning before she went into work. She was often up all night; he didn't like to be alone. Eventually he came to the hospital's intensive-care unit. The fevers were too high for her to manage at home. She used to sit with him every night after her shift, sometimes staying until the following morning. It was all so upsetting, she couldn't manage much other personal contact. A swelling was pressing on his brain stem and he finally stopped responding to stimulation; he couldn't even breathe on his own. Carson was there by his bedside, "bagging him" by hand with black rubber bellows to push the air in and out. When, after two days, he still had zero neurological function, he was taken off life supports.

Before he died she had felt a special bond with AIDS patients. Because of her sensitivity she would just "get right into it." But after she returned from the ten days she took off on unpaid leave, Carson, twenty-two, just couldn't handle it. Every night the deaths keep going through her mind; it was all too close to home. She's requested a transfer. "I just can't come back to the floor. There's too much dying here."

For a nurse, there's always a lot of dying. Palliative care covers a range of patients from the "no codes" in hospitals, the aging in extended care, and those terminally ill or chronically ill patients gradually dying at home or in hospices. AIDS sufferers are extremely sick for a longer period of time than other palliative-care patients, and the stigma surrounding the disease makes AIDS a deeply personal challenge for nurses.

People with AIDS don't need treatment as much as they need caring; they don't need doctors as much as they need nurses.

Canada will not be able to continue to nurse AIDS patients in acute care. While AIDS patients must be tended by a professional when suffering from the acute respiratory and gastrointestinal opportunistic infections that need aggressive treatment, they don't have to be in general hospitals. The most logical places, given their kinds of disabilities, are extended-care facilities. Out-patient AIDS clinics like the one at St. Paul's by using an array of social-service support workers will take some of the heat off acute-care hospitals. And unless governments expand homecare to include around-the-clock supervision, families will be encouraged to keep AIDS sufferers at home to reduce costs. AIDS is going to blur the boundaries between a professional like Carson and a volunteer like Griffin. We are going to need a lot more volunteers like Griffin.

The real battle against AIDS, however, cannot be waged inside the system; by the time a person with AIDS gets there, his fight against the disease has already been lost. When there is no cure, the focus must be on prevention. Jackie Barnett is a "Bleach Street" nurse hired by the Vancouver public-health department to minister to needle drug addicts. She and the other "Bleach Street" nurse get their nickname by handing out the AIDS street-survival kit: a Zip-Lock plastic bag containing one Street Clinic calling card with names and telephone numbers for free, confidential testing and counselling, one square pink AIDS information card, three lubricated condoms, an alcohol swab sealed in foil, two cotton batting balls, a one-ounce plastic bottle full of bleach, and a smaller plastic vial-size bottle of sterile water to prevent their "patients" from using their own blood as the "shaker."

Barnett "is not there to save anybody." If they want to kill themselves, that's fine by her, she says. Lack of authoritarian "bullshit" is one of the major reasons for the nurses' reputation on the street; the young drug user will tell a nurse things he would never say to a police officer or youth worker.

The majority of Barnett's patients are hardcore drug users who already test HIV positive and see AIDS as a death sentence. Barnett's "clinic" is the Vancouver streets, the bars, restaurant hangouts, and neighbourhood hotels where the nurses shove large bright-pink pamphlets under bedroom doors and put up posters advertising the next free on-site AIDS test. At night the two nurses carry syringes to take blood for AIDS testing in the doorless hotel bar bathrooms. The nurses trade new needles for old. "It's imperative to make sure they have enough rigs all the time so that they never share with anybody," Barnett says.

The Bleach Street nurses, a pilot outreach project funded by the provincial Ministry of Health, also operate a little office out of the Downtown Eastside Youth Activities Society, with an examining room where they can do complete testing for sexually transmitted disease. But most of the time they walk. Initially, program co-ordinators discussed using existing resources such as social workers and educators. They changed their minds. What is really needed out there, they said, are nurses who can do the HIV testing on the spot and who would not be expected to do any policing.

Nurses will need a legislated, expanded role to continue to carry out community-based AIDS prevention in areas so marginal that public-health programs are ineffective and medical supervision irrelevant. Soon, governments may have to give this role to them. Soon, governments may actually have to pour money into community-based health care instead of just talking about it.

12

The Health-Care Armageddon

A once-in-a-lifetime opportunity dropped into the lap of Canadian nurses in 1983. All the major players on the health-care field were at war; the future of medicare was at risk. Fresh from a highly praised agenda for reform presented to a royal commission inquiry three years earlier, the Canadian Nurses Association set out to save the Canada Health Act. It was "the most vocal, massive, concerted effort in Canadian nursing history."

What is now known as Canada's medicare crisis began in 1977 when Ottawa replaced its fifty-fifty cost-sharing agreement with the provinces by block funding tied to the gross national product. That left the provinces with less money for health care but more freedom to raise it in the way they saw fit. They began to sanction hospital user fees and medical-insurance premiums, and doctors interpreted these measures as permission either to opt out of medical insurance or to extra bill. The Liberal government knew it had a national crisis on its hands on February 27, 1979, when Ontario Health Minister Dennis Timbrell called Monique Bégin in Ottawa. He was testing the federal health minister's reaction to a $9.80 daily user fee for each chronically ill person in Ontario after the sixty-first day in hospital.

Medicare was under siege.

The Conservative minority goverment had appointed Mr. Justice Emmett Hall to head a Royal Commission of Inquiry into the health-care system before they were defeated. By the time the Canadian Nurses Association, at that time representing nurses in all ten provinces, jumped into the fray in February 1980, the Liberals were again in power. Mr. Justice Hall called the CNA's *Putting "Health" Into Health Care* "one of the most impressive [of the 450] briefs presented to me. Well-structured and carefully documented, it was affirmative and forward looking . . . it has been impossible for me to give the time that a comprehensive analysis of the whole submission demands."

In their brief to the Emmett Hall Special Commission, Canada's 169,000 registered nurses condemned extra billing, coming out squarely in opposition to the nation's doctors. But the CNA also did something else; it called on all provincial governments to legitimize nurses acting *under supervision* in an expanded role in hospital out-patient departments, community clinics, and doctors' offices. The new expanded-duty nurse was now no longer called a nurse practitioner, although many people still used that label. Now, the CNA promised, *all* nurses trained in degree-granting institutions would be well-prepared to function in an expanded role. If the CNA had its way, all nurses after the year 2000 would be trained in degree-granting institutions. Thus the new role for the nurse, the expanded-duty nurse, would eventually apply to *every* registered nurse in Canada. The expansion of her duties was going to be an expansion of her unique function as a nurse, not assisting doctors or substituting for doctors.

The idea was to put nurses on the front lines of advancing health care for all. Once they were sanctioned by law to do so, nurses in every local community could be consulted by anyone – the well, the infirm, and the indigent – on health education, childcare, immunization, treatment of common diseases and injuries, mental health, and provision of essential drugs. They would also use all their counselling and education skills to prevent health problems. What the CNA was encouraging governments to do was to send every registered nurse in Canada out into a primary health-care setting as the gatekeepers to health care for all.

When the Boudreau committee studied the nurse practitioner concept in 1972 it defined primary health care as the "common entry point" or "that section of the health-care system which most of the people use most of the time for most of their health problems." The impetus "to continue this extension of the role of nurses and nurse practitioners in caring for the chronically ill and the mentally ill at home, in family counselling on preventive health measures, and in the abatement of environmental hazards and self-imposed risks," had received unprecedented support in Canada from a man who now must be considered to have given birth to a vision before its time. Marc Lalonde, the federal minister of health and welfare, issued a report, *A New Perspective on the Health of Canadians*, in 1974 which is still new, seventeen years after its release.

Lalonde took great pains to suggest that the first point of contact with the health-care system must no longer be in hospital, where prevention is already too late. He pointed to the tremendous number of at-risk Canadians not being serviced by the system. These people could be reached, Lalonde said, if only "care could be elevated to the same level of importance as cure." Too much emphasis is being placed on "the medical solution to health problems," Lalonde said. "There can be no doubt that the traditional view of equating the level of health in Canada with the availability of physicians and hospitals is inadequate . . . . The existence of a generous supply of hospital beds and of increasing numbers of physicans makes it [too] easy for patients to seek care even for minor conditions and for physicians to hospitalize more patients, particularly when there are no financial barriers."

Universally accessible health care is also being seriously eroded by allowing doctors complete freedom to practise where and what they wish, Lalonde went on to say, and professional licensing patterns and the fee-for-service system encourage doctors to carry out tasks that could be done "by others as well or *better* and often at a lower cost." Health-care administrators obviously prefer "to see services provided by staff trained only to the level of skill needed for the task performed." To pay a director of the board to do a job that can be done as well *if not better* by an executive secretary doesn't make sense. And there is, Lalonde said, no reason why ordinary citizens cannot be trained to take more responsibility for caring for themselves.

The costs of not using available health-care personnel to their best advantage are high. A 1982 analysis of the cost-saving potential of nurse practitioners indicated that if nurse-practitioner time had been substituted for doctor time in 1980 for all the medical services already demonstrated to be safe and feasible for nurses to carry out, the total savings in medical costs would have been $300 million.

Nurses are cheaper than doctors, much cheaper; what used to be a three-to-one income differential forty years ago is now five-to-one. Hospital nurses, delegated by doctors, often offer a cheaper substitute. "If they go and see a patient, they come back and make a little touch like this, beside the visit." Anne Marie Poitras, a nurse at Montreal's Cardiology Institute, makes a clucking noise at the "like this". "If he prescribes an IV line, *I* go in and put it in, but the doctor turns the patient's chart, takes its blue page, and marks beside it 'IV line.' He gets paid for what he prescribed, but I'm the one who went to do it."

Delegated medical acts are the mechanisms used by provincial professional associations to deal with the blurring of professional boundaries in times of expedience. Doctors, too busy to take blood pressures in Toronto and unavailable to write prescriptions in Labrador, delegate those tasks to nurses; nurses under stress in hospitals delegate nursing acts to nursing assistants. In each case, the person performing the function must be supervised because the person delegating the task still retains legal responsibility for its outcome.

This system is haphazardly administered and inconsistently interpreted. What is a delegated medical act in one hospital is a nursing act in another, and the criterion for categorizing it one way or the other is based either on whether there are any doctors around or how the ones who are around want to define it. A nurse in a non-teaching hospital will be asked to do many intricate procedures that a medical intern or resident would never let her do in a teaching hospital. Mental-health nurse Leith Nance had perfected a way to relax patients in Vancouver General Hospital's burn unit until doctors decided she was doing "hypnosis" and called in a physician hypnotherapist. Nance later learned to call her technique "deep breathing."

Doctors determining what nurses can do to help out is not what the expanded-duty nurse is all about, explains Valerie Gilbey, a University of New Brunswick associate professor who helps run a screening clinic to train nurses in primary health-care skills. Gilbey's student nurses, shielded by a small university-fed clientele and university teaching funds, enjoy unimpeded access to the patient. But because of the provincial law on delegated medical acts, there is no place in the community for them to use their primary health-care expertise once they graduate.

In its 1980 brief to the Hall commission, the CNA called on the provinces to put Canada's underused registered nurses into service by revising current provincial laws on delegated medical acts.

The CNA brief also exhorted governments to revamp medical-insurance plans to include nursing services out of hospital in order to pave the way for nurses to be the first point of entry. Section 2 of the Canada Health Act defines insured physician's services as "any *medically required* service rendered by a *medical* practitioner," and hospital (insured) services as "any of the [following] services provided to inpatients or outpatients *at a hospital*, if the services are *medically necessary* for the purpose of maintaining health, preventing disease or diagnosing or treating an injury, illness or disability." (My italics.)

In its brief the CNA also recommended that "remuneration of all health personnel be by salary," dismantling fee-for-service payments and destroying the doctors' near monopoly as gatekeepers. The prospect of putting doctors on salary was too much for Mr. Justice Hall. The desire of the majority of Canadians to have "a doctor of their own" is strong, he said, and the 1964 Health Charter for Canadians is based upon free and self-governing professions. Nonetheless, the judge unequivocally supported the other proposals in the CNA's primary health-care package, berating governments for the tremendous "manpower waste" in preventing nurses from working at their full potential in the community. "The whole submission of the Canadian Nurses Association demands close study by all Governments, and I recommend that this be done in a serious and objective way."

It never was.

In his final report, tabled in the House of Commons in September 1980, Mr. Justice Hall came down hard, as did the CNA, against extra billing, insurance premiums, and user fees. He also expanded the health-care war on two more fronts by calling for binding arbitration in the event of stalemated negotiations between doctors and a provincial government, and, the ultimate red flag, immediate action to reduce enrolment in faculties of medicine, "as there were too many doctors."

Bégin responded by opening the Canada Health Act, throwing down the gauntlet to the provincial governments and doctors across the country to do battle with Ottawa and prompting the CNA to launch its first-ever national political campaign, called the Canada Health Act Project.

The Canadian Medical Association, determined since 1981 to break the government monopoly on health insurance, was gaining increasing momentum and support from its member organizations and provincial governments: in 1982, annual user fees in British Columbia totalled $50 million; 44 per cent of Alberta doctors were extra billing; and the Ontario Medical Association had announced rotating strikes to support a 72 per cent fee increase.

The stakes for the nurses rose even higher when it became clear Ottawa was simply going to clarify conditions and reformulate penalties rather than initiate any kind of meaningful overhaul of national health insurance. CNA president Helen Glass was quoted in the *Ottawa Citizen* on December 13, 1983, as expressing deep disappointment that the fee system continued to recognize only hospitals and doctors. Two months later the CNA voted funds from its membership dues to mobilize nurses around the medicare issue.

It hired Registered Nurses' Association of Ontario staff member Diana Dick to become full-time national co-ordinator of the CNA's Canada Health Act Project. She modelled the fourteen-month campaign on the earlier high-profile fight by Canadian women's groups for equal rights under Canada's new Charter of Rights and Freedoms. Eliciting the support of provincial member associations from coast to coast, women's groups, teachers' federations, health coalitions, consumers' groups, and labour organizations, the project, which Dick called a "radical departure" for nurses, launched a regular bilingual newsletter, an intricate network of delegates to lobby MPs, a part-time research team including a well-known local health economist, a full-time national committee, and a flood of petitions, telegrams, letters, and telephone calls. The nurses went as far as arranging a private meeting with Bégin.

It was their finest hour.

But the Canada Health Act lobby was flawed by a lack of clarity over the issue of salary – an issue that haunts the profession to this day. Ginette Rodger, then CNA executive director, insists there was no backing down on the question of salary. "What we said was that salary was the best mode of remuneration, but it was obvious from 1980 to 1984 that society was not willing to put in a salary for everybody. No, we did not back down."

The CNA, it is true, continued to criticize the fee-for-service system, but there was a clear if subtle shift in strategy following Mr. Justice Hall's negative reaction to the CNA's all-salary proposal. In its subsequent briefs on the subject, the thrust of the CNA's proposals for financial reforms was deflected into getting nursing included in the legal definition of insured services. "You see politically it's an act of defiance to say we want all health-care providers to be salaried, so we tried to come up with a different way of saying it," says Dick. "We decided to bury it. It is an awkward wording. We were very unhappy with it. When we said nursing service should be an insured service, we didn't know what we meant by that quite frankly, and neither did anybody else . . . . We never got a chance to re-interpret to people what we really meant."

In hospital settings, nursing services are already insured, although no one has separated out what they cost (and hence, what they are worth). Provincial medicare was designed for fee-for-service payments; salaries do not require amendments to medical-insurance plans.

The idea of putting all health-care personnel on salary was to provide a financial incentive to move health care out of hospitals. On paper, the community-based insurance for nurses the CNA requested could mean salary payments. Most consumers, politicians, hospital administrators, doctors, and nurses, in short the people who count, have understandably interpreted the CNA's push for nursing as an insured service to signify their desire to plug in to the fee-for-service-system as private entrepreneurs like doctors. The fear was that this would escalate costs, create a climate for a two-tier system, if not out-and-out privatization, and erode medicare's potential for providing health for all even further.

The CNA didn't win nursing as an insured service; the medical profession and provincial governments wouldn't stand for it. Helen Glass, then CNA president, attended a medical association convention in 1983 and reported back to the CNA that doctors were concerned that there would be less work for them. Provincial health ministers were "worried about [the] serious dissatisfaction from doctors and unreasonable salary demands by nurses" they thought would inevitably result from insuring nursing services, Bégin reports in a book on the medicare crisis.

Although the federal health minister claimed to be "in complete agreement" with the nurses, Bégin had promised her provincial colleagues she would not include anything in the bill that would put "expansionist pressure on the system, so I could not accommodate the nurses' demand." Bégin, nonetheless, has described the CNA's January 1984 brief to the Standing Committee on Health, Welfare and Social Affairs as raising "the most important and best-fought points" in the debate.

The result, however, was that, "Given the limited time frame," as Eleanor Adaskin writes in a nursing textbook, "the CNA decided at its February 1984 board meeting to focus all its energies on the achievement of one key clause." The one key clause (there were eleven in the CNA's January brief), added at the suggestion of Conservative committee member Jake Epp, was, according to the CNA's March brief to the Senate Committee, going to be "the conceptual breakthrough." It says: "The health care insurance of a province must insure all insured health services provided by hospitals, medical practitioners or dentists, and *where the law of the province so permits*, similar or additional services rendered by other health care practitioners." (My italics.)

The CNA admitted in its brief to the Senate that this "compromise" neither "alters the definition of insured services" nor expands "the comprehensiveness of existing services." Feebly reiterating its support for salaried health professionals, the CNA went on "to recognize that society has the right to determine fair and equitable methods of reimbursement."

The other health-care practitioner clause, referred to as "enabling legislation," was a foot in the door; if provincial governments followed through, nurses would be first-line practitioners in the community. If medical insurance were changed to health insurance, which would include nurses, nurses would no longer be the drones of the health-care system, the perennial employees, the civil servants. Then they would have an opportunity to be self-employed entrepreneurs, as they were before the 1930s. That, however, would not accomplish the same kind of overwhelming reform as putting all health-care personnel on salary.

But no province in Canada has enabled "other health care practitioners" to provide insured services. There is no single hamlet, town, village, or city in Canada where that is now possible. Remote northern communities come the closest. Nurses there are gatekeepers; they see the patients first before the patients see a doctor, if patients need to see a doctor at all. But their practice is not nursing practice; it is supervised medical practice. Elsewhere in Canada, as Greg Stoddard and Jonathan Lomas wrote in 1982, the nurse practitioner "now works with physician supervision over every encounter and performs services which are largely spin-offs from everyday physician functions."

The location of nursing practice, the perceived need for supervision, while demeaning to nurses, is not as significant as the content of nursing practice. Doctors have had a hundred years to concentrate on prevention; by and large, they haven't done it. Let nurses do it. The doctor can diagnose osteoporosis and prescribe medication, but it is the nurse who has the skills to help someone with osteoporosis deal with the limitations on mobility and with what the patient can accomplish *safely* during the course of a day. When an allergic child has an asthma attack, the nurse should be the professional on hand to help the parents tough it out – at home. Whether it's teaching a diabetic child to administer his own insulin injections or an ailing grandmother to flush out her own intravenous tube, non-institutional care is dependent on nurses. Government homecare does not now provide for either prevention or health promotion. But during the next decade, the homecare nurses would have an ideal opportunity to pick up on clues about overeating, or drinking and drug abuse. Nurses would be able to help people help themselves.

Nurses are trained to deal with the whole person, to help a client cope and grieve and manage stress. Nurses *want* to do such peripheral non-medical tasks as counselling and teaching, services not often offered by doctors. Hospital nurses are already involved in everything from marital counselling to family fights to mediating for people wracked with anxiety. Community nurses helping a new mother with her baby or teaching someone to adapt to living with a chronic illness are counselling on a regular basis.

Nurses in private practice carrying out diet, nutrition, or substance-abuse counselling sometimes call themselves nurse-therapists, and "therapy" performed by anyone other than a medical practitioner is not covered by medical insurance. But if the proper adjustments were made, medical insurance could turn into health insurance.

Some nurses are trying to make it on their own, charging clients directly for their services. Lawyers and professional associations have warned them to buy adequate malpractice insurance; the liability risk of self-employed nurses, governed by the same professional accountability as employed nurses, is a huge grey area. But because nursing is not paid for by public insurance, nurses in private practice are not likely to attract the attention of provincial health ministries. As a result, they do not need to prove they are being medically supervised in the same way nurses working in an expanded role in hospitals and clinics do. The logical rationale, if there were one, would be that nurses in private practice are performing only nursing acts.

But there is no logical rationale. Registered nurse Phyllis Jensen runs a stop-smoking course out of her home. Is helping somebody to stop smoking a billable medical service? "Well, I should think so, if a doctor does it," says Jensen. "But doctors won't do it. That's why I'm doing it. Doctors give people nicotine gum. And then they come to me and I get them off nicotine gum."

Almost twenty years after the Boudreau report, there are fewer than five places in the entire country, apart from the north, where nurses have direct unsupervised clinical access to patients. One is a Montreal CLSC that is less than two years old, and another is at Valerie Gilbey's screening clinic at the University of New Brunswick. There are also selected communities on the southeast coast of Newfoundland, a joint effort of the provincial nursing association and Danish nurses sponsored by the World Health Organization, where primary health care provided by nurses is just getting started. It is, however, another research project with no long-term funding.

The revised Canada Health Act enabled private nursing practice, but it did nothing to implement it. Strenuous opposition from doctors, hospitals, and provincial governments, who all fought on the same side of the medicare crisis, remains, and nurses who practise in an expanded role still do so without any structural, financial, legal, or professional support. The restraints imposed by health-care legislation since its inception in Canada has meant the change and restructuring that might have occurred naturally in an open environment have not been permitted.

There is a history of opposition to government support for the expanded-duty nurse. The resistance to nurses acting in a primary health-care role started more than a century ago when midwives hung on as the "last holdouts of the old people's medicine." In eighteenth-century England, doctors protected their turf by getting obstetrical forceps legally classified as a surgical instrument at a time when women were legally barred from surgical practice. When medicated childbirth expanded its techniques, introducing pain-killing drugs and special surgical instruments, public-health nurses, threatened by medical opposition, reduced the amount of direct care they gave to pregnant women and new mothers, redefining their roles as health educators. By 1935, half the births in Canada took place in hospital, and after this critical point was reached, it took only a little more than a decade to get most of the rest into hospital as well. With the advent of medicare, there was no more place for the traditional birth culture in hospitals.

A midwife is now defined as "a person (usually a woman) trained to *assist others* in giving birth" (my italics), and even at that, she must operate in a shadowy area of the law; Canada is one of two industrialized countries in the world where midwives do not have legal status. Women who want to give birth at home attended by a midwife have to find a doctor who is willing to supervise. Such doctors are rare. Sometimes the women resort to calling an ambulance, to protect themselves legally, and then wave it away. But highly publicized cases of home births attended by midwives in British Columbia and Ontario in the last few years have led to a series of reports designed to provide a framework for licensing a new health professional to act in an expanded role for women in childbirth.

Legal sanction for midwives to assist women in childbirth supervised by doctors in publicly administered facilities, however, is not the breakthrough into primary health care that nurses seek. In the age of rapidly proliferating technology, an alarming growth in the aging population, AIDS, environmental and chronic illnesses, and the impending collapse of the traditional ways of delivering health care, the new arena of battle is much larger.

No one is saying non-medical people should practise medicine, nor should medical practice be restricted. Nurses acting as gatekeepers have to know the limits of their skills. The boundary between nursing and medicine is not going to be determined by artificial definition; it is going to evolve out of practices developed to meet new and changing conditions.

When Marvin Moore, the former Alberta minister of health, announced at the annual general meeting of the Alberta Association of Registered Nurses in 1986 that one-third of the province's doctors could be scrapped and replaced by nurses, the nurses weren't pleased. "We know that's nonsense," said Phyllis Giovannetti, association president in 1990. "It pits one organization against the other. The last thing we are attempting to do through our primary health-care model is to say we want to be doctors."

But there remains a great deal of confusion on the subject, and nurses need to clarify their position, not only on where they want to practise but also on what they want to be allowed to do. Some twenty years after the Virginia Henderson definition of nursing passed at the International Council of Nurses, the American Nurses Association put out a social policy statement defining nursing "as the *diagnosis and treatment* of human responses to actual and potential problems" (my italics) and looking suspiciously akin to the medical model that nurses say they are trying to flee.

The North American Nursing Diagnosis Association, a voluntary organization based in the United States, tries to promote nursing as a separate science. It puts out a list widely circulated in Canada of diagnoses nurses could make, such as anxiety, activity intolerance, hopelessness, hyperthermia, parental role conflict, chronic pain, and urinary retention, just the kind of diagnoses that are least likely to threaten doctors. In a 1987 article in *Nursing Research*, U.S. nursing scholar Rozella Schlotfeldt points to this definition as "not only incomplete and in part illogical, but also in conflict with the long-standing conceptualization of the nature of nursing."

The line between a medical diagnosis and nursing diagnosis is a very fine distinction; more research is needed to evaluate its effect on patient outcome; and nursing practice still gravitates around the medical act in spite of the nursing diagnosis on the patient's chart.

As Toronto nurse Deborah LeBaron puts it, "What's the use of making a diagnosis when you have no power to use it?" Nobody needs pay any attention to it. A poster describing a nursing diagnosis forum hadn't been up in the corridors of the Wellesley Hospital for long before a doctor crossed out the "nursing" and replaced it with "MD." "This was a lesson learned," says vice-president of nursing Virginia Sinnott, who knows it's going to take more than the "airy fairy lingo and jargon developed by a few nurses" to implement the new theories. "That's their [doctors'] territory; we've got to help them understand."

The Joint Ministerial Task Force on Nursing Education in Manitoba warned nurses in December 1977 of the pitfalls of "attempting to delineate practice boundaries by statute." Such action is not only likely to provoke confrontation with medical doctors but may also "lead to unsuitable restrictions being imposed on the practice of nursing." This has already occurred in some U.S. states where laws using euphemisms like "assessment" rather than diagnosis confine rather than expand the scope of nursing practice.

Legislation proposed by Ontario's Liberal government, before it lost power, to regulate health professions in the province defines "diagnosis" as "communication to a patient or his or her representative of a conclusion as to the cause or identification of a disease, disorder or dysfunction," and reserves this function for doctors, dentists, and chiropractors.

Nurses "communicate" this information all the time. "People make a distinction between assessment and diagnosis," explains Jean Daziel, director of nursing practice for the Ontario College of Nurses. "This [definition] will have to be changed. It is unacceptable."

Nurses haven't been able to convince even reasonably sympathetic outsiders of what the basics and the basis of nursing are, says Dr. Walter Spitzer, a biochemist and epidemiologist who spent several years as a young physician working for the Grenfell association in Newfoundland. That, indeed, is part of the problem. Shirley Wheatley, a graduate of the University of Toronto nurse-practitioner program in 1973, says she has never yet met a doctor who understands what a nurse does.

It is still not clear if the demand for nursing as an insured service would be a community-based initiative leading the country to health for all or if it is nursing's ticket out of the white-collar working class into middle-class private enterprise. Do nurses support medicare or do they simply want a piece of the action? Some provincial nursing associations such as the one in Ontario reiterate the principle of salary payments for all health-care professionals; others simply say "a single source of funding is necessary." Nurses pushing to be insured on a fee-for-service basis like doctors are not doing much to save a beleaguered medicare system.

Governments, already having a hard enough time controlling medical fees and desperate to contain spiralling health-care costs, aren't anxious to set a precedent by expanding the fee-for-service system to include nurses; what would stop social workers, physiotherapists, and psychologists from wanting the same privilege?

On the other hand, doctors can't be expected to continue to lose money by hiring expanded-duty nurses, especially when government action to ensure fewer doctors is the logical corollary. And while limiting the expansion of insurance regulations to "supervised" nurses in offices and clinics may motivate doctors to hire them, it does so only at nurses' expense, burying the worth of her services under doctors' billing.

There is another financial alternative and nurses must now take the opportunity Diana Dick said they missed ten years ago by restating it. All health-care personnel could be paid by salary.

Health policy experts at the end of the decade were quick to point out that nurse practitioners would be put to much better use in clinical settings outside fee-for-service. Everyone has more time to spend with patients when remuneration is not based on how many of them can be seen in one day, and doctors don't have to worry about financial incentives to delegate services to nurse practitioners when their wages come out of a global budget rather than out of their own pockets. Even a capitation system – monthly payments for every patient rather than reimbursement for every medical act – has hidden long-term cost benefits.

But government financing of community clinics, in fact, hasn't turned out to be politically any less sensitive than introducing third-party insurance for nurses. Local doctors organized a massive boycott of the Sault Ste. Marie centre in the years after it opened in 1963, and private medical practitioners are apparently still hostile to the clinic. Most doctors view community health centres as a threat. Medical associations have lobbied hard against their expansion, and medical associations have the ear of government. Entrenched in the more traditional funding priorities of institutional care, government support of community health centres has always been limited. It would take an inordinate amount of courage and vision to reroute funds from fee-for-service medicine to pay nurses a wage commensurate with their expertise, even if the changes resulted in better health for all. Quebec remains the only province in Canada with a significant number of community health centres, and some provinces, like New Brunswick, have none at all.

Cost effectiveness is not what launched the nurse-practitioner concept; nurse practitioners arose out of a need to live up to the principles of Canadian medicare by making the health-care system more accessible. "The family practice nurse was never intended to provide cheaper medical care for the citizens of our country, but rather comprehensive care that the Canadian public would soon learn to appreciate," the president of the Canadian College of Family Physicians, Dr. Hollister F. King, wrote in *The Canadian Nurse* in 1978.

The public does appreciate it. When a recent TVOntario talk-show asked viewers if they had enough confidence to consult a nurse rather than a doctor, twice as many did as didn't. It's just that they can't now do so. With the proper legislative support, health-care consumers could have the option to consult a nurse first before going to a general practitioner, if at all. Presumably, those who made that choice would do so not because the nurse is cheaper but because, for what they need, she is better.

A federal document released by federal health and welfare minister Jake Epp in 1986 reiterated the concepts promoted by Lalonde by calling on provinces to redirect their health-care dollars into community health services, bolstering voluntary organizations and nourishing self-help groups. Epp characterizes the new era of health promotion as "a multi-faceted exercise which includes education, training research, legislation, policy coordination and community development . . . . In the past, when infectious disease was the predominant cause of illness and death, health was defined in terms of the absence of disease. By the mid-1900s, we had reduced the incidence of these infections, and health had come to mean more than simply not being ill. It was now defined as a state of complete physical, mental and social well-being."

Dr. Peter Roberts, the director of Grenfell Regional Health Services, earns a salary, as do all the doctors in St. Anthony; the community isn't large enough to support a fee-for-service practice. "Personally I think that one of the changes that has to occur is that there has to be a lot more salaried service," he says. "That's the only way to solve this." Walter Spitzer also favours salaried doctors but only on the basis of capitation – the fixed sum per regular patient – because capitation payments afford an opportunity for doctors' incomes to rise in proportion to the number of patients they see, not the number of medical acts they perform.

Hospitals aren't going to go that route without being pushed. "Hospitals aren't particularly attracted to paying doctors on salary," says Gordon Cunningham, president of the Ontario Hospital Association. "The fee-for-service system is really one designed by the government and I don't think a hospital would get very far in trying to convince its medical staff to go on salary. If the government wants salaried doctors, it's going to have to do something."

Some provincial governments, notably Ontario, are coming out with high-profile incentives to woo doctors away from fee-for-service. "There won't be a momentous breakthrough," says Ginette Rodger. "That's not how social change is made. Social change takes decades. The CNA is not out to abolish fee-for-service. The CNA has as one of its beliefs that salary is the best mode of remuneration and, therefore, urges government that when they develop those clinics, they implement a salary base. It is not the doctor holding it back. It has nothing to do with doctors. The extension for insured services has to do with government, [and] they are too concerned with the delivery of medical care and the political actions of the medical profession. They will progressively do it, like they are doing it right now, probably low key so that it raises the least dust possible."

There are others, however, who predict the change will not be gentle. "I suspect that sometime in the future, there's going to be something that I call the Health-Service Armageddon," says Dr. Spitzer, "where mid-course corrections are no longer going to be possible. Costs are going to go up to the point where it will be possible for the political system to make politically unpopular decisions that will shift alignments in a major way, and it's in that kind of context, of a revolution rather than an evolution, that I think health professionals have a chance of redefined roles."

Nurses are the most underused professionals in the health-care system. They must be put to use. Our health and the health of our universally accessible health-care system are at stake.

The decade of the 1990s is the point of no return for nursing. The revolution in medical technology, the explosive increase in the need for palliative care and chronic care, and the crushing financial constraints now putting a premium on nursing services have not translated into control, money, or respect. Despite a relentless increase in responsibility, nurses remain employees whose legal authority is so limited, they are perceived to need close supervision, a misperception that has characterized nursing as a second-string semi-profession ever since the Depression. But now medical realities are driving doctors to delegate more tasks to nurses as doctors' assistants and nursing assistants are having to take on the bedside caring.

Why do we need to allow nurses a greater role, an independent role, in our health-care system? Because primary health care either isn't getting done or is being done by nurses who haven't been formally trained to do it. Because the failing hospital system is becoming so expensive and focused on the critically ill that the locus of health care must move into the community. Because the demands that AIDS and the aged will put on the health-care system by the year 2000 cannot possibly be met when one group's creativity and potential is thwarted by subordination to another profession. Because more than 80 per cent of our country's nurses minister to less than 10 per cent of the country's population – in hospital. Because developing nursing is society's best cure for an ailing health-care system.

Health education, self-care, self-help, and non-medical intervention at the primary level clear the only sure path to health for all by the year 2000. And health for all by the year 2000 is going to at least begin, if not end, with the nurse.

Bibliography

Aikin, Linda H., and Mullinix, Connie Flynt. "The Nurse Short-age: Myth or Reality?" Special Report in *The New England Journal of Medicine*, Vol. 317, No. 10. (September 3, 1987), pp. 641–646.

Akyeampong, Ernest. " 'Involuntary' Part-time Employment in Canada, 1975 to 1985." Ottawa: Labour and Household Sur-veys Analysis Division, Statistics Canada, reprint from *The Labour Force*, 1986.

Alberta Association of Registered Nurses. *Concerns of Registered Nurses Employed in Alberta Hospitals and Nursing Homes*. Brief to the Premier's Commission on Future Health Care for Albertans. Edmonton, March 14, 1988.

Alberta Courts. Transcripts of testimony on the death of Can-dace Taschuk sworn at the fatality inquiry before the Alberta Provincial Court in July 1983 and the disciplinary appeal before the Court of Queen's Bench of Alberta in May 1984 in Edmonton. Courtesy of the Staff Nurses' Association of Alberta.

Alberta Hospital Association. Two briefs to the Premier's Com-mission on Future Health Care for Albertans: March 1988 and June 1988; Comments on the Commission's Interim Report, October 1988; and summary and highlights. Edmon-ton, November 1988.

———. *Nursing Manpower: A Study of Factors in Nursing Supply and Demand in Alberta Hospitals and Nursing Homes*. Edmonton, November 1980.

Alberta Society of the Friends of Medicare. "Submission to the Premier's Commission on Future Health Care for Albertans." Edmonton, Fall 1988.

Adaskin, Eleanor. "Organized Political Action: Lobbying by Nurses' Associations." In *Canadian Nursing Faces the Future*, edited by Baumgart and Larsen, pp. 475–487.

Alexus, Lillian. "HIV Testing: To Test or Not To Test"; and "Counselling: Tips for Nurses." *RNABC News*, Vol. 21, No. 4. (July/August 1989), pp. 13–16.

Allen, Margaret. "Women, Nursing and Feminism: An Interview with Alice J. Baumgart, RN, PhD." *The Canadian Nurse*. January 20, 1985.

Applied Management Consultants. *Final Report: A Review of the Quality of Worklife Issues of Nurses in New Brunswick*. Fredericion, July 15, 1988.

Armstrong, Esther, and Hewitt, W. E. "AIDS: The Knowledge and Attitudes of Nurses." *The Canadian Nurse*, June 1989, pp. 29–31.

Ashley, Jo Ann. *Hospitals, Paternalism and the Role of the Nurse*. New York: Teachers College Press, 1976.

Attridge, Carolyn and Callahan, Marilyn. *Women in Women's Work: Nurses' Perspective of Quality Work Environments*. Research Report No. 1, Faculty of Human and Social Development, University of Victoria, 1987.

———. *What Nurses Want: B.C. Nurses Redesign Their Work and Workplace*. Research Report No. 2, Faculty of Human and Social Development, University of Victoria, 1988.

Baumgart, Alice. "Nurses and Political Action: The Legacy of Sexism." *Nursing Papers*, Vol. 12, No. 4, (1980), pp. 6–15.

———. "The Conflicting Demands of Professionalism and Unionism." *International Nursing Review*, Vol. 30, No. 5. (1983), pp. 150–155.

Baumgart, Alice and Larsen, Jenniece, eds. *Canadian Nursing Faces the Future*. Toronto: C.V. Mosby Company, 1988.

Bazowski, Peter. "Report on the Vancouver General Hospital by Peter Bazowski, Public Administrator, to the Hon. R. H.

McClelland, Minister of Health, October 16, 1978." Unpublished. Courtesy Library of the Registered Nurses Association of British Columbia.

Bégin, Monique. *Medicare: Canada's Right to Health*. Translated by David Homel and Lucille Nelson. Ottawa: Optimum Publishing International, 1988.

Brown, Laura. "Taking to the Streets." *RNABC News*, November-December 1988, pp. 10–12.

Calamai, Peter. "The Nurses Find Their Bastille in B.C." Southam News Services, 1977.

Campbell, Marie. "Accounting for Care: A Framework for Analysing Change in Canadian Nursing." In *Political Issues In Nursing: Past, Present and Future*, Vol. 3, edited by R. White. London, England: John Wiley and Sons, 1988.

———. "Information Systems and Management of Hospital Nursing: A Study in Social Organization of Knowledge." PhD dissertation, University of Toronto, 1984. Courtesy of author.

———. "Productivity in Canadian Nursing: Administering Cuts." *Health and Canadian Society: Sociological Perspectives*, 2nd ed. edited by D. Coburn, C. D'Arcy, G. Terrance, and P. New. Toronto: Fitzhenry and Whiteside, 1987.

Canada Health Act, Ottawa, 1984. Chapter C-6, s.1.

Canada's National-Provincial Health Program for the '80s. The Hon. Emmett M. Hall Special Commission. Chapter 7, "Nursing Proposals." Ottawa, September 1980.

Canadian Broadcasting Corporation. Videotape of *Man Alive* interview with Susan Nelles. Audiotape of *Sunday Morning* interview with five Hospital for Sick Children nurses. Toronto, January 1985. Courtesy CBC.

Canadian Nurse, The. "Why Nurses Leave Nursing." March 21, 1987, pp. 21–23.

———. "The Nurse Practitioner – What Happened?" An interview with Dorothy Kergin by Mona Callin. April 1978.

Canadian Nurses Association. *The Leaf and the Lamp: The Canadian Nurses Association and the influences which shaped its origins and outlook during its first sixty years*. Ottawa, 1968.

———. *Health for All Canadians: A Call for Health-Care Reform*. Ottawa, September 1988.

————. *Brief to the House of Commons Standing Committee on Health, Welfare and Social Affairs in Response to the Proposed Canada Health Act*. Ottawa, January 1984.

————. *Putting "Health" into Healthcare: A Model for Change*. Submission to the Health Services Review. Ottawa, February 1980.

————. *Brief to The Senate Committee on Social Affairs, Science And Technology in Response to The Amended Bill C-3* (the Canada Health Act). Ottawa, March 1984.

Chinn, Peggy, and Wheeler, Charlene. "Feminism and Nursing: Can Nursing Afford to Remain Aloof from the Women's Movement?" *Nursing Outlook*, Vol. 33, No. 2 (1985), pp. 74–77.

Coburn, Judi. "A Short History of Nursing in Ontario." In *Women at Work*. Toronto: Canadian Women's Educational Press, 1974.

Department of National Health and Welfare. *Report of the Committee on Nurse Practitioners* (Boudreau Report). Ottawa, 1972.

Denton, Frank; Gafni, Amiram; Spencer, Byron; and Stoddart, Greg. "Potential Savings From the Adoption of Nurse Practitioner Technology in the Canadian Health Care System." Quantitative Studies in Economics and Population Research Report No. 45, Faculty of Social Sciences, McMaster University, July 1982.

Dick, Diana; Harris, Barbara; Lehman, Allie; and Savage, Roslyn. "Getting into the Act: a Canadian Nurse's Experience." *International Nursing Review*, Vol. 33, No. 6 (1986).

Ehrenreich, Barbara, and English, Deirdre. *Witches, Midwives and Nurses: A History of Women Healers*. Brooklyn: The Feminist Press, 1976.

Epp, Jake. *Achieving Health for All: A Framework for Health Promotion*. Ottawa: Minister of Supply and Services Canada, 1986.

Fédération Des Infirmières et Infirmiers du Québec, Negotiation Sector. *Report on Nursing Manpower*. February 26, 1988.

————. *The Rochon Commission: Decisive Social Changes*. Response to the Parti Québécois Quebec government's inquiry into provincial health care set up on June 18, 1985.

Ford, Ann. *A History of the College of Nurses of Ontario*. Toronto: College of Nurses of Ontario, 1988.

Gibbon, John, and Mathewson, Mary. *Three Centuries of Canadian Nursing*. Toronto: Macmillan Company of Canada, 1947.

Giovannetti, Phyllis. "Staffing methods – Implications for Quality." In *Measuring the Quality of Nursing Care*, edited by L. Willis and P. Linwood, pp. 123–150. London: Churchill Livingston, 1984.

———. "Patient Classification Systems in Nursing: A Description and Analysis." United States Department of Health Education and Welfare Publication No. HRA 78–22, Johns Hopkins University, Baltimore, July 1978.

Glass, Helen. "The Sleeping Giant." Speech at the Canadian Nurses Association Annual Convention in St. John's, Newfoundland, reprinted as an editorial in *The Canadian Nurse*, September 1982.

Goldstone, Irene. "The Origins and Development of Collective Bargaining by Nurses in British Columbia, 1912–76." MSc thesis, University of British Columbia, October 1981. Courtesy of author.

Goldstone, Irene; Beaufoy, Ann; and Riddell, Rosemarie. "HIV Disease and AIDS." *The Canadian Nurse*, August 1988, pp. 17–30.

Government of Quebec. *The Remuneration of Nurses: External and Internal Market Comparison*. Research Institute, Quebec, March 1988.

Grand, N.K. "Nightingalism, Employeeism, and Professional Collectivism." *Nursing Forum*, Vol. 10 (1971), No. 3, pp. 289–99. Cited in Goldstone.

Grange, Samuel. *The Royal Commission of Inquiry into Certain Deaths at the Hospital for Sick Children*. Phase I: May 31, 1983 to June 25, 1984. Phase II: July 9, 1984 to September 27, 1984. Transcripts courtesy Registered Nurses Association of Ontario Library.

Grissum, Marlene, and Spengler, Carol. *Womanpower & Healthcare*. Boston: Little, Brown and Company, 1976.

Gottlieb, Laurie, and Rowat, Kathleen. "The McGill Model of Nursing." *Advanced Nursing Science*, Vol. 9, No. 4 (July 1987), pp. 51–61.

Haines, Judith. "AIDS: New Considerations in Caring." A special news report in *The Canadian Nurse* (June 1987), pp. 11–13.

Hannah, Kathryn J. "Computers in Nursing Practice." In *Canadian Nursing Faces The Future*, edited by Baumgart and Larsen.

Helmstadter, Carol. "Some Nineteenth Century Perspectives on Four Current Issues in Nursing." Unpublished paper, Toronto, June 1988. Courtesy of author.

Hibberd, Judith. "Militancy and Organizational Culture in a Nurses' Union." Paper presented at the First National Nursing History Conference, Charlottetown, May 16, 1988.

———. "The Labour Disputes of Alberta Nurses: 1977–1982." PhD dissertation, Department of Educational Administration, University of Alberta, Spring 1987. Courtesy of author.

Iglehart, John K. "Health Policy Report: Problems Facing the Nursing Profession." *The New England Journal of Medicine*. Vol. 317, No. 10 (September 3, 1987), pp. 646–652.

Jensen, Phyllis. "Collective Bargaining of Nurses in Canada." PhD dissertation, University of Toronto, 1984. Courtesy of author.

Kalisch, Beatrice J., and Kalisch, Philip. "Nursing Images: The TV News Picture." *Nursing Management*, April 1985.

Kerr, Janet Ross. "The Organization and Financing of Health Care: Issues for Nursing." In *Canadian Nursing: Issues and Perspectives*, edited by Kerr and McPhail.

———. "A Historical Approach to the Evolution of University Nursing in Canada." In *Canadian Nursing: Issues and Perspectives*, edited by Kerr and McPhail.

Kerr, Janet Ross, and McPhail, Jannetta, eds. *Canadian Nursing: Issues and Perspectives*. Toronto: McGraw-Hill Ryerson, 1988.

LeBaron, Deborah. "Insurgent Sisters." Toronto, 1988. Courtesy of author.

Labelle, Huguette. "Nurses as a Social Force." Keynote speech at the International Council of Nurses 1985 Congress, opening ceremony, Tel Aviv, September 1985.

Lalonde, Marc. *A New Perspective on the Health of Canadians: A Working Document*. Ottawa: Minister of National Health and Welfare, April 1974.

Larsen, Jenniece. "Report on a Think Tank in Nursing Leadership." 1982.

Lipovenko, Dorothy. "Canada's AIDS Care Bill Will Reach $508 Million by 1992, Conference Told." The *Globe and Mail*, November 30, 1988.

Lomas, Jonathan, and Stoddart, Greg. "Estimates of the Potential Impact of Nurse Practitioners on Future Requirements of General Practitioners." Quantitative Studies in Economics and Population Research Report No. 48, Faculty of Social Sciences, McMaster University, August 1982. *See also* Research Paper No. 2 of the Council of Ontario Universities Task Force on Medical Manpower by the same authors.

Lovell, Verna. *"I Care That VGH Nurses Care!" A Case Study and Sociological Analysis of Nursing's Influence on the Health Care System.* Vancouver: In Touch Publications, 1981.

Mantle, Jessie. "Nursing Practice in Long-term Care Agencies." In *Canadian Nursing Faces the Future*, edited by Baumgart and Larsen.

McCormick, K.A. "Preparing Nurses for the Technologic Future," In *Contemporary Leadership Behavior: Selected Readings*, 2nd. ed., edited by E.C. Hein and M.J. Nicholson. Boston: Little, Brown and Company, 1986.

McLeod, Michelle, and Silverthorn, Kelly. "AIDS and the ICU Nurse." *The Canadian Nurse*, August 1988, pp. 28–30.

Medicus Canada. *A Review of Management Processes and Operations at the Wellesley Hospital*. Vols. 1–4. Toronto, March 1988. Courtesy of the Wellesley Hospital.

Meltz, Noah, with Marzetti, Jill. "Sorry No Care Available Due to Nursing Shortage," *The Shortage of Registered Nurses: An Analysis in a Labour Market Context*. Registered Nurses' Association of Ontario, November 1988.

Muff, Janet, ed. *Socialization, Sexism and Stereotyping: Women's Issues in Nursing*. St. Louis: C.V. Mosby Company, 1982.

Murray, Michael, and Frisina, Angela. Reports to the Nursing Manpower Task Force of the Hospital Council of Metropolitan Toronto. University of Toronto.
  What Do Nurses Want? A Review of Job Satisfaction and Job Turnover Literature. August 1988.

Agency Nurses In Toronto: Who Works for Supplementary Nursing Services, and Why? August 1988.

Nursing Morale In Toronto: An Analysis of Career, Job, and Hospital Satisfaction Among Hospital Staff Nurses. August 1988.

Morale Among Registered Nursing Assistants In Toronto's Long-Term Care Hospitals. October 1988.

Nurses Resigning Their Hospital Jobs in Toronto: Who Are They, Why Are They Resigning and What Are They Going To Do? September 1988.

Newman, Peter C. "The Private Hospital Revolution." *Maclean's,* February 8, 1988.

Nightingale, Florence. *Notes on Nursing: What it is and What it is Not.* New York: Dover Publications, 1969. (First U.S. edition, 1860.)

Nursing Québec. "Disaffiliation: A Step Towards Equilibrium." Special edition, August 1985.

O'Brien, Patricia. " 'All a Woman's Life can Bring': The Domestic Roots of Nursing in Philadelphia, 1830–1885." *Nursing Research,* Vol. 36, No. 1 (January/February 1987), pp. 12–17.

Obstetrics '87: A Report of the Canadian Medical Association on Obstetrical Care in Canada. Printed as a supplement to the *Canadian Medical Association Journal,* March 15, 1987.

Ontario Nurses' Association. *An Industry in Crisis; Ontario Nurses Speak Out on the Nursing Shortage.* Position paper, Toronto, April 1988.

Padmore, Tim. "Analysis" [of the Vancouver General Hospital crisis]. *Vancouver Sun,* June 7, 1977.

Premier's Commission on Future Health Care for Albertans. *Caring and Commitment, Concerns of Nurses in the Hospital and Nursing Home System.* Interim Report. Edmonton, June 1988.

―――. *Rainbow Report: Our Vision for Health.* Final Report. Edmonton, December 1989.

Price Waterhouse. *Operational Review of the Ontario Home Care Program, Final Report.* Toronto: Ontario Ministry of Health, February 1989.

Pringle, Dorothy M. "Nursing Practice in the Home." In *Canadian Nursing Faces the Future,* edited by Baumgart and Larsen.

Pringle, Dorothy M.; Mousseau, Johanne; Mohide, E. Ann;

Coates, Randall; and Weaver, Lynda. "Visiting Nurses' and Their Male Partners' Knowledge, Attitudes and Concerns Regarding the Care of Patients With AIDS." Ottawa: Victorian Order of Nurses of Canada, April 1988.

Public Archives of Ontario. Videotapes of Rogers Cablevision telecast of Grange inquiry. April 1983–June 1984.

Registered Nurses Association of Ontario. *RNAO RESPONDS: A Nursing Perspective on Events at the Hospital for Sick Children and the Grange Inquiry*. Toronto, April 1987.

Report of the Task Force on the Implementation of Midwifery in Ontario. Toronto, 1987.

Report of the CMA/CNA Joint Committee on the Expanded Role of the Nurse: Statement of Policy. Ottawa, 1973.

Report of the Joint Ministerial Task Force on Nursing Education in Manitoba. Chapter IX: "A Mechanism for Certifying Competence in Post-Basic Specialties." Winnipeg, December 1977.

Reverby, Susan. *Ordered To Care: The Dilemma of American Nursing, 1850-1945*. Cambridge: Cambridge University Press, 1987.

Ryten, Eva. "Women As Deliverers of Health Care." Unpublished paper for the Canadian Association of University Schools of Nursing, June 1988. Courtesy of author.

Schlotfeldt, Rozella M. "Defining Nursing: A Historic Controversy." *Nursing Research*, Vol. 36, No. 1 (January/February 1987).

Schroeder, Andreas, "Emergency! Vancouver General Hospital's Power Struggle is a Warning to Us All." *Toronto Star*, April 14, 1979.

Spitzer, Dr. Walter. "The Nurse Practitioner Revisited: Slow Death of a Good Idea." *The New England Journal of Medicine*, April 19, 1984.

Spitzer, Dr. Walter; Kergin, Dorothy, *et al*. "The Burlington Randomized Trial of the Nurse Practitioner." *The New England Journal of Medicine*, January 31, 1974.

Smith, Donny Lynn. "Nursing Practice in Acute Care Hospitals." In *Canadian Nursing Faces the Future*, edited by Baumgart and Larsen.

Staff Nurses' Association of Alberta. *Submission to the Premier's Commission on Future Health Care for Albertans*.

Statistics Canada. *Nursing in Canada, 1986*. Ottawa: Health Division, April 1988.

Stein, Leonard I. "Male and Female: The doctor-nurse game." In *Conformity and Conflict*, edited by Spradley and McCurdy. Boston: Little, Brown and Company, 1971, pp. 185–193.

Taylor, M.G. "The Role of the Medical Profession in the Formulation and Execution of Public Policy." *Canadian Journal of Economics and Political Science*, Vol. 26, No. 1 (February 1960), pp. 108–127.

Trapp Bulbrook, Mary Jo. "Background Paper to the Study 'Documentation of the Nature of Occupational Stress among Newfoundland and Labrador Nurses' Union Membership.'" Submitted to Newfoundland and Labrador Nurses' Union, St. John's, September 1987.

United Nurses of Alberta. *Brief to the Premier's Commission on Future Health Care of Albertans*. Edmonton, March 18, 1988.

University of British Columbia. *The Nurse Manpower Study*. Vancouver: Health Manpower Research Unit, February 1988. Vol. I, *Report of the Nurse Manpower Advisory Committee*; Vol. II, *A Synthesis of the Nurse Manpower Data in British Columbia*; Vol. III, *Influence of the Workplace On Nurse Manpower Supply in British Columbia: An Exploratory Study*.

Vachon, Mary L.S. "Are Your Patients Burning Out?" *Canadian Family Physician*, Vol. 28 (September 1982), pp. 1570–1574.

Vance, Connie; Talbott, Susan; McBride, Angela; and Mason, Diana. "An Uneasy Alliance: Nursing and the Women's Movement." *Nursing Outlook*, Vol. 33, No. 6 (November/December 1985), pp. 281–285.

Wagner, David. "The Proletarianization of Nursing in the United States, 1932–1946." *International Journal of Health Services*, Vol. 10, No. 2 (1980).

Wallace, Joan. *Part-Time Work in Canada: Report of the Commission of Inquiry into Part-Time Work*. Ottawa: Supply and Services Canada, 1983.

Wiebe, Sherry. "Legal Issues in Nursing Practice." In *Canadian Nursing Faces the Future*, edited by Baumgart and Larsen.

Witter Du Gas, Beverly; and Casey, Alberta. "Baccalaureates for RNs." *The Canadian Nurse*, February 1989, pp. 31–33.

York, Geoffrey. *The High Price of Health*: *A Patient's Guide to the Hazards of Medical Politics*. Toronto: James Lorimer and Company, 1987.

Young, Judith. "Attitudes and Practices Towards Families at the Hospital for Sick Children from 1935 to 1975." Paper presented at the First National Nursing History Conference, Charlottetown, May 16, 1988. Courtesy of the author.

Zwarun, Suzanne. "Nurses in Revolt." *Chatelaine*, November 1984.

Index

Acute-care nursing, 69, 155,
177, 184, 191, 200, 202, 204,
206, 207, 211, 212, 220. *See
also* Intensive care
Adaskin, Eleanor, 230
Administration:
Hospital, 47, 51, 53, 57, 58,
59, 72, 76, 77, 79–81, 82,
83, 92, 99, 101, 105, 166,
224;
Nursing, 58, 69–70, 79, 80, 83,
98–99, 104–5, 106, 121,
155, 172
Agencies, 65, 66, 69, 87. *See also*
Private-practice nursing
AIDS, 106, 123, 169, 213–21
AIDS Vancouver, 218
Alberta;
Court of Queen's Bench,
139;
Labour Relations ruling, 138;
Nursing in, 54, 55, 62, 73–74,
75, 76, 84, 85, 91, 96–98,
107, 114–19, 132–44, 150,
151, 153, 169, 171, 227, 234
Alberta Assoc. of Registered
Nurses (AARN), 73, 91, 101,
107, 117–18, 119, 131,
138–39, 141, 160, 170, 171,
234
Alberta College of Physicians
and Surgeons, 118, 138
Alberta Hospital Assoc. (AHA),
87, 91, 124, 138
Alberta Medical Assoc., 138
American Nurses Assoc., 127,
159–60, 234
Anderson, Molly, 212
Andrews, Noelle, 130
Anti-Inflation Board, 142
Apprenticeship, 48–49. *See also*
Nurses, student
Armstrong, Elva, 83
Ashley, Jo Ann, 104
Assoc. of Canadian Medical
Colleges, 161
Assoc. of Registered Nurses of
Nfld., 178
Associations, nursing, 52, 53,
54, 58, 60–62, 98, 105–11,
117, 119, 150, 153, 157, 158,
159–60, 166, 167–68, 170–71,
172, 187, 190
Auffrey, Lucille, 120

Avery, Nancy, 94, 190–94, 196

Baker, Dilin, 209–11, 212
Banning, Judith, 41
Barfoot, Grace, 164
Barnett, Jackie, 150, 220–21
Baumgart, Alice, 21, 32, 35, 41, 43, 111, 162
Bazowski, Peter, 81, 83
Beaufoy, Anne, 169, 216
Bed closures, 11, 42, 63, 69, 70, 72, 148
Bégin, Monique, 67, 131, 222, 227, 228, 229
Bell, Bertha, 36–37
Bellevue Training School for Nurses, N.Y.C., 47
Besel, Lorine, 66–67, 104, 110
Bill 11, 136–37, 142–43
Bill 37, 137
Bill 44, 143–44
Bill 160, 147–49, 153
Binding arbitration, 136, 143, 146, 152, 227
"Bleach Street" nurses, 220–21
Boggs, Denise, 172–73, 174, 188
Boissoneault, Helen, 146–47
Boothby, David, 34
Bossé, Raymonde, 110, 149
Boudreau, Thomas, 183
Boudreau committee, 224, 232
Bourassa, Robert, 113, 137, 148
Bowley, Suzanne, 17–24, 119–20, 150
Brault, Hélène, 87
Britain, nursing in, 45–47
British Columbia, nursing in, 55, 78–84, 85, 91, 92, 105, 125, 128, 132, 136, 145–46, 149, 151, 153, 162, 171, 180, 199–200, 213, 214–15, 216, 217, 218–21, 226, 227, 233

B.C. Nurses' Union (BCNU), 85, 128, 145
Browne, Carol, 28, 31, 36–37, 39, 103
Burnout, see stress
Buzzell, Mary, 188–89

Cambrian Community College, 171
Cameron, Donna, 85–86
Campbell, Marie, 36, 75, 111
Canada Health Act, 222, 226, 227, 232–33
Canada Health Act Project, 227–29
Canada West Foundations, 150
Canadian Assoc. of Critical Care Nurses, 155
Canadian Assoc. of University Schools of Nursing, 54
Canadian College of Family Physicians, 200
Canadian Council on Hospital Accreditation, 79
Canadian Hospital Assoc., 67
Canadian Labour Congress, 151
Canadian Medical Assoc. (CMA), 49, 54, 102, 183, 227
Canadian National Assoc. of Trained Nurses, see Canadian Nurses Assoc.
Canadian Nurse, The, 21, 24, 35, 41, 106, 110, 238
Canadian Nurses Assoc. (CNA), 24, 36, 52, 54, 55, 60, 77, 103, 109–11, 117, 127, 136, 157, 158, 160–61, 164, 166, 167–68, 170, 171, 183, 207, 216, 222, 223, 226–30, 239
Canadian Nurses Foundation, 169

Canadian Red Cross Society, 165, 180, 191

Canadian Union of Public Employees, 151

Capitation, 237, 238–39

Cardiology Institute, Montreal, 225

Carson, Cindy, 218–19, 220

Casey House, Toronto, 214, 218

Casgrain, Abbé, 45

Casual nurses, 63, 73. *See also* Nurses, part-time

CEGEPS (community colleges), 55, 146

Centenary Hospital, Toronto, 89

Central and Marine Hospital, St. Catharines, 47

Certification, 13, 20, 40, 54, 61, 69. *See also* Licensing

Chapman, Yvonne, 171

Charles S. Curtis Memorial Hospital, St. Anthony, 11, 71

Chicago Hospital Assoc., 48

Children's Hospital, Montreal, 122, 158

Chronic care, *see* Long-term care

Clinical "laddering", 169

Clinical nurse specialists, 65, 169–74, 199. *See also* Specialty nurses; Expanded-duty nurses

CLSCs, 185, 212–13, 232

Cobourg, Dr. Ann, 183

Coburn, Judi, 48, 58

Code of ethics, 19–20, 36, 44, 77, 82, 85, 117, 118, 136, 153

Code 25 (cardiac arrest), 26

Collective bargaining, 59–61, 84, 108, 152

College of Nurses of Ont., 37, 54, 62, 67, 93, 103, 107, 108, 160, 167, 182, 234

College of Physicians and Surgeons of Ont., 103, 107

Collins-Nakai, Dr. Ruth, 138

Community colleges, *see* Nursing schools

Compassion trap, 44–45, 48–49, 51, 120, 123

Connors, Kathleen, 107, 141, 151, 153

Cooper, Austin, 35

Cooper, Shari, 161

Co-practitioner nurses, 184. *See also* Expanded-duty nurses

Coulson, Kathy, 27, 28, 31, 34, 36–37

Credentials, 170, 172

Critical-care nursing, *see* Acute care; Intensive care

Crocker, Lynn, 173–74, 187

Cunningham, Gordon, 77, 88, 239

Cutshall, Pat, 76

Danson, Wendy, 143

Daziel, Jean, 236

Degree-prepared nurses, *see* Nursing schools

Delegated medical acts, 100, 102, 103, 178, 184, 187, 190, 224–26

deVette, Pauline, 176–77, 180–81

Dick, Diana, 29, 131, 163, 228–29, 237

District nurses, 96–97

Doctor-nurse game, 13, 14, 21, 22–23, 25, 26, 127, 163

Doctors, 11, 14, 15–17, 19–24, 27, 39–41, 50, 59, 66–72, 82, 96, 100, 102, 119, 120, 166,

182, 183–84, 186–90, 193–95,
198, 208–9, 212, 220, 222–26,
229–40
Donahue, Bob, 141
Donner, Gail, 93, 95, 108, 162,
164
Downtown Eastside Youth
Activities Society, Vancouver,
221
Drugs, *see* Medications
Dubin, Charles, 39–40, 77
Dubin Inquiry and Report,
39–40, 88, 101, 159
Dufour, Justice Jacques, 149
Dunphy, Cathleen, 214, 217–18
Dymond, Dr. Matthew, 107

Edmonton General Hospital,
73, 96, 98, 132
Education, 40, 45–49, 54–57, 60,
68, 156–74 *passim*, 223;
financial support, 165–66,
169;
in-service, 89, 90, 92;
post-RN programs, 55, 157,
159, 168–74, 183, 184, 185.
See also Nursing schools;
Certification
Elderly, *see* Extended-care
Éloy, Martine, 213
Emergency medicine, 11, 209
Employeeism, 28, 41, 59–60, 70,
83–84
Entry to practice, 52, 156–68,
171; *See also* Nursing Schools
Epp, Jake, 230, 238
Erickson, Penny, 99, 194
Ethier, Margaret, 131, 135–36,
142, 143, 144, 151, 153–54
Euthanasia, 115–18, 120
Evans, Anne, 27, 28, 38
Expanded-duty nurses, 94,

96–97, 172, 190–96, 223–24,
226–27, 232, 233–35, 236–38.
See also Nurse practitioners
Extended-care nursing, 128–29,
156, 199–208, 220. *See also*
Long-term care
Extra billing, 222, 223, 227
Extra-Mural Hospital, Moncton,
191–96

Falk, Dorothy, 139
Family-practice nursing, 179
Fatality inquiries, 76, 114, 115,
116–17
Fédération des Infirmières et
Infirmiers du Québec (FIIQ),
60–61, 76, 146–49, 152
Fee for service, 222, 224, 226,
227, 228, 236–39
Feminism, 34, 40–41, 113,
121–23, 128, 131, 142
Ferguson, Dr. Gordon, 194–95,
207
Firings, 78, 80, 82
Flaherty, Josephine, 88, 118
Float nurse, 13, 22, 73
Frise, Meredith, 38
Fry, Dr. Hedy, 166

Gal, Dr. Nachum, 115–16, 118
Gallagher, Laverne, 74
Gallant, Jeannette, 164
Gatekeepers, *see* Expanded-duty
nurses, Doctors
Gaudet, Jessie, 165
Geriatrics, 156, 199–208. *See
also* Extended-care nursing
Getty, Don, 140
Gibbons, Joan, 179
Gilbey, Valerie, 226, 232
Giovannetti, Phyllis, 75–76, 163,
234

Glass, Helen, 227, 229
Glenrose Rehabilitation Hospital, 137
Global budget, 237
Gobel, Maria, 94
Goldstone, Irene, 41, 84, 111, 214–15
Gordon, Delrose, 176–79, 180, 191, 194
Grabham, Judy, 156, 201–2, 204, 205–6
Grange, Samuel, 29, 32, 33, 34, 35, 39
Grange inquiry and report, 25, 30–43, 119, 135, 155, 170
Grant, Bill, 124–27, 140–41, 163
Grenfell Regional Health Services, 11, 176–80, 183, 238
Grey Nuns, 45
Gribben, Anne, 65, 71, 111, 152
Griffin, Barry, 218, 220
Grissum, Marlene, 51
Guimond, Thérèse, 109–10

Hall, Mr. Justice Emmett, 103, 222–23, 226–27, 228
Hall Special Commission, Emmett, 103, 222–23, 226–27
Hancock, Dr. Trevor, 66, 67
Head nurses, 11, 12, 62, 72, 74, 124–25
Health and Welfare Canada, 183
Health care, primary, 161, 166, 173, 184–86, 190, 191, 197, 223–24, 226–27, 233–34, 240
  privatization of, 66, 72–73, 182, 195, 197, 201–2, 212, 229, 236
  rationing of, 72
Health insurance, 59, 64, 67, 100, 181, 182, 183, 188–89, 197, 207, 209, 212, 222, 226, 227–30, 232–33, 236–38. *See also* Medicare
Health Sciences Centre, Winnipeg, 187
Health Services Review, 207
Helmstadter, Carol, 123
Henderson, Virginia, 104, 234
Herbert, Sidney, 46
Heroic measures, 19, 115, 119, 205–6
Hibberd, Judith, 142, 171
High Prairie Regional Health Complex, 97
Holistic medicine, 46–47, 157, 211, 214
Homecare nurses, 49–50, 191, 194, 195, 196–98, 207–8, 210–13, 214, 215–16, 224, 231
Homemakers, 191
Homophobia, 125, 215–16
Hospices, 219
Hospital Council of Metro Toronto, 85, 87, 89, 90, 93
Hospital for Sick Children, Toronto, 25, 26–34 *passim*, 36, 38, 40, 41, 42–43, 66, 88–89, 103, 155, 162
Hospital hierarchy, 13, 14, 21, 22–23, 28, 40, 41, 43, 57, 59, 63–64, 83, 98, 99, 106; system failure, 33, 43; two-stream, 47, 50, 122
Hospital insurance, *see* Health insurance
Hôtel Dieu Hospitals: Montreal, 45; Quebec City, 45; Windsor, 55
Howell, Barbara Jane, 114–16, 117, 118, 119, 120

Immigrant nurses, 177, 232
Inquests, 76, 81
Institutionalization, 49, 52, 58–59, 98, 100
Intensive care, 27, 42–43, 66, 68, 70, 88, 89, 119, 155, 170, 216, 219;
cardiac, 42;
costs, 18, 42;
neonatal, 17–24 *passim*, 79, 88–89, 155, 169;
neurological, 121;
pediatric, 42, 155
International Council of Nurses, 104, 213, 234
International Grenfell Assoc., 180

Jensen, Phyllis, 43, 232
Johnstone, Lynn, 36–37
Juan de Fuca Hospitals, 169, 199–200, 201–6
Judd, Valerie, 211–12

Kelly, Rick, 89
Kergin, Dorothy, 184, 185
Kilgour, Maureen, 129
"Killer Nurse," 120
King, Dr. Hollister F., 238
King, Martin Luther, Jr., 133–34
Kitely, Fran, 32–33

Labour Relations Act, 137
Lalonde, Marc, 224–25, 238
Lamek, Paul, 31, 32, 33
Lantz, Bonnie, 79, 80, 81, 82
Larsen, Jenniece, 43, 121–22
Laurentian University, 171
Law, *see* Regulations affecting nursing
Lay helpers, 192–94, 196, 208, 214, 218
LeBaron, Deborah, 28, 29, 30, 235
Legislation, *see* Regulations affecting nursing
Le Riche, Dr. Roy, 138
Lévesque, Susan, 181–83, 187
Lewis, Pat, 194
Licensing, 51, 52, 53, 57, 62, 100, 105, 107–8, 167, 224, 233
Live-in students, 48–49
Lomas, Jonathan, 189, 231
Long-term care, 69, 137–38, 199–208, 213–21, 224, 240. *See also* Extended-care nursing
Lovell, Verna, 120
Lynch, Yvonne, 216

Macgregor, Donald, 123–24, 138, 141
Mack Training School, St. Catharines, 47
Male nurses, 21, 124–27, 128; gay stereotype of, 124, 125
Malloy, Heather, 140, 144
Malowany, Evelyn, 122, 158
Manitoba:
Joint Ministerial Task Force on Nursing Education, 172, 235;
nursing in, 55, 62, 85, 87–88, 93, 125, 129, 130–31, 136, 160, 172, 187, 235
Manitoba Assoc. of Registered Nurses, 187
Manitoba Nursing Review Committee, 187
Manitoba Nurses' Union, 35
Mann, Tom, 93
Mantle, Jessie, 158, 164, 199–200, 203, 204
Martin, Linda S., 75

Matrons, 47, 50, 51, 52, 53, 98–99
Mayer, Susan, 95, 121
McCaskell, Lisa, 160
McClelland, Bob, 82, 83
McGee, Marian, 32–33, 42, 99, 103–4, 172
McGee, Robert, 35
McGill University, 169, 172
McGrath, Briget, 179, 183
McIntyre, Liz, 33
McIvor, Vera, 200
McLaughlin, Audrey, 140
McMaster University, 169, 173, 184, 186, 188
McMurtry, Roy, 29, 38
McPherson, Dr. Alex, 102
Medicare, 58, 59, 222–23, 228, 229, 232–33, 236, 237. *See also* Health insurance
Medications:
   administration of, 13, 15, 30, 34, 39, 114, 115, 118, 178–79, 194, 202–3, 210, 218–19, 231, 233;
   Demerol, 15, 115;
   Digoxin, 30, 35, 38;
   overdoses, 115–16, 119
Medicus Systems Corp., 68–74, 75, 82
Meltz, Noah, 86, 93, 94, 101, 102, 204–5
Memorial University, 177
Men In Nursing Interest Group, 125
Mercer, Marlene, 168
Metcalfe, Linda, 188
Metropolitan Demonstrations School for Nursing, Windsor, 55
Metropolitan Life, 197
Midwifery, 49–50, 108, 176, 233–34
Militancy, 66, 78–84, 141, 142, 150–51, 153. *See also* Strikes
Miller, Frank, 65
Miller, Win, 82
Mississauga Hospital, 129
Moncton Hospital, 70, 76, 86, 88, 92, 121, 209
Montreal, nursing in, 60, 71, 87, 111, 128, 212–13, 232
Montreal General Hospital, 128
Moore, Marvin, 140, 234
Mount Sinai Hospital, Toronto, 17–18, 20–24, 70, 89, 161
Mount Tolmie Hospital, Victoria, 156, 200, 201–6
Murray, Muriel, 113

Nadalin, Nancy, 55–56
Nakamoto, June, 206
Nance, Leith, 81, 226
National Advisory Committee on AIDS, 215
National Federation of Nurses' Unions (NFNU), 62, 107, 141, 151, 153
Nelles, Susan, 27–31, 33, 35, 37–38, 40, 41–42, 120
New Brunswick, nursing in, 55, 75, 84, 93, 94, 121, 136, 153, 167, 194–95, 201, 207, 209, 216, 226, 237
New Brunswick Nurses' Union, 93, 167–68
Newfoundland and Labrador, nursing in, 11–17, 53, 55, 60, 86, 90, 136, 165, 175–81, 183, 184, 202, 210, 225, 232
Newfoundland and Labrador Nurses' Union, 165, 179–80
Nightingale, Florence, 45–47, 50–51, 52, 54, 138, 149

Nightingale School of Nursing, Toronto, 55

Nightingalism, 28, 48, 49, 50–51, 104, 124, 125, 135–36, 138, 149

"No code," 115, 118, 218–19

North American Nursing Diagnosis Assoc., 234–35

Northern communities, nursing in, 173, 175–84, 230–31

Northwest Territories, 180

Nova Scotia, nursing in, 52–53, 55, 86, 106, 136, 153

Nurse practitioners, 65, 172–73, 175–90, 204, 223, 224, 225–26, 230–31, 236, 237–38

Nurse Practitioners' Assoc. of Ont., 173, 182

Nurses:
  control over work, 59, 69, 95, 99, 121, 133;
  duties of, 12, 13, 14, 50, 58, 59, 60, 73–74, 80, 98, 100–104, 223, 225;
  exodus of, 42, 94;
  full-time, 17, 57, 63, 64, 66, 69, 87, 90–91, 94;
  image of, 120–24, 125, 126, 127–28;
  legal obligations of, 15, 20, 36, 70, 71, 75, 84, 104, 117, 118, 225, 240;
  part-time, 63, 64, 73, 87, 91, 92;
  proletarianization of, 59;
  recruitment of, 48, 66, 86, 88, 92–93, 155, 159, 177, 181;
  retention of, 88, 92, 172;
  safety of, 86, 132, 135, 144;
  self-employed, 58, 59, 60, 230, 232;
  shortage of, 11, 18, 24, 26, 27, 42–43, 57, 65, 70, 72, 75, 77, 78, 91–93, 100, 106, 111, 146, 165, 168, 170, 173, 180–81, 204, 212;
  student, 51, 53, 76, 79, 123, 127, 156, 226;
  supervision of, 182, 187, 204, 223, 225, 232, 233–34, 236, 240;
  supply of, 52–53, 63–66, 72, 151, 164, 166;
  surplus of, 65
  See also Matrons, Registered Nurses, Nursing assistants

Nurses' aides, 57, 60, 100, 101, 102, 164, 202, 206

Nurses Assoc. of N.B., 120, 167–68

Nursing Alliance of Montreal, 60

Nursing assistants, 193, 202, 225, 240;
  duties, 12, 14, 100–102;
  Registered (RNA), 73, 98, 100–102;

Nursing homes, 130, 201–6

Nursing leaders, 57, 101–2, 135, 157, 162, 173

Nursing managers, see Administration, nursing

Nursing Research, 235

Nursing schools, 54, 63, 100, 107, 127, 156–74 passim;
  Community Colleges, 55, 156, 157, 158, 160, 161, 163, 171, 173;
  Diploma, 54, 55, 56, 65–66, 92, 98, 157–68 passim, 173;
  Hospital-based, 13, 47–48, 50, 54, 56, 57, 60, 92, 96, 114, 156–57, 158, 160, 163, 171, 173, 197;

University level, 54, 55, 56, 65, 66, 111, 128, 157–74, 183, 184, 223, 226. *See also* Education

Nursing sisters, 45

Olts, Glenys, 194
Ontario:
Health Disciplines Act, 53, 166;
Health Insurance Plan, 188–89;
Hospital Act, 106;
Ministry of Health, 54, 128;
Nurses' Act (1921), 107;
nursing in, 29, 53, 54, 55, 61–62, 64, 65, 66, 67, 69–70, 74, 84, 90, 91, 93, 101, 106–8, 111, 117, 121, 129–31, 132, 135, 136, 146, 151–52, 153, 162, 166–67, 171, 172–73, 181–82, 184, 185–86, 188, 196–97, 205, 208, 209–11, 213, 222, 227, 233, 235–36, 239. *See also* Toronto, nursing in

Ontario Home Care Program, 208
Ontario Hospital Assoc. (OHA), 77, 88, 107, 166, 239
Ontario Medical Assoc., 50, 107, 227
Ontario Nurses' Assoc. (ONA), 28–29, 62, 65, 106–7, 108–9, 152
Orderlies, 76, 101, 102
Ordre des Infirmières et Infirmiers du Québec, 60, 105–6, 109–11
O'Reilly, Ros, 127
Ottawa Civic Hospital, 71
Ouellette, Shelly, 86

Overtime, 145, 147

Padmore, Tim, 83
Paech, Gail, 31–32, 33, 42, 108, 152
Pain management, 115, 116, 118–19, 214, 218–19
Paish, Hazel, 96–98, 144
Palliative care, 193–94, 196–99, 213–21, 240
Paperwork, 15, 27, 76, 102
Parent, Madeleine, 140
Patients:
classifications, 72–76, 82–83;
completes, 12, 15–17;
death of, 19–20, 26, 81, 182, 205–6, 217, 218–19;
health of, 24, 27, 66–68, 69, 70, 74;
safety of, 25, 53, 78, 81–82, 84–85, 133, 136, 138, 144, 150, 151, 152, 182, 208
Pay equity, 66, 128–31, 162
Pelland, Jennie, 109–10
Percival, Barry, 31
Petitions, 78, 81–88
Picherack, Frances, 67
Poirier, Norma, 168, 216
Poitras, Anne Marie, 87, 225
Popadiuk, Shirley, 35
Power, Chrissie, 11–17, 24
Premier's Comm. on Future Health Care for Albertans, 92, 102, 140, 170
Prentice, Dawn, 94, 196–97
Press, Jack, 35
Prince Edward Island, nursing in, 53, 55, 62, 136, 166
Pringle, Dorothy, 49, 215
Private-practice nursing, 49, 57, 58, 65, 66, 85, 94, 211, 231–33

Professed nurses, 45, 49, 100, 107
Professional responsibility committees, 146
Project for Research in Nursing, 75
Prouse, Marney, 94
Public-health nursing, 62, 233

Quebec:
  Essential Services Council, 147, 148;
  nursing in, 45, 53, 54, 55, 60–61, 62, 75, 76, 87, 90, 91, 93, 105–6, 109–11, 113, 117, 136, 137, 146–49, 151, 152–53, 185, 201, 204, 212–13, 237;
  Superior Court, 149
  Treasury Board, 147
Quebec Federation of Labour, 60
Quebec Hospitals Assoc., 148
Quebec Professional Code, 109

Radojewski, Elizabeth, 36–37
Rae, Bob, 130
Rand formula, 141–42
Rankin, Nikki, 38, 155–56
"Reality shock," 163
Reardon, Mae, 121
Rebalkin, Helen, 134–35
Red Deer Community College, 171
Reed, Dr. John, 116
Registered Nurses (RNs), 53, 57, 58, 60, 61, 62, 64, 66, 68, 73, 90, 91, 93, 94, 95, 100–105, 109, 111, 113, 118, 206, 223, 225, 240. *See also* Nurses
Registered Nursing Assistants (RNAs), *see* Nursing Assistants

Registered Nurses Assoc. of B.C. (RNABC), 61, 62, 76, 79, 80, 81, 83–85, 105;
  RNABC News, 84
Registered Nurses Assoc. of N.S., 106
Registered Nurses Assoc. of Ont. (RNAO), 54, 55, 62, 86, 93, 101, 102, 106–9, 111–12, 159, 166, 170, 171, 228
Registrations, 52–53, 57, 93, 107
Regulations, Legislations and Laws affecting Nursing, 13, 20, 21, 39, 52–53, 61–62, 76, 96, 101, 104–5, 108, 129, 132, 134, 136–37, 138, 142–49, 153, 157, 158, 163, 168, 178, 182, 186–97, 207, 213, 221, 223, 225, 226, 228, 230, 233, 235, 236
Renouf, Simon, 143
Resignations, 78, 79, 80–81, 82, 84. *See also* Turnover
Reverby, Susan, 46, 48, 120
Riddell, Rosemarie, 86, 89, 113–14
Risk, Margaret, 108, 160
Roberts, Dr. Peter, 238
Rochon Commission, 90
Rodger, Ginette, 110, 111, 121, 228, 239
Rogers, Louise, 77, 144
Rolf, Judge Carl, 116–17
Ross, Eleanor, 102
Rothwell, Sue, 81–82
Rounds, 12–13
Royal Alexandra Hospital, Edmonton, 139
Royal Commission of Inquiry into Certain Deaths, *see* Grange inquiry
Royal Commission on Health

Services (1964), 55, 56–57. *See also* Hall Special Commission

Royal Commission on the Status of Women, 120–21

Royal Victoria Hospital, Montreal, 67

Ryerson Polytechnical Institute, 55, 95, 121, 169

"Ryerson Project," 55

Ryten, Eva, 90, 161, 168

St. Clair College, Windsor, 55

St. Joseph's Hospital, Comox, 145

St. Joseph's Health Centre, Toronto, 169

Ste-Justine Hospital for Children, Montreal, 87

St. Michael's Hospital, Toronto, 77

St. Paul's Hospital, Vancouver, 41, 89, 125, 213–15, 216–17, 218–19, 220

St. Thomas' Hospital, Eng., 46

Salaries, *see* Wages

Sandy Hill Community Centre, Ottawa, 211

Saskatchewan, nursing in, 55, 85, 104–5, 136, 144, 151, 153, 160, 165, 184, 187, 188, 204, 216

Saskatchewan Registered Nurses' Assoc., 61

Saskatchewan Union of Nurses, 144

Savage, Pat, 146

Schamborzki, Inge, 75

Schiff, Dr. David, 116, 118

Schlotfeldt, Rozella, 235

Schulze, Betty, 116, 117–18, 119

Scott, Lois, 209

Self-employed, *see* Private-practice nursing; Nurses, self-employed

Seniority, 147–48, 170

Service Employees International Union, 61

Sexism, 32–33, 40

Shifflert, Betty, 140

Shifts:
day, 103, 132;
night, 11, 66, 70, 85, 103;
12-hour, 11, 20, 86–87, 96, 102, 114

Scheiner, John, 149

Simms, Dianne, 71, 161, 163–64

Sinnott, Virginia, 70, 71, 74, 106, 235

Slattery, Glenna Cole, 43, 107, 111, 128, 151–52, 159, 170

Smith, Heather, 143, 144, 167

Snedden, J.D., 26

Snell, Sharon, 138, 170, 172

Specialty nurses, 65–68, 69, 170–74

Spitzer, Dr. Walter, 130, 236, 238–39

Staff Nurses' Assoc. of Alta., 77, 117, 119, 133, 144

Standards, *see* Certification; Entry to practice

Staley, Trudy, 83, 84, 129

Steeves, Madeleine, 167

Stinson, Shirley, 110

Stoddard, Greg, 189, 231

Stordy, Elizabeth Ann, 88

Stress, 26, 37, 39, 42, 85, 86, 88, 126, 165, 180, 215

Strikes, 60, 75, 84, 97–98, 128, 132–50, 152–53. *See also* Militancy

Stringer, Bernadette, 128

Suicide, 37, 200

Subsidiary workers, 57, 95, 101
Supreme Court of Canada, 38,
  61, 62, 137, 139
Symes, Beth, 33

Taschuk inquiry, 114, 115,
  116–17, 119
Team nursing, 11–17 *passim*,
  58, 100, 101, 102, 169
Technology, 99–100
Technologists, technicians, 18,
  20, 22, 100, 128, 130, 158,
  160, 191
Thatcher, Margaret, 122
Timbrell, Dennis, 222
Todd, Jack, 148
Toronto, nursing in, 17–18,
  20–24, 26–43 *passim*, 68–70,
  71, 77, 85-86, 89, 90, 92, 103,
  106, 123, 151, 209–11, 212,
  213, 214, 215, 218, 225, 235.
  See also Ontario, nursing in
Toronto General Hospital, 89,
  92
Toronto Street Health, 209–11
Training, *see* Education
Trayner, Phyllis, 27, 30, 37
Truitt, Larry, 80, 81, 82, 83–84
Turnover, 17, 24, 69, 89–90, 123,
  177, 180
Tynan, Mary Costello, 36–37

Unions, 28–29, 35–36, 43, 59,
  62, 66, 70, 75, 81, 84–85, 86,
  87, 91, 92, 97, 98, 100,
  105–11, 117, 119, 129–30,
  132, 134–51, 158, 159, 160,
  163, 167–68, 170
United Nurses of Alberta (UNA),
  73, 75, 97, 107, 131, 132–44,
  150, 167
United States, nursing in, 47,

53, 66, 67, 120, 130, 150, 152,
  184, 234–35
Universities Co-ordinating
  Council (Alta.), 54
University Hospital, Edmonton,
  74
University of Alberta, 171, 172
University of Alberta Hospital,
  114–16, 119, 133, 134, 139,
  171
University of British Columbia,
  57, 169, 171, 206
University of Manitoba School
  of Nursing, 121
University of Montreal, 111
University of New Brunswick,
  226, 232
University of Toronto, 56,
  157–58, 181
Upgrading, *see* Education, post-
  RN
User fees, 222, 227, 228, 229

Vachon, Mary, 86, 212
Vancouver General Hospital
  (VGH), 26, 27, 75, 76, 78–84,
  105, 120, 145–46, 171, 216,
  226
Vander Zalm, Bill, 145
Vanek, David, 30
Victoria General Hospital,
  Halifax, 106, 216
Victorian Order of Nurses
  (VON), 45, 49–50, 94, 98, 191,
  195, 196–97, 212, 215
Vivian, John, 179–80

Wadhams, Steve, 27, 38
Wages, 14, 52, 59, 60, 61, 64, 66,
  68, 69, 87, 91, 100, 105, 123,
  126, 128–31, 132, 140, 142,
  144, 145, 146, 147, 148, 163

Wagner, David, 58–59
Ward clerk, 11
Wards, 57, 133
Weir, Dr. George, 54
Weir Report, 54, 55, 157
Wellesley Hospital, Toronto, 68, 69–71, 89, 106, 160, 213, 235
Wheatley, Shirley, 112, 236
Wiebe, Sherry, 36
Wiens, Mattie, 217
Women's College Hospital, Toronto, 85

Women's Health Centre, Winnipeg, 173–74
Women's movement, 113–14, 140, 228
Working Woman, 113
Work-to-rule, 145, 146
World Health Organization (WHO), 123, 185, 232

York-Finch General Hospital, Toronto, 71

Printed in Canada